ALSO BY THE AUTHORS

BY PHILIP M. BOFFEY

The Brain Bank of America: An Inquiry Into the Politics of Science
Next: The Coming Era in Medicine (co-author)

BY WILLIAM J. BROAD

Star Warriors: A Penetrating Look into the Lives of the Young Scientists
Behind Our Space Age Weaponry
Betrayers of Truth: Fraud and Deceit in the Halls of Science (co-author)

BY LESLIE H. GELB

The Irony of Vietnam: The System Worked (co-author)
Our Own Worst Enemy: The Unmaking of American Foreign Policy (co-author)

BY HOLCOMB B. NOBLE

Next: The Coming Era in Science (co-author and editor)
Next: The Coming Era in Medicine (co-author and editor)
The New York Times Guide to the Return of Halley's Comet (co-author)

CLAIMING
THE
HEAVENS

CLAIMING THE HEAVENS

The New York Times

COMPLETE GUIDE TO THE STAR WARS DEBATE

PHILIP M. BOFFEY

WILLIAM J. BROAD

LESLIE H. GELB

CHARLES MOHR

HOLCOMB B. NOBLE

Times BOOKS

Grateful acknowledgment is made to the following to reprint previously published artwork:

Grumman Corporation: illustration of a Grumman artist's concept of a Grumman-designed space-based radar platform from *Horizons* magazine, Volume 21, No. 3, 1985. Used by permission.

The New York Times Company: "Elements of Proposed Strategic Defense Concept," by Jim Perry, November 3, 1985; "Present ABM System Around Moscow," March 6, 1985; artwork by David Redell, September 16, 1986; artwork by Steven Hart, February 5, 1985; "Free Electron Laser," and "Conventional Laser" by Dan Osyczka, August 19, 1986; "Without Atmospheric Distortion," June 22, 1985; "Target Mirror/Laser Beam," June 22, 1985; "Systems to Deploy and Maintain 'Star Wars,' " June 15, 1986. Copyright © 1985, 1986 by The New York Times Company. Reprinted by permission.

Simon and Schuster, Inc.: illustration on page 117 of *Star Warriors* by William J. Broad. Copyright © 1985 by William J. Broad. Rights in the United States and Canada administered by Simon and Schuster, Inc. Rights in all other territories administered by Sterling Lord Literistic, Inc., New York. Reprinted by permission of Simon and Schuster, Inc., and Sterling Lord Literistic, Inc.

Library of Congress Cataloging-in-Publication Data
Claiming the heavens. Includes index.
1. Strategic Defense Initiative. I. Broad, William, 1951–. II. New York times.
UG743.C58 1988 358'.1754 87-40196
ISBN 0-8129-1647-6

Manufactured in the United States of America
9 8 7 6 5 4 3 2
First Edition
Book Design: Jessica Shatan

TO
REAGAN AND GORBACHEV

ACKNOWLEDGMENTS

For guidance, counsel, inspiration or assistance extended generously in various forms at various times, the authors give grateful acknowledgment to Ronda L. Billig, Judy Gelb, Tanya Mohr, Norma Mohr and Carolyn L. Noble and to colleagues at *The New York Times*: Don Caswell, Robert J. Kanasola, Gary Cosimini, John Darnton, David C. East, Richard Flaste, James L. Greenfield, Sydney Gruson, Steve Hart, Warren Hoge, Bill Kovach, Peter H. Lewis, William P. Luce, Brenda Nicholson, Warren Obr, Jeanne B. Pinder, A. M. Rosenthal, Jack Rosenthal, Arthur Ochs Sulzberger, Seymour Topping, Nicholas Wade, Craig R. Whitney.

CONTENTS

INTRODUCTION

The "Star Wars" team of *The New York Times* that wrote this book was formed before it was formed. The book was completed, in a sense, before it was started. The events it describes have by their very nature been alternately so maddening, frustrating, contradictory, so inherently fascinating, inspiring, perplexing, so immensely important to us all, as writers, as readers, as parents, as children, as members of a relatively young nation still marveling at technology and science the way a child marvels at a new battery-driven toy, that they fairly etched themselves on the brains of some of the people who followed them closely. It was as if chapters were being created by compulsion simultaneously with the unfolding of history—a history that itself was somehow unfolding generations ahead of itself.

The assignment that officially drew the newspaper team together near the end of January 1985 resulted in a six-part series that ran in *The Times* on

Sunday, March 7, 1985, through Friday, March 12, led to a Pulitzer Prize in April 1986, and to the publication of this book by most of the original participants in greatly expanded form, as Star Wars moved steadily to the forefront of world attention and concern. The issue now of nuclear missile defense has become central in efforts to achieve nuclear-arms control. The idea then for the initial assignment seemed simple enough: What, after all, is Star Wars? Where did it come from? Whose idea was it? How did it get where it is? Where is it going? When? Why? And why do we care?

By then thousands upon thousands of words had already been written on this single subject over the course of the previous two years, week after week, month after month. So how was it possible that the editors of *The New York Times* still believed that such a basic primer was called for, indeed, at such length and with utmost urgency?

First, consider the night of March 23, 1983. That was when President Reagan announced to the world that he had a plan to make nuclear missiles impotent and obsolete. He would, he said, erect a great globe-circling shield in space that would protect the world from nuclear missiles, blocking them, destroying them, before they could carry out their irreparable devastation on the peoples and resources of the earth. "Up until now," the President said, "we have increasingly based our strategy of deterrence upon the threat of retaliation. But what if free people could live secure in the knowledge that their security did not rest upon the threat of instant U.S. retaliation to deter a Soviet attack; that we could intercept and destroy strategic ballistic missiles before they reached our own soil or that of our allies?"

Mr. Reagan acknowledged that it might be the year 2000 before the technology could be developed and launched into place in space to carry out his mission. "Yet current technology has attained a level of sophistication where it is reasonable for us to begin this effort. It will take years, probably decades, of effort on many fronts. There will be failures and setbacks just as there will be successes and breakthroughs. And as we proceed we must remain constant in preserving the nuclear deterrent and maintaining a solid capability for flexible response. But is it not worth every investment necessary to free the world from the threat of nuclear war? We know it is." So the President of the United States, leader of a nation that had pursued a course of nuclear deterrence from the time it developed and dropped the first atomic bomb on a hostile nation during warfare, on Hiroshima on August 6, 1945— this President caught the world by surprise and proposed a new era for nuclear policy:

"I call upon the scientific community who gave us nuclear weapons to turn their great talents to the cause of mankind and world peace; to give us the means of rendering these nuclear weapons impotent and obsolete."

Whenever the President makes this kind of speech, in which he does conceivably set in motion forces that may ultimately affect sweeping patterns of history, and when this possibility can be readily imagined, a switch is thrown and an old newspaper fire alarm goes off. Reporters and editors alike know they've got a good story. News, like history, is change. So, really, from the moment the words "impotent and obsolete" were out of the President's mouth, Star Wars became hot journalistic stuff: First, because the Pentagon was shocked by the Reagan speech, mainly because it hadn't known it was coming. The military planners who did were angered, too, because they believed they had had no chance to lay the groundwork for such a declaration and because their lifework, and by implication their jobs, were focused on the very thing the President said he was going to eliminate—nuclear missiles. Next, the Europeans were shocked. Wouldn't Star Wars make them more vulnerable to superior conventional forces of the Soviet Union? And the scientists were shocked. Wasn't the technology, after all, far from the point that would justify this kind of confidence on the part of the President? The news stories flowed virtually nonstop.

Still, despite this vast amount of already widely disseminated information, very few citizens of the world, either its leaders or the ordinary citizens, seemed to grasp the scope of what was going on. Certainly the author of this introduction, Holcomb B. Noble, who was deputy science editor of *The Times*, tells himself he never properly woke up, never felt his spine chill over Star Wars, never properly elevated the story in his mind to five alarms, until nearly two years after the celebrated speech. That happened in January 1985, after Mr. Reagan's landslide reelection to a second term, during the editing of an article for the Science Times section by William J. Broad, a science reporter for *The Times*. Scientists and military technical experts, he had written, were beginning to realize that they were embarking on what might prove to be one of the biggest technical research undertakings of all time, perhaps bigger than the Manhattan Project that produced the A-bomb, bigger than the Apollo program that put men on the moon. At almost the same moment, Seymour Topping, then managing editor, and Craig Whitney, an assistant managing editor, had come to the conclusion that extra effort was needed in covering the story, and they called a meeting of selected editors and reporters whose beats often cross one another in the coverage of America's military, foreign, scientific and political affairs. The meeting itself was surprising. Far more information existed collectively in the minds of the reporters than had somehow been conveyed. And taken together, expressed together under one roof, it created a far more vast, complicated, yet compelling picture than people generally understood.

It was decided therefore to package the whole story—its beginnings, middle and projected end—in a series that would run at whatever length necessary, but promptly, so as to be useful in advance of arms-reduction talks resuming in Geneva in the second week of March. There was not much time, actually, under the circumstances.

But a bit of luck intervened. At almost precisely the same moment as *The Times* decided to explore the subject more thoroughly than it ever had before, the Reagan administration decided that it wanted to talk about Star Wars in more detail. Robert C. (Bud) McFarlane, then Mr. Reagan's national security adviser, invited himself to New York to meet with a *Times* group; the President himself suddenly accepted a long-standing request to be interviewed at the White House by a team of *Times* reporters; and both the Pentagon and defense contractors became far more open and talkative in areas that had previously been carefully guarded. Clearly, the administration was seeking aggressively to promote Star Wars.

As a result, reporting skill and luck combined to produce a series that was able to go backward and forward at the same time, to uncover important new diplomatic and scientific history and to report significant new events. Les Gelb, then a valued foreign policy reporter and analyst and now deputy editorial page editor, wrote that the administration had, indeed, started to move the nation toward a new era in strategic thinking and nuclear competition; William Broad reported that the key man in persuading Ronald Reagan to take that step was the man who once had played a central role in developing the hydrogen bomb—Edward Teller, who, it turned out, had had four private meetings with the President before the speech. Wayne Biddle, who had long covered space technology and has since left *The Times* and is writing a book on defense spending, knocked on the door of Rockwell International Corporation and found it now willing and eager to display its chief contribution to the program: Code-named Sigma Tau, then the nearest thing to a laser base anywhere in the Western world, it was hidden in the rocky canyons of the Santa Susana Mountains high above Los Angeles. Charles Mohr, whose many years as a military affairs reporter included a term as Saigon bureau chief during the Vietnam War, reported that the Soviet Union was approximately equal to the United States in missile-defense research, but was trailing badly in developing the fine-tuned technology needed to put such weaponry in place. Philip M. Boffey, Washington-based science writer for *The Times,* disclosed an unsettling addition to the new missile "defense" equation: that the weapons envisioned for use in the President's antiballistic-missile shield could also be used, according to both friends and foes of the program, with devastating offensive effect as well. The proposed missile-defense system, if used offensively, could, as one laser expert and Star Wars proponent put it, "take an industrialized country back to an eighteenth-century level in thirty minutes."

Now, after years of scientific and military research, what are our government, our scientists, our military leaders, the Soviet Union and the United States really left with?

Have the United States and the Soviet Union really only embarked on a research program—or are they both in fact virtually committed in the end to deploying a defense system against nuclear missiles if such a system becomes technically feasible?

Is the President's goal of rendering nuclear weapons impotent really a desirable objective?

Would it stabilize world peace, or destabilize it?

Or, is it, after all, merely enhancing the old policy of deterrence, merely a way of providing greater assurance for mutually assured destruction, MAD—a purpose that would run exactly counter to Mr. Reagan's stated goal of making nuclear weapons obsolete?

Can Star Wars really be made to work at a cost any nation can afford?

How would each side deploy it? How would each side protect itself while it was going through the precarious business of putting the defensive system in place and dismantling its nuclear arsenal?

Are there better alternatives?

Those crucial questions and still others are in large measure what constitutes this book, chapter 1, 2, 6, 12 and 16 of which were written by William Broad; chapters 3, 4 and 13 by Leslie Gelb; 5, 7, 8 and 15 by Charles Mohr; 9 by Holcomb Noble; and 10, 11 and 14 by Philip Boffey. The issues, rather than becoming stale as time has passed, seem only to have become more pressing. In nearly every successive stage of arms talks between the Soviet Union and the United States, the issue of Star Wars and the research, development, testing and deployment of missile-defense systems in space have been a central issue. And it will continue to be for years to come, probably decades to come, perhaps generations. It is not an overstatement to say that the fate of the world depends on the resolution.

CLAIMING
THE
HEAVENS

1

THE BIRTH
OF STAR WARS

In a 1940 film, secret agent Brass Bancroft is engaged in battle with a band of Communist spies. American scientists have developed a powerful defensive weapon that paralyzes electric currents, allowing it to disable anything that runs on electricity, to blast enemy planes out of the sky. The Communists plan to steal the device, unless agent Bancroft can stop them.

"Well," says Brass at one point, "it seems the spy ring has designs on the greatest war weapon ever invented which, by the way, is the exclusive property of Uncle Sam." Another character, a Navy admiral, notes that the weapon "not only makes the United States invincible in war, but in so doing, promises to become the greatest force for world peace ever discovered."

The mission is to foil the spies, thus saving the world from Communist aggression. At the film's climax, Bancroft turns the ray on spies escaping with plans for the weapon. Their plane stops in midair, catches fire and plummets to earth. The film is called *Murder in the Air,* and secret agent Brass Bancroft was played by movie actor Ronald Reagan.

No one—perhaps not even Reagan—can definitively list all the factors that ultimately prompted him to make his celebrated "Star Wars" speech on March 23, 1983, which he gave in a televised address to the nation. Behind it lay a confluence of people and ideas, of forces and counterforces. According to many scholars, one notable influence was his movie career, especially *Murder in the Air* with its remarkable foreshadowing of Star Wars weaponry. Another was a persuasive aide who, in 1979, promoted the idea of strategic defense during the presidential campaign. Another was the encouragement of key confidants such as Dr. Edward Teller, the Hungarian-born "father" of the hydrogen bomb who lobbied vigorously during 1982 for a crash program of strategic defense. Still another powerful force was the approving collective influence exerted by Reagan's science adviser, his national security adviser, and members of the Joint Chiefs of Staff, all of whom in early 1983 said the time was ripe to try to defend the nation against enemy planes and missiles. A final factor was the sheer record of scientific progress of the twentieth century—as with many men of his generation, Reagan had developed a profound respect for the powers of technology.

Ronald Wilson Reagan was born in the small midwestern town of Tampico, Illinois, in 1911. In his autobiography, Reagan describes his boyhood as "a rare Huck Finn idyll" in which he explored the mysteries of the dark woods and enjoyed escapades with his friends. It was an age in which the Wright brothers still made dramatic flights and Henry Ford mass-produced motorcars, making them an increasingly common sight on roads once dominated by horses. It was a time when most Americans learned to believe that technology, optimism and progress were synonymous.

Young Reagan caught the spirit of the age. In the autobiography, Reagan recalled listening "with breathless attention" to a primitive radio, "a pair of earphones attached tightly to my head, scratching a crystal with a wire. I was listening to raspy recorded music and faint voices saying, 'This is KDKA, Pittsburgh, KDKA, Pittsburgh.'"

As an adult, Reagan went into commercial radio, making his living as an announcer from 1933 to 1937. He then moved on to motion pictures, which fascinated him. In 1937, after completing his first film, he wrote a series of

A still from the 1940s film *Murder in the Air*, in which Ronald Reagan portrays an American secret agent who battles Communist spies using a powerful electronic weapon that blasts planes out of the sky. Some scholars say Reagan's love of cinematic heroes and fascination with technology combined in the film to create a powerful image that stayed with him for decades. MEMORY SHOP PHOTO

articles for the Des Moines *Sunday Register* in which he described, in admiring detail, the technical intricacies of making a movie.

Reagan's love of technology seems to have found an artistic outlet in *Murder in the Air*. The hero is clearly a technological sophisticate, and the plot is thick with scientific images. At one point, secret agent Reagan explains to a friend that the revolutionary weapon is known as the Inertia Projector.

"The nervous objector?"

"The Inertia Projector," Bancroft-Reagan responds dryly. "It's a device for throwing electrical waves capable of paralyzing alternating and direct currents at the source." The hero goes on to explain that the principle behind the machine had been witnessed in public, telling his friend to recall "that news story that broke sometime ago and then was hushed up about the amateur radio operator in Kansas, who was stopping automobiles and street cars and electrical appliances for miles around."

According to some scholars, Reagan's love of cinematic heros and fascination with technology combined in *Murder in the Air* to create a powerful image for him that endured for decades.

"There's no question that it influenced the President's views," Dr. Michael Rogin, a political scientist at the University of California at Berkeley, said in an interview. "When I saw the movie, it just jumped out at me. I was stunned." In scholarly papers Dr. Rogin argues that *Murder in the Air* helped inspire not only the President's antimissile plan but his general presidential outlook. The film, he writes, shows an "obsession with intelligence agents as the means to national security, and, most strikingly, the existence of an airborne defensive superweapon that will make America invulnerable. All these look forward to the Star Wars militarization of space and the Reagan presidency."

The frequent intermingling of Hollywood fiction with Sacramento or Washington reality has often been noted. Dr. Rogin cites the many times Reagan has relied on films during his presidential campaign. "I am paying for this microphone," Reagan told rivals during the 1980 presidential primary debate in New Hampshire. It was a line from the old movie *State of the Union.* For his inauguration, Reagan chose the music from his own favorite movie, *King's Row.* Responding to criticism of his tax plan, Reagan challenged critics to "Make my day," a line delivered by Clint Eastwood in *Sudden Impact.* In a speech defending his antimissile plan, Reagan said "The Force is with us," an allusion to the movie *Star Wars.*

The serious question here is not just how much Reagan was influenced by movies in general but whether a 1940s film might indeed have provided key inspiration for what eventually would bring a profound reconsideration of the nuclear arms policy of the United States. The question cannot really be answered, even of a movie as remarkable as *Murder in the Air.* Nor could anyone establish with certainty that Brass Bancroft provided some sort of role model for Ronald Reagan. But it does seem clear that the notion of clean, swift and simple national defense against sinister foreign invaders was firmly planted in the mind of the President-to-be.

In the genesis of Star Wars, other forces and factors stand out, especially the long line of conservative advisers to Reagan who hailed the merits of strategic defense. Preeminent among these was Dr. Teller. Before the President gave his famous Star Wars speech, Reagan consulted with Dr. Teller on four occasions, in 1982 and early 1983, to learn of new ways of trying to destroy missiles and warheads during an enemy attack.

Dr. Teller, a physicist whose strident anti-Communist views have long made him a suspect figure to liberal scientists, had played a central role in developing the hydrogen bomb in the 1950s. But almost as soon as the Soviet Union matched that achievement (which came far more quickly than many American scientists had dreamed possible), Dr. Teller began searching for technologies that could protect the nation from a nuclear threat. "It would be wonderful," he wrote in his 1962 book, *The Legacy of Hiroshima*, "if we could shoot down approaching missiles before they could destroy a target in the United States." At the time, technology was far too feeble for the job, but Dr. Teller nonetheless warned that the West should be watchful lest the needed breakthroughs were made elsewhere. "If the Communists should become certain that their defenses are reliable and at the same time know that ours are insufficient," he wrote, "Soviet conquest of the world would be inevitable." His fear was veiled, but nonetheless clear. An aggressor with a good shield might be tempted to use his spear, confident he could deflect the weapon of his opponent.

Reagan first met Dr. Teller when the physicist was at the height of his power and popularity, an international celebrity who had long advised Presidents, politicians and the Pentagon. Sworn in as governor of California in 1967, Reagan visited him during his first few months in office, going to meet him at the Lawrence Livermore National Laboratory, one of two federal facilities for the design of nuclear weapons. Although the laboratory had been founded in 1952, mainly at Dr. Teller's behest, Reagan was the first California governor to visit the sprawling lab, located in a dry valley about forty miles east of San Francisco. Of course, it was packed with intriguing computers, lasers and other technical wonders that made the weapons of *Murder in the Air* look much less futuristic or fictional.

"We showed him all the complex projects," Dr. Teller recalled in an interview. "He listened carefully and interrupted maybe a dozen times. Every one of his questions was to the point. He clearly comprehended the technology. And there was no skimping on time. He came in the morning and stayed over lunch. He quite obviously is one of the really few politicians who takes a detailed interest in technical subjects." At Livermore, for the first time, Dr. Teller shared with Reagan his dream of protecting the nation from the onslaught of enemy missiles.

As Reagan's political career advanced, he often made statements that disparaged the nuclear status quo and praised the goal of creating defenses for the United States. In 1976 during his unsuccessful presidential bid, Reagan questioned the doctrine of mutual assured destruction, or MAD, saying it was like two men pointing pistols at each other's heads with one of them tightening his finger on the trigger. During a radio speech in 1978, Reagan described the grim implications. "If the Soviets should push the button," he warned, "there is no defense against them—no way to prevent nuclear devastation of their targets here in the United States."

In 1979, during the presidential campaign, Reagan had an opportunity to visit the site dedicated to warning of nuclear attack. The North American Aerospace Defense Command, or NORAD, is a top-secret military facility inside a hollowed-out mountain in Colorado whose mission is to track the trajectories of all objects in space, including any missiles or warheads that should suddenly appear on radar screens. Reagan went there with Martin Anderson, one of his policy advisers for the campaign.

"It's an experience," Anderson recalled in an interview. "It's just like the movies. There's a big steel door into the mountain and a huge subterranean complex carved inside. In the war room there's a map of the United States that can show the paths of incoming planes and missiles. We got the full briefing. At the end we went back to the general's office. All day long I had wanted to ask the question: What would happen if they launched just one? The answer was that there was nothing we could do. Reagan joined in and we pressed it further, going into different scenarios. We could do nothing. On the plane coming back, Reagan was clearly struck by the fact that we had spent billions on national defense, with all the weapons, yet we were totally helpless."

Later on in the campaign, Reagan recalled his NORAD visit, telling a reporter that it worried him. "They actually are tracking several thousand objects in space, meaning satellites of ours and everyone else's, even down to the point that they are tracking a glove lost by an astronaut," he told Robert Scheer, as recounted in *With Enough Shovels*. "I think the thing that struck me," Reagan continued, "was the irony that here, with this great technology of ours, we can do all of this, yet we cannot stop any of the weapons that are coming at us. I don't think there's a time in history when there wasn't a defense against some kind of thrust, even back in the old-fashioned days when we had coast artillery that would stop invading ships."

In addition to worrying Reagan, the NORAD experience made a deep impression on Anderson, a senior fellow at the Hoover Institution on War, Revolution and Peace at Stanford University who had worked in Reagan's unsuccessful 1976 campaign and later became President Reagan's special assistant for domestic policy. In August 1979, Anderson sat down in his Los Angeles office and wrote "Policy Memorandum No. 3 on Foreign Policy and National Security, Reagan for President." It was a remarkable document. His memo listed three campaign options: stick with President Carter's policy of relying on good Soviet intentions ("dangerous folly," Anderson interjected), embark on a big arms buildup ("apt to frighten as many people as it consoles"), or start to build a system to shoot down enemy missiles ("far more appealing to the American people than the questionable satisfaction of knowing that those who initiated an attack against us were also blown away"). "Of course," Anderson noted, "there is the question of feasibility, especially with the development of multiple entry warheads, but there have apparently been striking advances in missile technology during the past decade or so that would make such a system technically possible." He added that defenses should be constructed "in conjunction with a reasonable buildup in our conventional forces, and an acceleration in development of cruise missiles, and conventional nuclear missiles like the MX."

Anderson noted in the memo that "we should be able to get evaluation of the concept from the group of national defense experts we have working with us." One of these was General Daniel O. Graham of the Army, who in 1976 retired from the government as head of the Defense Intelligence Agency. Another was Dr. Teller, whom Anderson had known since 1975 when the physicist took a position at the Hoover Institution in addition to his duties at the Livermore weapons lab. The memo itself was written for Reagan and his dozen top campaign aides, people such as Richard V. Allen, Michael K. Deaver, Peter Hannaford and Edwin Meese. These men played important campaign roles, perhaps more so than their counterparts among other politicians. John P. Sears, who served as campaign manager in two of Reagan's presidential campaigns but was fired before the election in 1980, once said of his boss, "He can be guided. His decisions rarely originate with him. He is an endorser. It is fair to say that on some occasions he is presented with options and selects one, but it is also true that in other instances he simply looks to someone to tell him what to do."

It would be unfair to say the Star Wars idea did not originate with Reagan himself, given his long abhorrence of MAD and his equally long interest in the idea of antimissile defense. But many others played strong roles in what was ultimately to take place, and when. In 1979, Anderson was by no means alone in trying to persuade Reagan to take a strong public stance for strategic defense. Senator Malcolm A. Wallop, Republican of Wyoming, embraced the missile-defense idea and urged it on Reagan. That summer Wallop sent the candidate a typewritten draft of an antimissile article for *Strategic Review*, a journal devoted to military affairs. Reagan returned it with notations. In the finished article, which ran in the fall 1979 issue, Wallop said: "It is high time that we lay the phantom of MAD to rest and that we turn our attention to the realistic task of affording maximal protection for our society in the event of conflict." At a barbecue that fall, Reagan and Wallop discussed the coming campaign. "They talked about space-based defense, and Reagan said he was going to make a big issue of it," Angelo M. Codevilla, a Wallop aide, recalled. "Later, I was asked to give Deaver some material on it, but he turned out to be very unenthusiastic—to put it mildly."

In fact, Reagan's top managers decided it would be political suicide to make strategic defense an issue in the campaign, despite Reagan's growing fascination. "The political people prevailed," Anderson recalled. "And I think they were right. Even as President, the roof fell in when he announced the goal. As a candidate, it would have been worse." Nevertheless, in July 1980 during the Republican convention in Detroit, Reagan did quietly approve an antimissile plank in the GOP platform. It called for "vigorous research and development of an effective antiballistic-missile system, such as is already at hand in the Soviet Union, as well as more modern ABM technologies." The platform also called for a new round of nuclear weapons and missiles, the ultimate goal being "overall military and technological superiority over the Soviet Union."

As planned, however, the issue of strategic defense was not raised during the Presidential campaign. Soon after his resounding electoral success in November, Reagan's interest in the subject reemerged. In December, the President-elect questioned Republican Senator Harrison H. Schmitt, a former astronaut and chairman of the Senate Subcommittee on Science, Technology and Space, about the feasibility of modern antimissile technologies, in particular lasers. "The meeting lasted about twenty minutes," Schmitt said. "We were talking about science and technology in general. Then, about halfway through the session, he made a statement that he was concerned that we could not just keep building nuclear missiles forever, that ultimately their proliferation would get us into serious trouble. He asked what I thought about the possibility of strategic defense, especially with lasers. My response was that the potential was there but a great deal of research needed to be done. We spent half the conversation talking about it. When I later heard his speech, the phrases sounded very familiar. The words had the same ring."

In the years between the inauguration and the Star Wars speech, Reagan's talks with his technical advisers came to be dominated by the question of feasibility. The President himself needed no convincing. He was morally committed to defense. He admired "this great technology of ours" and personally thought the goal of strategic defense could be achieved. More than forty years had passed since *Murder in the Air*. The clean, simple notion of plucking an advancing enemy out of the sky persisted, and Reagan's hunch was that technology had progressed to the point where science fiction was now ready to become strategic fact. The main question, according to former aide Anderson, who left the White House in 1982, was whether it could be done: Was it technologically, economically and politically feasible?

With Reagan committed to the vision, three distinct groups lobbied the White House with particular plans for its realization. The difference among the groups was the level of sophistication they envisioned for antimissile arms. The high-technology option would be possible only in the distant future; medium level would stem from the best current research; and low would use off-the-shelf equipment already available. In 1981, the three groups refined their agendas and attitudes toward one another, and in 1982 they accelerated their attempts to persuade the President how to move ahead.

The most influential advocate of all was Dr. Teller, who lobbied for a variant of high technology. His message was that he and his colleagues at the Livermore weapons lab had come up with a technical breakthrough in late 1980 that would end the MAD era once and for all. The top-secret device was known as the nuclear X-ray laser, code-named Excalibur. For decades, physicists had dreamed of creating X-ray lasers. Now it seemed theoretically possible for Excalibur to channel the energy of an exploding hydrogen bomb into beams of intense X-rays that would flash through space and destroy enemy missiles. In practice, however, it might take years or even decades to discover if it could work as envisioned.

In February 1981, Dr. Teller, seventy-three, and his protégé at Livermore, Dr. Lowell L. Wood, Jr., forty, began briefing leaders of the House and Senate on details of the secret weapon. Rumors of a breakthrough first reached the public in the February 23, 1981, issue of *Aviation Week & Space Technology*, a trade publication known in military circles as "Aviation Leak." The X-ray news was attributed to anonymous government and congressional officials. When the magazine hit the streets, Reagan had been in office exactly one month.

In May 1981, Dr. Teller's campaign to influence the White House picked up speed when a good friend of his, Dr. George A. Keyworth II, was named the President's science adviser. A nuclear physicist from the Los Alamos National Laboratory in New Mexico, the birthplace of the bomb, Dr. Keyworth was intimately familiar with the X-ray secrets. At forty-one years of age, Dr. Keyworth was also typical of the bright young scientists that had long been groomed for positions of power by Dr. Teller. In Washington, the science adviser told new friends he considered Dr. Teller a father figure, often referring to him as "my dad."

In the late summer of 1981, a group of influential scientists, industrialists, military men and aerospace executives began to meet in Washington, D.C., at the Heritage Foundation, a conservative think tank, to weigh antimissile options. Among the nearly two dozen participants were Dr. Teller, Dr. Wood, General Graham and such members of the President's "kitchen cabinet" as Joseph Coors, sixty-eight, a brewer; Jacquelin Hume, eighty, a foods magnate; and William A. Wilson, seventy-one, a rancher and trustee of the Reagan finances. Those meetings were also attended by members of Dr. Keyworth's staff from the White House Office of Science and Technology Policy. The group's top officer was Karl R. Bendetsen, seventy-eight, once Under Secretary of the Army, later chairman of the board of the Champion International Corporation, and a longtime overseer of the Hoover Institution. He had known Dr. Teller since the 1940s and eventually became a close friend of Dr. Keyworth's. All group members received security clearances so they could learn about and discuss the secret details of new technologies and weapons.

The leaders of the group briefed White House officials for the first time on September 14, 1981, according to Anderson, who was then President

Reagan's special assistant for domestic policy. "We got a clear message that what we'd been talking about was feasible," Anderson recalled.

Despite such high-level access, the group soon split over the issue of which research path was best. Bendetsen, Dr. Teller and the Reagan "kitchen cabinet" separated into a small group to investigate proposals for advanced lasers and other technologies that required a long period of gestation. General Graham, on the other hand, formed a group known as the High Frontier to promote systems built primarily with existing equipment, such as small rockets that could be based in space to destroy targets by simply smashing into them. The Boeing Company, maker of jumbo jets and advanced weaponry, was the main technical force behind High Frontier, providing General Graham's group with advice and assistance. In 1980, the company had set up a special office to line up antimissile contracts that investment experts said were on the horizon.

At odds philosophically, the two groups also differed on what role, if any, the X-ray laser and other advanced nuclear arms should play. General Graham, who advocated nonnuclear systems, recalled that Dr. Teller "wanted very much to leave in the nuclear options. The man is carrying a load and has taken a lot of abuse as the 'father' of the H-bomb. Now he wants to see nuclear technology turn out to be the answer in the opposite direction, to save the Western world." The split had vast implications in terms of presidential access. Bendetsen and his colleagues, many of them old friends of Reagan, could visit the White House with ease to press the high-technology approach. General Graham, champion of the low road, had no such access.

By the fall of 1981, the smoke of quiet dispute threatened to become an open blaze. The problem was that the middle technological path was attracting fairly broad congressional support, raising the prospect that antimissile policy would be dictated by the legislative branch of the federal government. Congressional advocates of this middle path were known as the "laser lobby." Their weapon of choice was the space-based laser powered by chemical reactions, prototypes of which had been under investigation by the Pentagon since the 1970s. A group of lobbyists known on Capitol Hill as "the gang of four" that included representatives of defense contractors TRW, Perkin-Elmer, Charles Stark Draper Laboratory, and Lockheed Missiles & Space Co. made up the strongest force promoting this option. The leader was Maxwell W. Hunter II, a shrewd, self-confident vice president of Lockheed—the man who had won Senator Wallop to the defensive vision in the late 1970s.

During 1980 and 1981, Senator Wallop and his congressional allies, including Senator Schmitt, sponsored measures intended to speed up the Pentagon's work on space-based chemical lasers and to create support for deploying these weapons in space.

Seeing a threat to White House flexibility in proposing other options, science adviser Keyworth prepared to fight the congressional moves and shape the increasingly volatile debate in Washington himself. Angering antimissile advocates, Dr. Keyworth in September 1981 hired a skeptic, Dr. Victor H. Reis, to be his assistant for national security. Later that year, Dr. Keyworth also charged a panel of the White House Science Council, made up of prominent scientists outside the government, to embark on a secret study of the feasibility of antimissile technologies.

In October 1981, at a breakfast gathering, Keyworth told a group of aerospace executives that he was spending most of his time in Washington trying to resist congressional pressure to build and operate space-based laser battle stations. The main technical problem with this approach, as he saw it, was that chemical lasers, at least at that stage of their development, had wavelengths that were too long: Their mirrors and associated optics for focusing the laser beam would have to be gigantic, and their beams consequently would be only mildly concentrated. Futuristic lasers with smaller wavelengths would be much better at focusing an intense beam of light on a speeding missile thousands of miles away in space. The shorter a laser's wavelength, the more destructive energy it could pour onto a target. The laser that held the record for the shortest wavelength of all was the nuclear X-ray laser.

The dispute between the low-road traveling High Frontier, the middle-road Laser Lobby and the high-roaders came to a head when Bendetsen and his high-tech advocates in the Star Wars kitchen cabinet met privately with Ronald Reagan for the first time. The meeting with the President, in the Roosevelt Room of the White House on January 8, 1982, was scheduled to last fifteen minutes. It went on for an hour.

Edward Teller was present, as was Bendetsen, Keyworth and a few others. "The President expressed great interest," recalled a group member, who spoke later on the condition of anonymity. The conversation focused on directed-energy weapons that might be used to destroy aircraft as well as missiles, and there was much talk of lasers. "Our little committee frankly told the President that the Pentagon was experimenting with lasers that might have only limited capacity because the wavelengths were too long." Reagan wondered whether a system for strategic defense would be used to save missile silos or cities, the latter being much more difficult to protect. Bendetsen told him it was too early to make a distinction. The important thing, he said, was to get on with the job. In summary, Bendetsen said the time was ripe for the President to make a speech announcing the start of a crash antimissile program similar to the 1942 Manhattan Project that produced the world's first atomic bomb. More specifically, the group's recommendation was to start a stepped-up program of advanced research rather than to embark on a program of building defenses with off-the-shelf or the current generation of lasers.

"Can we do it?" the President asked.

Yes, absolutely, was the group's collective reply.

General Graham, his request for presidential access denied, took his case to the public. In February 1982 he issued the High Frontier report, a 175-page book filled with a detailed description of his faction's vision, as well as futuristic color sketches of battles in space. With surprising candor, General Graham recalled in its foreword that his group had originally searched not for a way to create antimissile defenses but for "a technological end-run on the Soviets" and noted it had "led inexorably to space. The U.S. advantage in space is demonstrated in its most dramatic form by the space shuttle," he wrote. "More fundamentally, the ability of the United States to miniaturize components gives us great advantages in space where transport costs-per-pound are critical. Today a pound of U.S. space machinery can do much more than a pound of Soviet space machinery. It also happened that the technologies immediately available for military systems—beyond intelligence, communication and navigation-aid satellites—are primarily applicable to ballistic-missiles defense systems."

General Graham personally delivered the recommendations of the High Frontier panel to General John W. Vessey, Jr., who soon after became the chairman of the Joint Chiefs of Staff. "He was pretty positive from the very beginning," General Graham said. Most Pentagon officials, however, greeted High Frontier with derision. Indeed, after the idea was studied exhaustively in early 1982 by the Air Force and the Army, Defense Secretary Caspar W.

Weinberger wrote General Graham to say that "with the substantial risks involved, we do not foresee 'cheap and quick' solutions to support the shift in policy you seek."

So, too, the President's science adviser was becoming increasingly negative about the antimissile quest. In April 1982, George Keyworth visited Senator Wallop on Capitol Hill and told him that to deploy space-based defenses during the 1980s, before the technology was ripe, would damage national security in the long run. "When peoples' expectations get built too high, budgets suffer greatly," Dr. Keyworth said. Dr. Keyworth was also having difficulties reining in his mentor, Dr. Teller. As a member of the Bendetsen group, Dr. Teller had already seen Reagan once and would do so two more times prior to delivery of the Star Wars speech. But Dr. Teller was getting frustrated by a situation in which others controlled the time and agenda. The old physicist repeatedly asked Dr. Keyworth for a private meeting with the President, one in which he and Reagan, both in their seventies, could reason together.

It was the kind of situation officials in the Reagan White House avoided at all costs. The President was far too impressionable. Reagan was a man of charm and warmth. A personal bond meant everything and could result in almost anything. His aides therefore usually made sure that virtually no visitor saw the President alone, especially one as controversial as Dr. Teller. The science adviser gave his old teacher the bad news: A private meeting was impossible.

Not to be deterred, Dr. Teller went public to complain. On June 15, 1982, he taped a segment of *Firing Line*, the nationally televised program hosted on the public broadcasting network by William F. Buckley, Jr. The physicist said lack of funds was inhibiting work on antimissile weapons and warned that in such areas the Soviet Union was forging ahead.

BUCKLEY: Are you telling me that the Soviet Union is currently engaged in defensive work of the same kind that you recommend to America, which would have the effect of making it safe for them to launch a first strike?
TELLER: I am not telling you that. I am only telling you that I have reason to suspect it. I have strong reason to suspect it.

Later in the show Buckley suggested that Dr. Teller should take an urgent message on antimissile matters to President Reagan, the talk-show host drawing a parallel to the warning Einstein took Roosevelt in 1939 about the danger of Nazi Germany developing the atom bomb.

TELLER: May I tell you one little secret which is not classified? From the time that President Reagan has been nominated I had not a single occasion to talk to him.

BUCKLEY: Have you sought out such an occasion?

TELLER: I have talked to people to whom I am close and who in turn are close to the President. I have tried what seemed to be reasonable to get action on these things. I may have been clumsy in one way or the other, but I am deeply grateful for any opportunity to speak about these things. I have lived through two world wars. I don't want to live through a third one.

While the program was being aired, Reagan watched it at his ranch in Santa Barbara. Later, the White House sent the scientist an invitation. Dr. Teller met with Reagan on September 14, 1982. The physicist was seventy-four, the President, seventy-one. Among other things, Dr. Teller warned that the Soviets were forging ahead in development of the nuclear X-ray laser, a situation that could, as he warned two decades earlier, bring about "Soviet conquest of the world." When Dr. Teller went on to appeal for a dramatic increase in funds for X-ray laser work at Livermore, White House aides cut the meeting short.

The September twentieth issue of *Aviation Week & Space Technology* noted the White House visit but not its abrupt ending. The magazine, read widely in the technocratic realms of official Washington, said Dr. Teller asked for increases in X-ray laser funding of $200 million a year "over the next several years." Dr. Teller then embarked on a vigorous, three-month campaign to win over key individuals in the federal bureaucracy. From October to January, he had several meetings with senior civilian officials in the Pentagon as well as Admiral John D. Watkins, the Chief of Naval Operations. Admiral Watkins, a devout Catholic, was troubled by the American Bishops' Pastoral Letter on War and Peace, drafts of which were circulated and widely debated in 1982. Nuclear weapons, the bishops wrote, were immoral because they were so indiscriminate and so destructive. Admiral Watkins and the other service chiefs, who met twice a month for a prayer breakfast, had discussed the letter. "Most of us agreed that we had never approached our responsibilities from what you might call a moral direction," he recalled. He added that the letter prompted him to go back to fundamentals, not the "Soviet threat," to deal with the nuclear status quo. He said he found MAD morally flawed.

It was during this period that Dr. Teller won the admiral to the antimissile vision. Admiral Watkins then wrote a top-secret Navy report endorsing the

Teller approach. Known to insiders as the "Freedom from Fear" paper, it was produced in consultation with Robert McFarlane, the President's deputy national security adviser who had been briefed by Dr. Teller on the X-ray laser and who rose rapidly in the White House after endorsing the Star Wars vision.

Despite Dr. Teller's growing list of converts in Washington, approval for his antimissile vision was far from universal, especially among fellow scientists—those best qualified to pass judgment on the technical merit of his ideas. After nearly a year of study, the panel of the White House Science Council called together by Dr. Keyworth had found that new types of nuclear weapons would play no role in the near future and that antimissile technology might forever remain too feeble for the job of protecting the nation's cities from enemy missiles and warheads. Members of the panel included such respected scientists as Dr. Harold M. Agnew, former director of the Los Alamos weapons lab, and Dr. Solomon J. Buchsbaum, a vice president of AT&T Bell Laboratories.

In November 1982, Dr. Teller appeared before the panel to criticize its conclusions and argue that X-ray lasers could be ready for deployment in as little as six years. The panel was unmoved. When its final report was presented to Dr. Keyworth in January 1983, the conclusions were the same: No "breakthrough" during the next decade would alter the balance of terror that had already kept an uneasy peace between the superpowers for a third of a century. The X-ray laser, though interesting, was seen as a long-term research project whose ultimate usefulness had yet to be determined. Now, some five months before the effective inauguration of the Star Wars research program, a key group of White House science advisers were still very much against the whole idea.

"Edward had a fuss, and we went back and did it again, and it came out exactly the same way," said a participant, who spoke on the condition of anonymity. So too, the science adviser himself in the fall of 1982 voiced public doubts about aspects of the antimissile drive—if not about his mentor's favorite weapon, the nuclear X-ray laser. George Keyworth appeared on *Braden and Buchanan*, a nationally syndicated radio talk show, and said that the space-based High Frontier system proposed by General Graham would cost not $10–$15 billion, as estimated by the group, but hundreds of billions of dollars. The President's adviser also said that Soviet lasers and particle beams posed no threat to the United States.

On January 14, 1983, Dr. Keyworth went further in his public comments and broke the official silence surrounding the nuclear X-ray laser. For years it had been a government secret, no official allowed to admit that it even existed. But in January Dr. Keyworth "declassified" the breakthrough in a public lecture at the Livermore Laboratory, where the device had been invented. With his mentor looking on, Dr. Keyworth hailed the nuclear "bomb-pumped X-ray laser" as "one of the most important programs that may seriously influence the nation's defense posture in the next decades." Although upbeat, it was no call for deployment. After the talk Dr. Keyworth backed off even further, telling reporters that missile-attacking lasers were the wrong way to counter the current Soviet "threat."

Meanwhile, Dr. Teller, widening his search for prominent scientists who would hail his X-ray "breakthrough," approached Dr. Hans A. Bethe, a Nobel laureate and longtime advocate of arms control. The two scientists were old friends turned foes. Both were in their seventies. Both had fled Europe because of the Nazis. Both had played pivotal roles in the birth of the nuclear era. Both had advised Presidents. What divided them was how to deal with the Soviet Union. For decades Dr. Teller had put more faith in technology than in diplomacy to protect the United States from Soviet expansionism and the danger of nuclear war.

In February 1983, the two men met at the Livermore lab, and Dr. Teller revealed the top-secret details of what he considered the ultimate solution to the problems of MAD and the age of deterrence.

"You have a splendid idea," Dr. Bethe recalls telling Dr. Teller, complimenting him on the physics of the device. But physics was not enough for the Nobel laureate. After the Star Wars speech, he became a key opponent of the X-ray laser and its exotic brethren, arguing that any defensive shield could easily be outwitted by an enemy. All it would take would be simple countermeasures.

Although influential scientists were skeptical of Dr. Teller's vision, many laymen were not. Indeed, Teller's ideas played a key role in a pivotal decision reached by the Joint Chiefs of Staff in February 1983. Admiral Watkins, impressed by Dr. Teller's news of technical breakthroughs, spoke approvingly of the antimissile idea at a meeting of the Joint Chiefs, who agreed to bring it up with the President. On February 11, 1983, in the Roosevelt Room of the White House, the group sat down at a luncheon meeting with Reagan. The focus was to be the MX missile and the President's program for strategic modernization. For years the government had been trying to find a safe place to deploy the MX, considering more than thirty basing modes. The latest plan was known as Densepack. Throughout the nation, however, opposition to the administration's goals had been steadily mounting, most visibly in the letter of the Catholic bishops and the "freeze" movement.

The Joint Chiefs told the President that the MX was in trouble but that, with luck, it might be the last major missile system to get through Congress. "He realized that his successors were going to face an uphill battle to retain a strategic deterrent," Dr. Keyworth recalled in an interview. Now, by prior arrangement with the other chiefs, Admiral Watkins brought up the topic of antimissile defense and is said to have ended his presentation by asking: "Wouldn't it be better to save lives than to avenge them?" That line later appeared in Reagan's Star Wars speech. After Admiral Watkins finished, General Vessey, chairman of the Joint Chiefs and friend of High Frontier director General Graham, led a discussion with the President. Altogether, the antimissile session is said to have lasted half an hour. In a real sense Star Wars was born.

Still, the Joint Chiefs were vague in their recommendations. The Pentagon, they said, should step up its investigation of the long-range possibilities of antimissile defense—something it was already doing, if in a limited way. There was no talk of deployment or of a crash program of research. And to a man, despite their own urgings, the chiefs have said they were surprised by the urgency of the Star Wars speech and by the President's claim, made repeatedly, that the February meeting with the Joint Chiefs was a critical turning point in the genesis of the antimissile program.

Unknown to the Joint Chiefs, the White House policymaking apparatus swung into high gear within hours of their meeting. In great secrecy, the deputy national security adviser, Robert McFarlane, assigned three staffers to start weighing antimissile options and considering how they might affect the current strategic program. Soon, the inner circle of the White House was drafting passages for what was variously described as the "insert" for an upcoming presidential speech on the Soviet menace.

On Saturday, March 19, Keyworth was called into McFarlane's office and told of the "insert." Dr. Keyworth has said he had no idea a major policy initiative was afoot. He was shocked, he says, but reacted cautiously. McFarlane clearly wanted Keyworth's blessing, and asked whether the time was not ripe for strategic defense.

During the next few days, the President's science adviser underwent a crisis of conscience, according to Gregg Herken, a scholar at the Institute on Global Conflict and Cooperation of the University of California who has studied the origins of Star Wars. Herken says Keyworth, an antimissile skeptic despite the long advocacy of his mentor, was one of the few White House officials who might have killed the "insert." Instead, Herken says, Dr. Keyworth underwent a conversion and became a key advocate.

Precisely what changed Keyworth's mind is far from clear. He had had good reason to have doubts, certainly. His White House Science Council had misgivings about strategic defense, as did many of his scientific peers and assistants. During the previous eighteen months, his deputy, Dr. Reis, had vigorously fought the wilder proposals. Dr. Keyworth himself had gone on a nationally syndicated radio show to challenge the antimissile lobby. Indeed, if there was a scientific consensus, it was that strategic defense was costly, futile and dangerous.

Nevertheless, on that Saturday, Dr. Keyworth told McFarlane that, yes, the time could be considered ripe to embark on a stepped-up program of antimissile research. But during the next few days as he worked on the President's speech, Dr. Keyworth fought to dissuade those who wanted to quickly develop and deploy low- and medium-technology weapons. And, in fact, the high road of pursuing futuristic research prevailed in the President's speech.

Dr. Keyworth "clearly went through a conversion," said a former White House official. "He felt very strongly about the need to support the President on things the President felt strongly about, and he worked hard those few days to ensure that the program would be directed toward research."

In his conversion, Dr. Keyworth was perhaps more the political pragmatist than the technical visionary. What he seemed to have learned during his White House tenure was that strategic defense was going ahead whether he liked it or not. Gregg Herken is of the opinion that Dr. Keyworth had deeply held beliefs about the limits of technology but that, as it turned out, key

Star Wars decisions had little to do with the maturity of antimissile systems. "Keyworth was tired of being the nay-sayer in the administration on things like the space station," Herken observed. "There's no question in my mind that Keyworth's decision to become a cheerleader had a large element of wanting-to-join-the-team behind it."

On the evening of March 23, 1983, President Reagan shared his private vision with the American people. He proposed that the nation set forth on a research plan to see if it was feasible to erect a great defensive shield, one that would block incoming intercontinental ballistic missiles, one that would be designed, ultimately, to make nuclear weapons "impotent and obsolete." It would be "a formidable technical task," the President said, that "may not be accomplished before the end of this century. Yet current technology has attained a level of sophistication where it is reasonable for us to begin this effort." It was a call for stepped-up research, not for the deployment of off-the-shelf systems. Among the dozen scientists invited to the White House to hear the news was the clear winner among key antimissile advocates, Dr. Teller. The seeds of a strategic revolution had been nurtured by a handful of ardent advocates, most notably by the elderly physicist.

The speech hit like a bombshell. High officials of the Department of State and Department of Defense—those most knowledgeable about the feasibility and wisdom of strategic defense—had been excluded from the White House deliberations and were aghast. Shock waves registered in Congress and abroad, allies fearful that Star Wars would upset the delicate balance achieved between East and West during the second half of the twentieth century.

Two days after the speech, on March 25, Reagan was asked at a White House news conference why he had chosen this time to propose a missile-defense system. "What better time?" he responded. It seemed "inconceivable," Reagan added, "that the great nations of the world will sit here like people facing themselves across a table each with a cocked gun, and no one knowing whether someone might tighten the finger on the trigger." An alternative, he said, was for the scientists who gave us nuclear arms to "turn their talent to the job of perhaps coming up with something that would render these weapons obsolete."

Edward Teller, a principal architect of the hydrogen bomb, at the White House in June, 1983. The President held four meetings with Dr. Teller before his Star Wars speech in March, and Dr. Teller's counsel is believed to have played an important role in that historic speech. UPI/BETTMANN NEWSPHOTOS

Dr. Teller, of course, was one of the scientists he had in mind. In an article that appeared in *The New York Times* on March 30, Dr. Teller hailed the Reagan plan: "Today," he wrote, "a wide range of good and ingenious technical plans, ranging from simple to extraordinarily complex, challenges the widespread opinion that practical defense cannot be obtained. Mr. Reagan did not lightly accept the idea that these can be made to work. He wanted to know a vast number of details. He asked questions of his science adviser, George Keyworth, and of many other scientists, myself included. He then decided that something must and can be done."

In May 1983 during a White House ceremony, Reagan awarded Dr. Teller the National Medal of Science, the country's highest scientific award.

On Saturday, July 23, 1983, exactly four months after the Star Wars speech, Dr. Teller wrote the President to urge accelerated work on the nuclear

X-ray laser, which he still claimed was the only weapon needed to inaugurate the antimissile age. Advances in nuclear weaponry, he wrote, "by converting hydrogen bombs into hitherto unprecedented forms and then directing these in highly effective fashions against enemy targets would end the MAD era and commence a period of assured survival on terms favorable to the Western alliance."

It is entirely possible that this letter helped President Reagan understand for the first time that the key breakthrough behind the antimissile quest was to be composed of nuclear weapons—the very things he had just publicly vowed to make "impotent and obsolete." According to several individuals, Dr. Teller's secret briefings on the X-ray laser often glossed over the nuclear dimensions of the device. "It's not a bomb, is it?" Defense Secretary Weinberger asked in reference to the X-ray laser shortly after Reagan's speech. An aide suggested he refer to it in upcoming congressional testimony as "a nuclear event."

In 1984, the President gave his Star Wars vision firm dimensions, outlining a five-year, $26 billion plan to investigate the feasibility of antimissile defenses. The big winners, at that stage, were not so much the aerospace firms, such as Lockheed and Boeing, as the barons of basic research, most especially the nation's federal laboratories. By 1986, Lawrence Livermore, over which Teller still exerted enormous influence, emerged as one of the top contractors receiving Star Wars funds.

Dr. Teller's long, lonely quest had, against formidable odds, begun to succeed. President Reagan, born into an era of technological magic, influenced no doubt in a small but subtly important way by an obscure 1940s movie, had been obviously ripe for the idea of strategic defense. And Dr. Teller, an old friend with news of more amazing American technological breakthroughs, offered reason enough to forge ahead.

But for many other scientists, doubts would fester, especially over the promise of the X-ray laser. "I can see how Edward was attracted to all this," said a scientific colleague and friend of Dr. Teller's who long respected him. "The X-ray laser was elegant. It was technically sweet, just like Oppenheimer said. But is Edward an engineer? No. Is he a systems designer? No. Is he a military planner? No. He was enthralled with the principle and rightly so. The principle is in fact that beautiful. But he is not the kind of guy who ever got hooked on building things. His first H-bomb was the size of an apartment house. Edward is a physicist with a fantastic creative mind. He understands the beauty of a piece of music. But for God's sake, don't ask him to design a trumpet."

Why had Dr. Teller pushed so long, so hard? And why had he so strongly advocated the X-ray laser, a weapon that would be triggered in space by a nuclear explosion? General Graham suggested it had something to do with Dr. Teller wanting to "save the Western world" from his own creation, the hydrogen bomb. But what of the scientists actually making the nuclear breakthroughs for the X-ray laser? Did they share Dr. Teller's confidence about the dawning of a new strategic era?

2

THE HERTZ FOUNDATION
AND THE YOUNG GENIUSES

In *The Child Buyer,*
John Hersey portrayed turmoil among the citizens
of Pequot as they discovered that a mysterious organization was trying to
force a young genius to work on secret defense projects for the government.
The novel opened with the mother of the gifted ten-year-old saying a strange
man was offering to buy her son for tens of thousands of dollars. The state
senate held an inquiry, and learned that the man worked for a shadowy firm
in the southwestern United States known as Lymphomilloid.

"I buy brains," the company representative told the hearing. "When a
commodity that you need falls in short supply, you have to get out and
hustle. I buy brains. About eighteen months ago my company, United
Lymphomilloid of America, Incorporated, was faced with an extremely difficult problem, a project, a long-range government contract, fifty years,
highly specialized and top secret, and we needed some of the best minds in
the country, and we looked around, and we found some minds that had
certainly been excellent at one time, but they'd been spoiled by education.
By what passes for education."

The firm's solution was to provide its own schooling to the gifted children it had bought. The education started with the child being locked naked in a small cell and given a drug that produced complete amnesia. Allowed no contact with nature or people, the child was instructed by films, tape recorders and computers. After being presented a problem related to Lymphomilloid's fifty-year government contract, the child underwent major surgery in which all five senses were tied off, allowing complete concentration.

The parallels are by no means exact, but the fictive world of *The Child Buyer* has curious relevance to the Star Wars project, according to some scientists who work on it. In real life rather than fiction, the recruitment of reluctant young scientists to work in isolation on top-secret projects happens frequently at the Lawrence Livermore National Laboratory.

Surrounded by barbed-wire fences and armed guards, the young scientists of Livermore work in a milieu of blue jeans, soft drinks, science-fiction novels and seemingly endless, all-night bouts of secret research. Their goal is to channel the power of nuclear explosions into beams of radiation that flash across the heavens at the speed of light. The wizards of Livermore range from gung-ho enthusiasts who hail President Reagan's call for an antimissile shield to skeptics who voice doubts about its feasibility and harbor inner visions of horror about the possible effects of their own work.

No matter what their views, the young scientists usually have no intention of working on nuclear weapons when they first arrive at Livermore. They tend to view such work as "evil" and talk of bomb makers as having "dirty hands." What initially brings them to the lab is the search for a high-powered graduate education, paid for by the lab's chief recruiter and educational agent, the Fannie and John Hertz Foundation. In an interview, a Hertz Fellow at Livermore drew the parallel between the foundation and Lymphomilloid. "I've toyed with the notion that Hertz operates on the model of *The Child Buyer*," Andrew H. Weisberg said. "Let's face it, no one in industry is giving away these kinds of scholarships."

Hertz has assets that fluctuate between $11 million and $14 million, according to the foundation's tax returns. Each year the foundation gives $12,500 annual fellowships to exceptionally bright young graduate students who want to work toward doctorates in the applied physical sciences, the Livermore weapons lab being the largest single employer of Hertz Fellows and alumni. Among the foundation's directors are Dr. Teller and his Livermore protégé, Dr. Lowell Wood, as well as two other Livermore officials. When first recruited to Livermore, some Hertz Fellows are literally teenagers, others in their early twenties. What often attracts them is sheer scientific glitter, especially the lab's collection of big computers, lasers and exotic scientific tools. It dazzles them just as it did Governor Reagan. In university laboratories, aspiring young scientists face years of dull apprenticeship if they are lucky enough to get scientific jobs at all. But at the weapons lab they suddenly find themselves free to try their brightest ideas on the best scientific equipment in the world.

In 1979, one Hertz Fellow, Peter L. Hagelstein, then twenty-four, discovered a way to create the nuclear X-ray laser. Successfully tested in 1980, his breakthrough was heralded by top government officials as the most innovative idea in nuclear weaponry since the hydrogen bomb. For him, it was strangely anticlimactic when in 1981 he received his Ph.D. from the Massachusetts Institute of Technology for unclassified aspects of his work at Lawrence Livermore. His thesis made no mention of nuclear breakthroughs. But it did acknowledge the financial aid he received from the Hertz Foundation.

Like other Hertz Fellows at Livermore, Peter initially was loath to work on nuclear weapons. Slowly, however, he found himself very deeply involved—personally as well as professionally.

The story of the Hertz Foundation and its recruiting of bright young scientists for weapons work starts in the 1940s. John D. Hertz, a poor boy made rich by his many business ventures, including Yellow Cab and Hertz rental cars, created the foundation to help students who were financially unable otherwise to attend good technical schools. His goal was to help train a generation of young scientists who could cope with what he saw as threatening technical advances by the Soviet Union. It was not until the 1950s that Dr. Teller became connected to the foundation, as a board member and interviewer for the fellowship program. Teller made sure that at least a few Hertz Fellows did their graduate research at the Livermore weapons lab. Over the years he worked with a remarkable spectrum of men on the board: Floyd B. Odlum, the financier who paid for development of the Atlas missile, the first intercontinental rocket meant to drop bombs on Russia; J. Edgar Hoover, director of the Federal Bureau of Investigation; General Curtis E. LeMay, head of the Strategic Air Command and chief of staff of the Strategic Air Forces when the first atom bombs were dropped on Hiroshima and Nagasaki; Dr. Arthur R. Kantrowitz, a physicist who helped develop the first reentry vehicles for the nation's nuclear missiles; Dr. Charles Stark Draper, a pioneer of inertial guidance for missiles and founder of the 2,000-employee laboratory in Cambridge, Massachusetts, that bears his name; and Hans Mark, former Air Force Secretary.

Once located in Chicago, home of John Hertz, the foundation shifted its office in the early 1980s to the town of Livermore, California, a move that reflected the growing influence of the weapons lab. At Livermore, the foundation has no building or suite, only a post office box. Wilson K. Talley, president of the Hertz Foundation during the period of accelerated antimissile research in the middle 1980s, was interviewed in 1985 about the foundation's Star Wars role. He said it came as no surprise to him that Hertz Fellows made major contributions to the Star Wars plan. "We've been supporting people for years all over the country in computer science, materials science and nuclear physics," he said. "We've attempted to be elitist. Only one out of fifteen who apply gets a fellowship. And those fifteen have A-minus averages. So it's not surprising that some of the brightest brains in the Strategic Defense Initiative happen to be Hertz Fellows."

Dr. Talley was then chairman of the Pentagon's Army Science Board and the only Hertz board member actually associated with a university—a professor at the University of California graduate division that Teller established at Livermore in 1963 in his quest for a place to train young recruits. Known as "Teller Tech," or more formally as the laboratory's Department of Applied Science, the graduate school is situated just inside barbed wire surrounding the weapons lab. Its $1 million building, Hertz Hall, was built with a matching grant from the Hertz Foundation. According to the foundation's directory, the weapons laboratory is the largest single employer of Hertz Fellows and alumni, having at least twenty-nine of them.

Peter Hagelstein came in contact with the Hertz Foundation in 1975 and was immediately viewed by its board as an ideal candidate. He had grown up in the Los Angeles area, poor, smart and eager to make his mark. In high school, he excelled in history, music—he played the violin and viola—languages and athletics, as well as science and mathematics. In 1972, Hagelstein graduated from Canoga Park High School with a National Merit Scholarship and headed for the Massachusetts Institute of Technology. After only two years, he was ready to graduate with a degree in electrical engineering and computer science. He began graduate school at M.I.T., looked for a graduate fellowship and hit upon a brochure from the Fannie and John Hertz Foundation, which stood out starkly from among others. The annual Hertz stipend for an unmarried graduate student was then $10,000 in addition to a tuition allowance of up to $5,500—substantially more than most graduate fellowships. But the award had two unusual conditions. First, unlike most other fellowship sponsors, which evaluated candidates on academic performance and financial need, the Hertz Foundation in addition demanded at least one personal interview. Second, according to the Hertz brochure, the foundation had an "express interest in fostering the technological strength of America" and required "all Fellows to morally commit themselves to make their skills and abilities available for the common defense, in the event of national emergency."

The Hertz interviewer who met with Hagelstein was Lowell Wood, the protégé of Dr. Teller. Holding the title Coordinator, Fellowship Project, Dr. Wood received some $8,000 a year for his Hertz work. "Peter still stands out in my memory," Dr. Wood recalls. "People coming for Hertz interviews are generally quite serious about it and very eager to please. Peter showed up in a sweatsuit that had obviously just been used." Dr. Wood, who usually fired dozens of technical questions at a candidate, was able to get in only one. The sweaty graduate student then proceeded to outline an answer in brilliant detail. "He made sure he sopped up the entire interview with it," Dr. Wood recalled dryly. "I think he was interested in establishing that he could break the norms and get away with it because he was exceedingly good."

In 1975, Hagelstein was offered not only a Hertz Fellowship but, at the age of twenty, a job at the weapons lab for the summer. Before the interview, Peter had never heard of the Livermore lab. At first he hesitated to take the job, but eventually accepted. He said later that Dr. Wood had been vague about Livermore: "He said that in some ways it was like any place else. He said they were working on lasers and laser fusion, which I had never heard of before, and he said there were computer codes out there that were like playing a Wurlitzer organ. It all sounded kind of dreamy."

Driving out through rural California, the young man found the area around the weapons lab sharply at odds with the green trees and blue ponds depicted in the brochures. "I got out here at the end of May," Peter recalled. "It was close to 100 degrees and the hills were burnt brown. The place looked disgusting. I was driving down the freeway and the sign said the population of Livermore was 35,000. It seemed there were more cows than people. I took some wrong turns. The first place I ended up was Dandy Dog, where I had some lunch. I got indigestion." But the lab itself was impressive—"especially the guards and barbed wire. When I got to the personnel department, it dawned on me that they worked on weapons here, and that's about the first I knew about it. I came pretty close to leaving. I didn't want to have anything to do with it. Anyway, I met nice people, so I stayed. The people were extremely interesting."

In 1976, Hagelstein received his master's degree from M.I.T. in computer science and electrical engineering and, though he still had no desire to work on weapons, he proceeded to take up full-time work at Livermore. Like other Hertz Fellows there, he also maintained his academic status, working toward a doctorate and receiving his yearly stipend from the foundation in addition to his Livermore salary. Perhaps what really induced him to go to the weapons lab on a full-time basis was his desire to win a Nobel Prize for creating the world's first laboratory X-ray laser, a device that he saw as having no use in war but wide application in biology and medicine. Such breakthroughs, he felt, would provide clues to the riddle of cancer. Peter pursued his X-ray project by learning physics, developing ideas and writing computer codes late into the night on his trusty computer terminal. His goal was to discover the electron transitions in atoms that could be used to create a laser of extraordinarily short wavelengths. "He was working fourteen or fifteen hours a day, night and day, seven days a week," recalled Lawrence C. West, a Hertz Fellow and friend of Peter's at Livermore. Young Hagelstein's hasty meals often consisted of peanut butter sandwiches and a Coke. "He'd run to the refrigerator," West said, "open the bread, slap down some peanut butter, and go right back to the computer terminal. He worked night and day calculating atomic energy levels. There were millions of things he had to do, all of which were very exotic and relied on the most advanced physical theory. He didn't even have a physics background. He learned the most advanced quantum physics by simply reading the technical literature, which was amazing. He worked that way for seven or eight years."

Eventually, this shy young graduate student hoped to try out his X-ray ideas on Livermore's huge, multimillion-dollar lasers that generated powerful beams of visible light. But at first the Livermore laser group had no time for him. The first laser had flashed to life in 1960, and ever since, researchers had vied to create ones that worked at increasingly short wavelengths, the rule being the shorter, the more powerful, generally speaking. All laser light is concentrated, or coherent; that is, its waves are in step with one another.

Peter Hagelstein, the young father of the nuclear-powered X-ray laser, had sought a biomedical use for lasers. Here he is seen in 1987 with a supercomputer at Lawrence Livermore National Laboratory in California, where he became involved in the development of Star Wars weapons.
© 1987 ROGER RESSMEYER/STARLIGHT

It has a synchronized, pounding rhythm. Regular light, on the other hand, such as that from an electric lightbulb, is incoherent; its helter-skelter waves mix together like those in a choppy sea. Over the years since 1960, scientists gradually were able to shift their attention in laser work from the reddish region of the electromagnetic spectrum, to the ultraviolet region, and finally to the X-ray region, always moving toward wavelengths that were shorter and shorter.

As Hagelstein pursued his peaceful X-ray studies, others at Livermore were trying to create X-ray lasers that were millions of times more powerful—and energized by nuclear bombs.

It took time, but the weapons designers at Livermore eventually persuaded him to join them. The temptation to triumph over a rival was too powerful to resist.

For decades, scientists at Livermore had envisioned nuclear weapons used to dig ditches, blast asteroids and "pump" all kinds of exotic beam weapons, including X-ray lasers. But their ideas for nuclear lasers never panned out. In 1977, however, a senior Livermore physicist named Dr. George Chapline came up with a novel (and still highly classified) idea for building an X-ray laser pumped by a nuclear bomb. The explosive test of Chapline's idea took place at the Nevada Test Site, the government's desolate tract for the underground detonation of nuclear weapons. Code-named Diablo Hawk, the test rumbled to life on September 13, 1978. Although the bomb indeed went off, the elaborate apparatus of detectors and sensors for measuring the output of the X-ray experiment broke down. No one knew whether Chapline's innovative idea was a success or failure.

As preparations and discussions intensified in advance of a second attempt in 1979, Dr. Chapline and the senior weapons scientists began to hold regular meetings. Hagelstein's views were eagerly sought because he knew the theoretics of X-ray lasers better than anyone else at the weapons lab, and he sat in on some of the discussions. But he says he still resisted making a contribution: He hated bombs. He wanted to avoid work on anything nuclear. This sentiment was reinforced by a woman he dated at the time, Josephine A. Stein.

Josie and Peter had met at M.I.T. during the early 1970s in the student symphony. She was a mechanical engineer who could talk comfortably with him about stress values or Schubert. During the summer of 1978 she moved from Cambridge to Berkeley to begin work on a master's degree at the University of California. She looked him up at Livermore and the two were soon seeing a good deal of each other. As Josie learned about the lab and what it did, she became vocal in her opposition. She said bombs were bombs, and would always be agents of death and destruction. She told Peter that Dr. Wood and Dr. Teller were using him for their own ends. At one point she marched with protesters outside Livermore's barbed-wire fences, and she encouraged Peter to quit.

In May 1979, Peter and Josie went to a concert in San Francisco. When they emerged from the concert hall, a riot was in progress in which police were swinging nightsticks and protestors were bleeding. Josie wanted to help. Peter wanted to get away. A bitter argument ensued in which Josie accused Peter of ignoring the inhumanity of his work. It would injure and maim just as surely as the riot police did, she screamed. Peter defended himself, denying that his labors had any application to weaponry. It was pure science, he insisted.

Because he did loathe the idea of working on weapons, he had usually done things at the lab that in his own mind had no relation to them. But there came a day when that all clearly changed. It was during the summer of 1979 at one of Dr. Chapline's meetings. In his typical way, Peter had just been on an around-the-clock working binge. Now, fatigued from work and lack of sleep, his subconscious seemed to take over. He appeared to be viewing himself from a distance, and there he was, saying something new in the arcane world of nuclear X-ray lasers. His superiors, startled at the novelty of the idea, pressed him to develop it. "I got my arm twisted to do a detailed calculation," Peter recalled. "I resisted doing it. There were political pressures like you wouldn't believe." He was asked to sit at his computer terminal day after day, pouring his special expertise into the calculation of what might happen when a certain setup was "pumped" by a nuclear explosion.

Despite his own fears and the protests of his girlfriend, Peter began to work on the problem. The enticements and pressures were too much. Among them were the intellectual challenge, a growing rivalry with Dr. Chapline, and a desire to win the approval of Dr. Teller and Dr. Wood. Perhaps most of all, there was the possible loss of his friends at the lab. Peter, after all, was being asked to participate in a regular part of the laboratory's agenda. If he refused, there probably would be no overt display of resentment on the part of lab officials. But it might spoil things enough so that eventually he would feel compelled to leave. This would mean giving up his association with people of whom he had become very fond. It would mean giving up what had become his home, leaving the only place in the world where he had ever really been understood.

Peter's design showed great promise as it evolved. Lab officials decided to include a test of it in Dr. Chapline's underground experiment. At this point, Peter's relationship with Josie started, predictably, to fall apart. "At first I tended to agree with her," Peter said, "but she was terribly adamant," and he became very depressed.

The nuclear test occurred on November 14, 1980. Dr. Wood and Dr. Chapline were at the Nevada Test Site, worrying about details of the setup. Peter was back in California, worrying about what he had done. It turned out to be a success for both experiments, although Peter's results were far superior. To celebrate, Dr. Wood took Peter and several other members of the group to Livermore for ice cream at Baskin-Robbins.

But there was no ice cream with Josie, the breakup having distanced their friendship. Peter, plunging deeper into depression, became elusive and brooding for a time, and, at the office, played nothing on his stereo but requiems by Brahms, Verdi and Mozart. Still, he continued working at the lab, and doors there began to open for him. Most important, he gained access to the laboratory's big lasers, allowing him to forge ahead on experiments with nonnuclear X-ray lasers. Ironically, however, his original reason for pursuing that research seemed to vanish. He felt that scientists working with electron microscopes and other advanced devices had improved their techniques to the point where these tools were better suited to achieving his long-sought biomedical goals.

As he continued to make important advances on the nuclear X-ray laser, Josie worked more vigorously than ever to promote public debate over nuclear arms. After the breakup with Peter, she returned to M.I.T. to work on her Ph.D. In Cambridge she played with a chamber music group known as the No Nukes Trio. She wrote an article in the M.I.T. biweekly student newspaper. Headlined "Fellowship for Work on 'Human Problems' Linked to Livermore," the article was a detailed account of how the Hertz Foundation recruited young scientists, and the central illustration was a picture of Dr. Teller. The thrust of her accusation was deception—that the foundation, ostensibly set up to fund graduate education, in truth recruited unsuspecting students to work on the design of nuclear weapons.

The newspaper article made no mention of Hagelstein. It dealt instead in generalities. But Josie clearly had strong feelings about why Peter had ended up at Livermore. It started off by noting that another M.I.T. newspaper, *Tech Talk*, had run ads from the Hertz Foundation soliciting applications to its fellowship program. A picture of one ad was printed. "The proposed field of graduate study" it read, "must be concerned with applications of the physical sciences to human problems, broadly construed." In her article Josie commented: "From the information in the announcements, one would never guess that the administration of the fellowship has close ties with the Lawrence Livermore National Laboratory, one of the two national laboratories dedicated to the research and development of nuclear weapons." She then drove the point home, noting Dr. Teller's place on the Hertz board, the foundation's address, and the fact that Dr. Wood was the foundation's chief recruiter as well as leader of the group of young weapon wizards, which "is largely composed of Hertz Fellows and Hertz alumni."

With a sharp eye, Josie noted shifting language in Hertz publications. Starting with vague statements about "the enhancement of the defense potential and technological stature of the United States," she traced a path to a statement that a candidate had to sign in the presence of two witnesses: "I acknowledge," said the statement, that Hertz "education and training will be of value to the United States in defense against any potential or actual enemy." Said Josie: "The wording is considerably stronger than anything in the previous literature." Josie then forged the final link in the chain. "The

Peter Hagelstein's girlfriend, Josie Stein, tried to dissuade him from working on nuclear weapons. Their relationship fell apart just about the time the successful test of his X-ray laser was made at the Nevada test site.

PHOTO BY GERALD L. EPSTEIN

personal interview," she wrote, "may be conducted by Livermore employees, who may use the occasion to recruit the students for summer employment and subsequent graduate work to be done at the laboratory."

At the end of the article she suggested that the Hertz Fellowship program was "in reality a deceptive campaign to recruit the most capable young technologists to work on nuclear-weapons-related projects at Lawrence Livermore" and warned prospective applicants "to carefully consider the implications of involvement with the foundation and Livermore." Not content merely to write about Hertz, Josie also put her feelings about nuclear weaponry to work in volunteer programs. She joined High Technology Professionals for Peace, a Cambridge-based group that ran an employment service for scientists and engineers seeking alternatives to work on weapons.

She wrote Peter from time to time. Though he was working on his M.I.T. doctoral thesis, he remained at the weapons lab. For her it seemed an ironic culmination of events when her friend, a young scientist who had not wanted to work on bombs, but who became highly praised in top-secret government circles for his nuclear X-ray laser breakthrough, submitted his thesis under the title "Physics of Short Wavelength Laser Design." It was a primer on the theoretics of making a laboratory X-ray laser, a goal he had so far failed to achieve. In its foreword Peter "gratefully acknowledged" the financial aid of the Fannie and John Hertz Foundation.

The 451 pages of the dissertation were thick with equations and scholarly references. At one point, however, it broke from its esoteric pace to suggest "future applications." Three works of science fiction were cited. In one of them, *Ringworld*, by Larry Niven, a spaceship was hit by beam weapons as it approached a foreign world.

"We have been fired upon," cried a crew member. "We are still being fired upon, probably by X-ray lasers. This ship is now in a state of war."

"An X-ray laser is invariably a weapon of war," shouted another crew member. "Were it not for our invulnerable hull, we would be dead."

For Peter, the reference to death rays bespoke a fear that his higher, peaceful ambitions for the X-ray laser would always be in danger of being subverted into instruments of war. "Writers of science fiction are supposed to look into the future," he said. "So I started looking to see what they had in mind for X-ray lasers. It turns out all the science-fiction references are to blowing things up. It's fairly discouraging."

In 1981 after winning his Ph.D., Hagelstein was presented an "Exceptional Ph.D. Dissertation Award" by the Hertz Foundation, which included a cash prize. As he ambivalently pursued work on nuclear weaponry at Livermore, Peter continued to try to ignore its military uses and focus instead on its scientific aspects. Nevertheless there was, in fact, a major shift in his thinking. "My view of weapons has changed," he said years later with a smile and what had to be construed as dry understatement. "Until 1980 or so, I didn't want to have anything to do with nuclear anything. Back in those days, I thought there was something fundamentally evil about weapons. Now I see it as an interesting physics problem."

On the issue of whether an antimissile shield was feasible, Peter shifted back and forth, clearly uneasy and tending to see limitations. "It would be very nice if we could develop a defense network that would blow away all Soviet ICBMs, but I don't think we can do that," he said. "We could take out some, but I don't think we could take out all of them. Even if we could, that would not stop war or get rid of the nuclear threat, people being what they are. Getting up a defensive system might help things somewhat. But it wouldn't keep cities from being obliterated."

Though he was now working on nuclear weapons, Peter also continued to pursue his original X-ray goal, although it had lost some of its original luster. And he eventually attained it. In October 1984, nearly a decade after he arrived at the lab, Peter had his work hailed by a team of Livermore scientists at the annual meeting of the plasma physics division of the American Physical Society. They announced that they and Peter had succeeded in creating the world's first laboratory X-ray laser. The breakthrough—in what the researchers described as the "soft" X-ray region of the electromagnetic spectrum—was obtained by focusing a flash of light from a large conventional laboratory laser onto targets made of yttrium, a rare silvery metal. Unlike the X-ray laser designed for space, the soft version would not be triggered by a nuclear explosion. Instead, it would require pumping by a

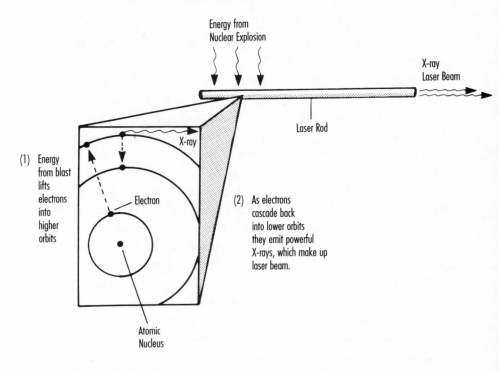

Peter Hagelstein's laser: How it works.   SIMON & SCHUSTER

conventional laser so large that the usefulness of the laser would be limited to science, industry and medicine, just as Peter originally envisioned. Indeed, the Livermore experiments had been carried out on the Novette laser, part of a huge $176 million laser system known as Nova.

In 1984, *Science Digest* named Peter one of the nation's brightest young scientists. In 1985, Peter's celebrity increased as tales of his nuclear break-throughs started to reach the public. He was the central figure in a book, *Star Warriors*, and was profiled in *The New York Times Magazine*. His picture appeared on the cover of *Science Digest*. His story was recounted in the pages of *Granta*, a British literary journal.

Then, at the age of thirty-two, while at the pinnacle of his atomic fame, Peter suddenly turned his back on it all. In October 1986, without so much as a hint of public explanation, he resigned from the Livermore weapons lab to take up a teaching and nonmilitary research post at Massachusetts Institute of Technology, his old stomping grounds. Newspapers and maga-zines around the country noted the move. "Troubled Laser Scientist Quitting Weapons Work," read the headline in the *Washington Post*. "A Crisis of Conscience," said *Newsweek*. "A Laser's Inventor Ending Arms Work," said

The New York Times. The Associated Press hailed Peter as "one of the top physicists" of President Reagan's Star Wars plan and quoted several scientists who said the loss dealt the program a serious blow.

When he left Livermore, Hagelstein turned down dozens of requests for interviews from journalists around the world. A colleague at M.I.T. said Peter had problems with the management style at Livermore but was also still troubled by weapons work. "He got caught up in the weapons program out there," said Dr. Richard Adler, associate head of the electrical engineering and computer science department at M.I.T. "Weapons troubled Peter in the past and when he went there he had trouble working on military things. He resolved that, but I think that's a component of his decision." Dr. Adler said, too, there was a desire to return to campus life: "Peter may fit better in an academic situation than in a monolithic, dedicated, mission-oriented activity."

The colleague noted, finally, that Peter's résumé submitted to M.I.T. had said he wanted to do work that would "benefit all mankind."

"He'll be missed greatly," said Dr. Steve Maxon, a senior physicist in Livermore's X-ray laser program. "Peter is essentially the basis of our ability to calculate X-ray lasers. I think he's the brightest physicist I've ever worked with, and I've been at the lab twenty-five years." Maxon added that he doubted Peter left the lab because of moral objections. "I've seen Peter operate on both sides, in the lab and in underground experiments, and I know he's interested in both, regardless of what people say."

"It will be a tremendous loss for our program," said Dr. Chapline. "You don't replace a Peter Hagelstein."

The White House refused comment. Army Lieut. Colonel Lee DeLorme, a spokesman for the Pentagon's Star Wars program, discounted the impact of Peter's resignation. "There are thousands of dedicated scientists and researchers across the country working on the Strategic Defense Initiative program, and the departure of any one of them does not have a significant impact on the overall program," he said.

Josie read of the resignation in the newspapers. Now a Ph.D., Josie worked for an arms control program at Princeton University, often informally counseling military scientists to seek alternatives to work on weapons. Her reaction was simple.

Hours before the office was open, she left a brief message that spoke volumes on a reporter's message-recording machine at *The New York Times*:

"Hooray!" she cheered. "He's out!"

3

THE ORIGINS
OF MAD

From that day in August 1945 when the atomic bomb exploded over Hiroshima, there has been a nuclear peace. Never once have those states possessing nuclear weapons—first the United States, then the Soviet Union, Great Britain, France and China—used them in combat. Perhaps only once, during the Cuban missile crisis of 1962, did the United States and the Soviet Union even come close to blows. It is a record of "peace" between great powers unrivaled in modern history.

Nuclear peace rested on the continuing recognition of a simple and overwhelming fact: Nuclear war meant mutual destruction. There would be no winners in any meaningful sense; all would be losers. Nuclear peace was founded on this bedrock of fear for over forty years. Winston Churchill captured the essence of the nuclear era: "It may well be that we shall, by a process of sublime irony, have reached a stage in this story where safety shall be the sturdy child of terror, and survival the twin brother of annihilation."

Military strategy had to be rethought, revolutionized. As Bernard Brodie, one of the founders of modern military strategy, put it: "Thus far the chief purpose of our military establishment has been to win wars. From now on its chief purpose must be to avert them." For those who had nuclear weapons and for those who felt threatened by them, the calculations no longer centered on whether to attack or to defend. The overriding goal of strategy in the nuclear age had to be deterrence or prevention of war.

The first step in developing a theology or doctrine or strategy was simple: Maintain sufficient and survivable nuclear force to absorb the first blow and still be able to respond with a devastating counterattack. In this way, a would-be attacker would always know that he could gain nothing of consequence by striking first, and so would be deterred. But how to do this was not self-evident. For almost four decades, political leaders and the cognoscenti of American national security policy struggled over how to maintain deterrence, what to do if deterrence failed, and how nuclear weapons would affect power politics and diplomacy. They debated bitterly over questions with enormous political explosivity.

Which side was ahead, Moscow or Washington? Was the Soviet Union about to gain nuclear superiority? Did it matter? If Moscow was stronger, would Soviet leaders feel they could strike first and win? Were new technology and new weapons undermining deterrence? Would mutual nuclear deterrence make nonnuclear or conventional war with the Soviet Union more likely? Would Moscow be tempted to use its nonnuclear or conventional military superiority in Europe in the belief that Washington would fear to redress the balance by employing nuclear weapons?

What if deterrence failed? Should Washington be the first to use nuclear weapons to break the back of a Soviet attack in Europe? If Moscow hit first with nuclear weapons, should the American response be total? Or should the President have alternatives short of all-out response? Would preparing to fight nuclear wars in this manner make such wars more likely in the first place? Could this kind of war be won or lost in any meaningful sense?

As political fortunes changed, as perceptions of Soviet intentions and might varied, and as new technologies appeared on the horizon, theories of deterrence waxed and waned. The Eisenhower administration fashioned the idea of the "massive retaliation" threat to dissuade Moscow from attack. The Kennedy team felt that this threat would not be credible to Soviet leaders. They regrouped around the concept of "flexible response," or responding at levels comparable to the level of attack. To this, they added the concept of "mutual assured destruction"—MAD, for short—or deterrence through the capability to absorb a first strike and still destroy the attacker's society. The Nixon administration seemed to reaffirm this by proclaiming that nuclear superiority provided little advantage, and that the United States therefore would content itself with forces "sufficient" to assure a devastating retaliatory blow. The Ford administration, however brief it was, pressed to marry sufficiency for deterrence to "limited nuclear options." The idea was to enhance deterrence and provide options for response should deterrence fail. The Carter administration carried this idea of deterrence through nuclear-war-fighting capabilities a step further in what it called a "countervailing strategy." President Reagan and his top advisers took the possibilities of nuclear-war-fighting far more seriously than their predecessors. In the early years of his administration, they carried the idea to the extreme of arguing that nuclear wars could be won or lost in meaningful ways, and that the American objective should be to "prevail."

From the early Truman administration to the present, every President has tried either to enhance deterrence or escape from the nuclear nightmare entirely. Enhancement was pursued by building better and more survivable offensive weapons. At times, survivability of weapons was to be achieved by protecting them with ballistic-missile defenses. Escape was, at times, sought after through arms-control arrangements including the elimination of nuclear arms, and sometimes through the idea of protecting people with ballistic-missile defenses. Uniquely, Ronald Reagan chased the goals of both enhancement and escape.

The story of deterrence began with President Truman at a time when the United States possessed only a handful of atomic bombs. Little pressure existed to increase that stockpile. Almost all pressures were in precisely the opposite direction. But enter a financier and philanthropist: Bernard Baruch. In 1946, Mr. Truman asked him to develop a plan for the control of atomic power. The Baruch plan was presented to the fledgling United Nations later that year. It called for the establishment of an International Atomic Development Authority to control "all phases of the development and use of atomic energy." This international authority, and not individual nation-states, was to have complete charge of all facilities for bomb making. It was also to have power to punish states seeking to acquire such bombs. The Soviet Union, without an atomic bomb of its own, rejected the proposal. It called on the United States to destroy its bombs and pledge never to use them again. In

1949, Moscow exploded its first atomic device, and a month later, the United Nations dropped the Baruch plan.

Periodically over the next decade, the two superpowers put forward grand schemes for escape, but got nowhere. They engaged in fruitless fights and propaganda battles over how to begin. Moscow demanded complete atomic disarmament followed by the creation of an international supervisory authority. Washington insisted on having the international authority in place to supervise disarmament. But meanwhile, stockpiles grew slowly, and American military planners made no special distinction between conventional forces and atomic bombs. The bombs were there as a deterrent, to be sure. But their main role was in battle, as a means of quickly destroying Soviet urban and industrial areas. The few bombs that were available were thought of as city-busters.

President Eisenhower introduced the idea of escaping the nuclear nightmare through arms control between the superpowers rather than through an international authority. Also, unlike the Baruch plan, he did not seek the elimination of strategic weapons. That goal seemed too remote and unrealistic, given the mistrust between the two sides. To chip away at that mistrust, the former Supreme Allied Commander proposed in 1954 Atoms for Peace. He hoped common ground could perhaps be found in the joint pursuit of peaceful uses of atomic energy. In 1957, he followed this with an Open Skies proposal. The idea here was for both sides to permit aerial inspection of their territories to guard against surprise attack. Mr. Eisenhower clearly realized that if an escape route were to be found, the two sides would have to work together in a step-by-step fashion over a long period.

While Mr. Eisenhower's two modest arms-control proposals foundered, his top national security aides focused on ways to enhance deterrence at the lowest possible cost to the federal treasury. Conventional forces cost too much, and soon Mr. Eisenhower moved away from Truman administration plans for expanding the Army and Navy and toward expanding atomic and nuclear striking power. "More bang for the buck," they called it. And the biggest bang resulted from the leap from atomic bombs to nuclear bombs and warheads. Atomic bombs were fission weapons with the explosion created by bombarding the nuclei of atoms. Nuclear or hydrogen weapons of up to one thousand times greater explosive power were the product of fusing nuclei, not splitting them. Destructive power was from then on measured in megatons or millions of tons of TNT, and not simply kilotons or thousands of tons of TNT, as with the approximately twelve-kiloton Hiroshima bomb. Perhaps some military planners thought of employing atomic weapons in warfare as a superconventional bomb. But it was virtually inconceivable to think of using the nuclear offspring.

■

Deterrence thus became an even greater imperative as the goal of national policy. The earliest Eisenhower strategic planning documents made explicit that the role of nuclear weapons was principally to prevent or deter wars. Communist attacks, Secretary of State John Foster Dulles announced in 1954, would be met with massive retaliation by American nuclear forces. Deterrence, he said, would be maintained by having "a great capacity to retaliate, instantly, by means and at places of our own choosing."

Eisenhower, however, began a substantial buildup of the nuclear stockpile. In addition, he deployed hundreds of much smaller, "tactical" atomic weapons to Europe. And, of equal significance, the U-2 spy plane began flying high above Soviet territory, bringing Washington the first highly reliable information about the deployed Soviet nuclear arsenal. The aircraft could snap pictures pinpointing the exact location of Soviet forces. For the first time, this permitted Washington to target Soviet strategic bombers and missiles. For the first time, nuclear weapons could be used against forces as well as cities. For the time being, the Eisenhower administration continued to plan for an all-out single-spasm war, hitting all targets, civilian and military, at once—the ultimate deterrent, they thought.

However, just when deterrence presented itself as absolutely necessary, it seemed to fall into question. Moscow's launching of a satellite named Sputnik generated nothing short of panic in the United States. Suddenly, the Soviets had swift intercontinental-range striking power, a missile that could hit American territory in thirty minutes in contrast to the four-hour flying time of a bomber. This put American bombers, the heart of Washington's retaliatory power, in jeopardy. Immediately, Mr. Eisenhower expedited programs to develop and deploy new American intercontinental ballistic missiles, or ICBMs, and submarines to fire submarine-launched ballistic missiles, SLBMs.

At a stroke, Sputnik seemed to threaten the basis of deterrence. Instead of clear-cut American nuclear superiority, it appeared that the Soviet Union was, or could be, on top—and soon. Instead of the United States having a secure retaliatory force, it seemed as if Moscow could wreck this in thirty minutes. Of almost equal alarm, it seemed as if massive retaliation was simply not a credible deterrent threat. Did it stop Communist adventurism, the critics asked, in Korea in 1950 or in Indochina in 1954? Perhaps such a threat could not be credible once the Soviet Union got the bomb. Perhaps as matters stood, Moscow would believe that only a direct, Pearl Harbor–style attack on the United States itself would call forth an American nuclear response.

One of President Kennedy's first acts was to reaffirm deterrence as the principal goal of his nuclear strategy. More so than Mr. Eisenhower, however, he worried about whether the United States still possessed a secure retaliatory force. His own campaign rhetoric in the 1960 presidential race primed him for this. "The missile gap" was transformed on Inauguration Day from a slogan to the driving force behind policy. It would take the young President and his formidable Defense Secretary, Robert S. McNamara, another year or two to act on the knowledge that the missile gap did indeed starkly exist—in America's favor.

In the full flush of 1961, though, the campaign rhetoric and fears were realities. In early testimony before Congress, McNamara put it this way: "In the age of nuclear-armed intercontinental ballistic missiles, the ability to deter rests heavily on the existence of a force which can weather or survive a massive nuclear attack, even with little or no warning, in sufficient strength to strike a decisive counterblow." So the preoccupation shifted smartly to survivability of forces to enhance deterrence. To this end, Kennedy and McNamara began full development of what came to be called the "strategic triad" of ICBMs, SLBMs and long-range bombers. The premise here was safety in numbers and variety. Moscow would be unable to mount an attack sufficient to knock out every leg of the triad at once. The Soviets might successfully strike at bombers not on alert and most of the ICBMs. But they would not be able to hit all of the ICBMs and SLBMs simultaneously. Thus, it became a cardinal principle of nuclear policy, holding to this day, that Washington must do whatever necessary to preserve each leg of the triad.

Bombers had been the backbone of the deterrent force for fifteen years, but not in the missile age. The mainstays became the ICBMs and SLBMs. Instead of intermediate-range missiles based in Europe, the United States would deploy intercontinental-range missiles based in the United States. This would give Washington more warning time to launch them in the event of attack. For added protection, the ICBMs, dubbed Minutemen, would be placed underground in hardened silos. There, they could withstand all but almost a direct hit. The submarines carrying SLBMs were named Polaris, and Kennedy accelerated their deployment and doubled their numbers from the Eisenhower program. Underwater, they would be safe from the prying eyes of spy aircraft and, soon thereafter, spy satellites. Beneath the seas, they would maintain their invulnerability and become the ultimate retaliatory force.

Then administration thinking on deterrence took a curious twist. In part, this resulted from the realization that the United States still retained nuclear superiority. Better intelligence showed that. Partly, it derived from the experience of the Cuban Missile Crisis of October 1962. Moscow surreptitiously deployed medium-range missiles in Cuba and lied about it. Kennedy threatened nuclear war unless the missiles were removed. They were, as part of a complicated deal in which Washington pledged not to attack Cuba and to remove American intermediate or medium-range missiles from Europe. But after the thirteen days of crisis with the two superpowers on the brink of nuclear war, leaders on both sides found themselves changed and chastened.

In 1963, McNamara announced that administration programs to build 1,000 Minutemen and 656 SLBMs were enough, and that further production would bring "diminishing returns." Even before this, he proclaimed the theory of mutual deterrence. "When both sides have a sure second-strike capability, then you might have a more stable balance of terror," he said. The statement was nothing short of revolutionary. Nuclear peace, he was saying, rested not on American superiority but upon something resembling parity. Rather than seeking an American first-strike capability, he was urging Moscow to develop a secure second-strike force. He was proclaiming the arrival of the age of nuclear stalemate. But neither he nor his successors would stick to that judgment. Something, a new weapon, a new fear, would always be on the horizon to unsettle thinking and destabilize the nuclear balance.

Logic might have taken this strain of thought down the path of minimum deterrence and away from overkill. Logic seemed to indicate that absolute power to destroy, not relative power, would be enough. But domestic political pressures and the march of technology took American and Soviet leaders in another direction.

Mr. McNamara had put together his first single integrated operations plan, or SIOP, for fighting nuclear war in 1961. Unlike the Eisenhower plan, the new SIOP called for holding nuclear forces in reserve even after the first retaliatory blow. There was to be no single-spasm war. And contrary to talk of stalemate, he even held out the possibility of winning. "We may seek to terminate a war on favorable terms by using our forces as a bargaining weapon—by threatening further attack. In any case, our large reserve of protected firepower would give an enemy an incentive to avoid our cities and to stop a war."

These ideas were to take further shape in June 1963 in a speech at the University of Michigan. There, he unveiled his no-cities, or counterforce, doctrine. Nuclear forces would be employed, so far as possible, to attack other nuclear forces and to spare populated areas. He was, in effect, asking the Soviets to cooperate in saving lives by avoiding strikes on cities, in the event deterrence failed. The idea was for both sides to cooperate to limit damage.

The speech found little warm welcome. Some domestic critics argued it would lead to a justification of American first-strike capability. European leaders felt that it would weaken deterrence in Europe. If Moscow felt that Washington would not hold Soviet cities to task in the event of a Soviet attack on Western Europe, such an attack might become more likely. Perhaps, some of them said, in the age of nuclear parity Washington would not put American cities at risk to save European cities.

McNamara retreated behind the doctrine of flexible and controlled response or graduated deterrence. There would be no more incredible threats to bomb Moscow in retaliation for guerrilla wars in Indochina. Attacks would be met by equal force where they occurred. That would be believable and thus enhance deterrence. Deterrence would hang on America's capacity to make equal and gradudated responses at any level on which a threat would be posed. And in the event Soviet conventional forces attacked and began to overwhelm Western forces in Europe, the United States would reserve the right to use nuclear weapons first, including against Soviet cities, and even at the risk of a counterattack on American cities.

The twin strategic pillars of flexible and graduated response were the concepts of assured destruction and damage limitation. Assured destruction meant that Washington would build its forces so that even after absorbing a full surprise attack, it could respond by destroying some 40 percent of Soviet society and industry. And by also deploying forces capable of destroying Soviet forces, Washington would be able to limit damage to the United States. Damage limitation was to be accomplished by developing missiles that could destroy Soviet missiles in their silos, that is, by having a counterforce capability. But there was another, much more technologically demanding way to limit damage always lurking in the background.

Air defenses had been around for a long time. None were ever wholly successful in thwarting an attack. Most bombers were able to penetrate them.

Nevertheless, Eisenhower had launched an even more ambitious program in 1956. Named the Nike-Zeus program, the idea was to use a missile to shoot down another missile in flight. Kennedy would later refer to this as "hitting a bullet with another bullet."

After a few years of increasing pressure to deploy what had become the Nike-X, McNamara pronounced the effort promising but unready to face the daunting operational problems of target acquisition, decoys and battle management. He said he would continue research and development, but not go forward with deployment. The program, however, received a further lift when Soviet leader Nikita Khrushchev boasted that he possessed defenses that could "hit a fly in the sky." Kennedy conceded one fly, but not "a thousand flies with decoys." That, he continued, "is a terribly difficult task," and "the offense has the advantage."

This decision to forgo ABM or antiballistic missile development held until 1967. President Johnson, faced with growing cries from conservative quarters, ordered McNamara to proceed with some antiballistic missile deployment. The Defense Secretary responded with the Sentinel program, aimed at protecting American cities from a small nuclear attack by a country such as China. Ballistic-missile defense against a Soviet attack, he said, would be impossible. Soon thereafter, however, McNamara modified, or better, transformed this into the idea of using the defenses to protect missiles in silos.

At this point, everything was a jumble. Doctrines were issued, ignored, modified and reinterpreted with unerring speed. But some elements stood out. One was the doctrine of flexible response, and the other was the concept of assured destruction. In 1967, McNamara said, "Damage-limiting programs, no matter how much we spend on them, can never substitute for an assured destruction capability in the deterrent role. It is our ability to destroy an attacker as a viable twentieth-century nation that provides the deterrent, not our ability to partially limit damage to ourselves." Then, in 1968, just before his resignation, he added: "For a 'damage limiting' posture to contribute significantly to the deterrent . . . it would have to be extremely effective, i.e., capable of reducing damage to truly nominal levels . . . we now have no way to accomplish this."

Without a way of limiting damage, McNamara reaffirmed his earlier idea of mutual assured deterrence or destruction, an idea that was to become the bane of conservative critics and the spur to new plans for ballistic-missile defenses. He also appealed to both sides "to try to halt the momentum of the arms race, which is causing vast expenditures on both sides and promises no increase in security."

Meanwhile, President Johnson decided to begin replacing single nuclear warheads sitting atop missiles with multiple independently targetable warheads, or MIRVs. This led to an enormous increase in the number of nuclear warheads and to important increases in accuracy as well. From this decision, nuclear arsenals on both sides were to grow from a few thousand each to over 10,000 strategic nuclear weapons and bombs each. Mr. Johnson's principal justification for this move was that more warheads were needed to overcome Soviet advances in the development of ballistic-missile defenses.

Presidents Kennedy and Johnson left a bewildering legacy through their Defense Secretary. There was the abiding faith in assured destruction, suggesting that enough was enough. There was the intellectual damning of damage limitation, coupled with a decision to begin deploying defenses to limit damage. There was the need to maintain flexible response capabilities, which was another way of saying that the United States had to be prepared to fight wars at different levels in order to deter them. Finally, there was the renewed call for arms limitation negotiations with Moscow. McNamara pushed hard to get those talks under way, only to have them canceled by the Soviet invasion of Czechoslovakia in August 1968.

During the Nixon and Ford presidencies, the major change in the strategic equation resulted from the vast growth in numbers of ballistic missile warheads. More warheads striking with greater accuracy meant more targets to hit, military and civilian. (Warheads did not need much accuracy to destroy cities.) All of this produced a steady accretion of war-fighting capabilities on both sides.

Inevitably, the principal concern became which side could do it better. Fear mounted that Moscow was either ahead or about to be. This, in turn, could lead to Soviet diplomatic advantages and to the Soviets having the edge in "blinking power" should the superpowers find themselves in another situation like the Cuban missile crisis. Maybe in the next crisis, so experts worried, it would be Washington and not Moscow that would blink first and give in.

Of growing and equal concern, American officials and experts feared American strategic power might no longer be able to deter a Soviet attack on Western Europe. With Moscow having substantial nuclear strength,

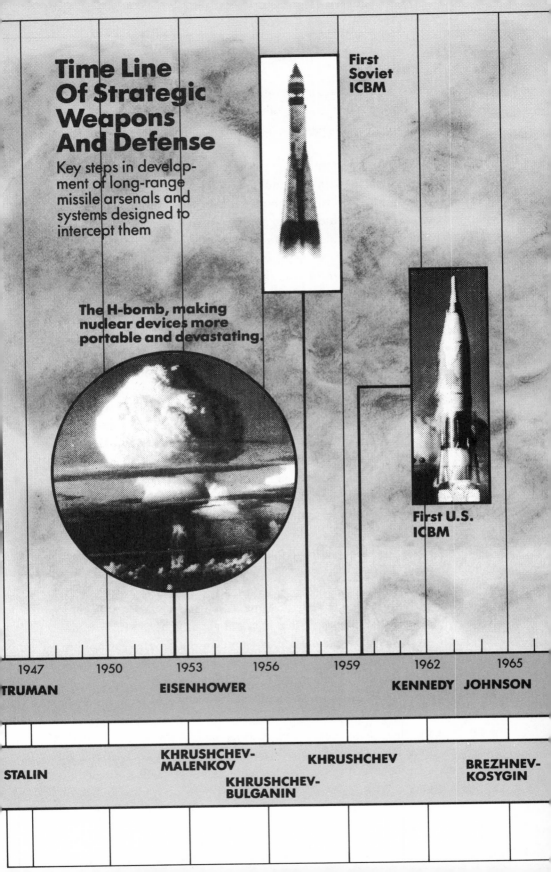

Time Line Of Strategic Weapons And Defense

Key steps in development of long-range missile arsenals and systems designed to intercept them

First Soviet ICBM

The H-bomb, making nuclear devices more portable and devastating.

First U.S. ICBM

1947	1950	1953	1956	1959	1962	1965		
TRUMAN		EISENHOWER			KENNEDY	JOHNSON		

STALIN		KHRUSHCHEV-MALENKOV	KHRUSHCHEV-BULGANIN	KHRUSHCHEV			BREZHNEV-KOSYGIN	

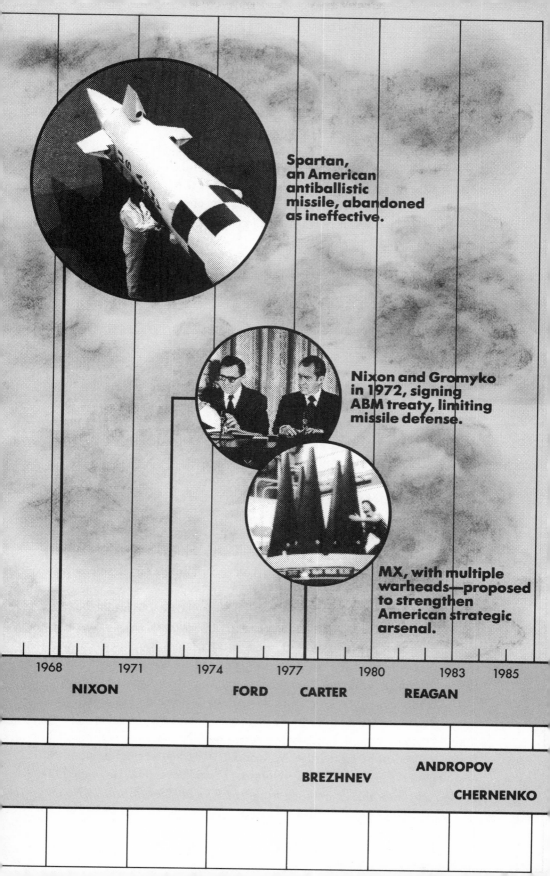

Spartan,
an American
antiballistic
missile, abandoned
as ineffective.

Nixon and Gromyko
in 1972, signing
ABM treaty, limiting
missile defense.

MX, with multiple
warheads—proposed
to strengthen
American strategic
arsenal.

| 1968 | 1971 | 1974 | 1977 | 1980 | 1983 | 1985 |

NIXON   **FORD**   **CARTER**   **REAGAN**

BREZHNEV   **ANDROPOV**

CHERNENKO

threats of nuclear retaliation would not be a credible deterrent. With Moscow having roughly equal war-fighting capability, threats to out-gun Moscow would not carry much weight either.

To overcome these concerns, the Nixon administration felt it had three choices: It could press ahead with an antiballistic missile system to defend cities or missiles. It could increase American forces to regain strategic superiority. Or it could settle for refinements, to create better, rather than more, forces. Mr. Nixon pursued all three routes and made considerable adjustments as he went along.

In one of his earlier decisions, Mr. Nixon opted for the Safeguard antiballistic missile defense system. Its aim would be to protect missiles, not people. Thus, it could redress or head off Soviet gains in being able to destroy American missiles in a war-fighting scenario. From the outset, however, strategists were plagued by doubts of Safeguard's technical feasibility and by even graver doubts of its wisdom. In other words, some critics opposed Safeguard because they argued it would not work, and some because they feared it might. The latter concerns revolved around the calculation that Safeguard might begin as a system to protect missiles but soon expand into population defense. The combination of defense and offense could prove dangerous or destabilizing, so the argument ran. One side might strike first with a small number of missiles and destroy almost all of the other side's retaliatory forces. The weakened retaliatory blow could then be blunted by the ABM system. The country that struck first would still have nuclear forces in reserve and would rule the world.

Even as the country debated the doctrinal and technical issues, Nixon moved to negotiate limits on ABM systems with Moscow. In 1972, he and Soviet leader Leonid I. Brezhnev signed an accord limiting each side to two defensive missile sites (later reduced to one), and severely restricting tests to develop new ABM systems. This was part of an agreement to limit offensive nuclear forces embodied in the strategic arms limitation talks, or what came to be called SALT I. In 1974, Defense Secretary James R. Schlesinger said that the ratification of the ABM Treaty "effectively removed the concept of defensive damage limitation from contention as a major strategic option."

The United States was essentially abandoning the option of limiting damage by defending itself. But this still left open the option of deterring and limiting damage by restoring strategic superiority. Nixon, however, rejected this as well when he signed the five-year SALT I pact freezing the number of superpower missile launchers. (Numbers of warheads, however, were not limited and both sides continued to put MIRVs on their missiles.) Nixon termed his doctrine one of "sufficiency." More was not needed. Strategic superiority was a thing of the past, never to be regained, his doctrine implied.

Meanwhile, the Nixon and Ford administrations moved ahead with available offensive technology and made refinements in striking power and doctrine. The driving force was still concern about war-fighting and perceptions of Soviet superiority. Schlesinger called for building new and more powerful ICBMs, including one to be named the MX. He had two purposes in mind. One was to avoid perceptions of Soviet superiority by building a weapon, the MX, as fearsome as the new large Soviet missiles. The second purpose was to initiate what came to be called the doctrine of limited nuclear options, or LNOs. He wanted to get away from massive strikes, and technology was about to make that possible. "Rather than massive options," he said, "we now want to provide the President with a wider set of much more selective targeting options." This was soon embodied in a document known as National Security Decision Memorandum 242.

The Nixon-Ford legacy represented a certain consistency. The two Presidents rejected ABMs and thoughts of regaining traditional superiority. They settled into beliefs of parity, sufficiency and mutual assured destruction or retaliation. Nixon, in particular, made the first serious starts on an arms-control dialogue with Moscow. These were small and practical steps, a chipping away at the problem rather than seeing arms control as an escape from the nuclear dilemma. Nixon treated arms control more as a political process for managing Soviet-American relations than as a means of solving security problems. The Nixon-Ford years, however, brought the United States further toward developing a war-fighting capability. There was no escape from the nuclear nightmare, Nixon and Ford seemed to say, only shoring up traditional deterrence by expanding options to fight if deterrence failed.

Jimmy Carter, for a brief and politically costly moment, flirted with more daring means of escape. He toyed with the idea of proposing that the superpowers eliminate all but some 200 submarine-launched ballistic missiles. Then he quickly dropped the idea when confronted with the problems of monitoring such vast reductions and maintaining deterrence in Europe in the face of Soviet conventional superiority. But he did go ahead and propose to Moscow that each side reduce its strategic arsenals by almost one-third. Moscow found this too adventuresome. In June 1979, both signed the SALT

II Treaty that reduced missile launchers slightly, set limits on the growth of nuclear warheads and made the first efforts to restrict modernization of missiles. The pact was less an escape from deterrence than its confirmation.

While SALT II negotiations were under way, Carter faced a steady drumbeat of criticism for doing nothing to counter large Soviet ICBMs, known as SS-18s and SS-19s. A portion of the SS-18s, with ten warheads each, and the SS-19s, with six each, purportedly could by themselves wipe out America's ICBM force, as well as submarines and bombers in base. If this were true, earlier fears about Soviet war-fighting capabilities had become a reality.

To counter this concern, Defense Secretary Harold Brown formulated what he called a "countervailing strategy." As contained in Presidential Directive 59, the doctrine brought the United States yet another step forward in thinking and planning for nuclear war-fighting. PD-59 visualized increased emphasis on targeting Soviet military assets, and, for the first time, political leadership as well. It also mandated developing the capability to fight a "prolonged" nuclear war, not just for days but for months.

The secret list of potential nuclear targets was expanded from about 20,000 to some 40,000, even though the total number of American strategic warheads would be no more than about 12,000. First priority would go not to economic targets, as in the past. Rather, new emphasis was placed on Soviet command and control facilities and Soviet leaders themselves on the theory that they feared nothing more than their own demise and loss of political control. New emphasis also fell not only on Soviet ICBMs, but on finer-grained targets such as military depots, airfields and large troop concentrations. The hallmarks of PD-59 were flexibility and endurance.

When word of the new doctrine leaked to the press, Brown responded with a speech keyed to the themes of continuity with modest change. "Deterrence remains, as it has been historically, our fundamental strategic objective," he said, trying to reassure doves. First priority went to deterrence of general war, but also to the need to deter "nuclear attacks on smaller sets of targets in the U.S. or on U.S. military forces" as well as against American friends and allies. American nuclear capability must "contribute to deterrence of conventional aggression as well." Then came the new punchline to reassure hawks: "In our analysis and planning, we are necessarily giving greater attention to how a nuclear war would actually be fought by both sides if deterrence fails. There is no contradiction between this focus on how a war would be fought and what its results would be, and our purpose of insuring continued peace through mutual deterrence. Indeed, this focus helps us achieve deterrence and peace, by ensuring that our ability to retaliate is fully credible."

Then, as if to take back most of what he had just stated and reassure moderates, he added that "we have no more illusions than our predecessors that a nuclear war could be closely and surgically controlled." The uncertainties of nuclear war, he continued, "combined with the catastrophic results sure to follow from a maximum escalation of the exchange, are an essential element of deterrence." In sum, the Carter administration was to ready the country to fight controlled and limited nuclear wars which it believed could not be controlled or remain limited or be won. In the end, Carter was not to flee from the nuclear dilemmas, but to embrace them, just as his predecessors did.

Ronald Reagan found this, and indeed, virtually all of the answers his predecessors gave on nuclear deterrence through the threat of retaliation to be intolerable. He would seek a way out of the nuclear nightmare.

4

MAKING NUCLEAR WEAPONS
IMPOTENT AND OBSOLETE

On the night of March 23, 1983, President Reagan shared with the world his vision of defensive systems to render nuclear weapons obsolete. "Tonight," he said, "consistent with our obligations under the ABM Treaty and recognizing the need for close consultation with our allies, I am taking an important first step. I am directing a comprehensive and intensive effort to define a long-term research and development program to begin to achieve our ultimate goal of eliminating the threat posed by strategic nuclear missiles. This could pave the way for arms-control measures to eliminate the weapons themselves. We seek neither military superiority nor political advantage. Our only purpose—one all people share—is to search for ways to reduce the danger of nuclear war. My fellow Americans, tonight we are launching an effort which holds the promise of changing the course of human history. There will be risks, and results take time. But with your support, I believe we can do it."

President Reagan before his Star Wars speech on March 23, 1983—an event that was to move the world toward a new era in strategic thinking and nuclear competition.
© NEW YORK TIMES PICTURES/D. GORTON

With that single speech, he began moving strategic thinking and nuclear competition toward a new era, for that vision did nothing less than assault the very core of present-day nuclear philosophy, namely deterrence based on the threat of retaliation. He and his senior aides were saying that the forty years of nuclear peace built on that threat could not last and that the premise itself was, in any event, immoral. Most experts said then, and continued subsequently to say, that perhaps decades of research would be required before they would know with confidence whether the vision could be translated into workable technology. Yet proponents and critics alike were well aware that the vision itself, along with accelerated research programs and the attendant debates, would shake the very foundations of American military policy—strategic doctrine, the shape of military spending, alliance relations and arms control.

The administration believed that the United States could not be sure that mutual assured destruction would work into the next century; it had to be replaced by mutual assured defense. Since it was signed in 1972, the Anti-ballistic Missile Treaty had formed the centerpiece of the nation's strategic thinking. The treaty limited the superpowers to no more than 100 defensive missiles, all defending one basic site. Washington interpreted this to mean that both sides accepted the doctrine of mutual deterrence through retaliation and that neither would do anything to take away the other's ability to retaliate devastatingly. Thus, Article V states, "Each party undertakes not to develop, test or deploy ABM systems or components which are sea-based, air-based, space-based or mobile land-based." This did not preclude research, which both sides continued to conduct, nor did it, or could it, make absolute distinctions between research and development.

Acceptance of the treaty was also predicated on the assumption that reductions in offensive arms would follow swiftly. Otherwise, Washington would reconsider its adherence to the treaty. But the administration was saying that quantitative and qualitative improvements in offensive weapons, particularly in the powerful and accurate Russian land-based missiles, threatened to neutralize the American retaliatory capacity. Officials contended that a few hundred missiles with multiple warheads could destroy virtually all American land-based missiles, submarines in port and bombers on air fields. This would leave future Presidents with only submarine-launched ballistic missiles of insufficient accuracy to destroy anything but Soviet cities. This, they said, was not a credible retaliatory threat because an attack on Russian cities would necessitate an attack on American population centers. To avoid this, Washington must build better offensive systems or defensive systems or both. The administration proposed to do both.

The critical factor in this decision was the belief of administration officials that new offensive programs were not enough. They argued that greater and greater offensive power would only make the nuclear balance more unstable. To them, defense against attacks—whether from small or accidental attacks or all-out attacks—was the only moral and practical answer.

Publicly, the administration claimed the Soviet Union already had the jump in missile defense, both in a deployed antiballistic missile system and in development of new technologies. Indeed, no one disputed that the Russians had a small ABM system around Moscow and that the United States had not deployed a system. Privately, however, the weight of opinion in the administration was that hard American knowledge of Soviet research in this area was negligible and that the United States probably led in most, if not all, areas of research.

National and world debate on the President's program soon grew intense. President Reagan's ideal was a defensive system that saved lives. But the reality could be new and more powerful offensive and defensive capacities that could be used for a decisive nuclear first strike. Thus, the debate centered on how far the reality was from the ideal: Was Star Wars well-conceived to save countless lives and enhance deterrence, or was it more likely to lead to an ever more precarious nuclear balance? The questions about the proposal were legion. What, in fact, was the Soviet technical ability? Could missile defense, abandoned as costly and ineffective a full decade ago, be made to work now? Could these defensive abilities also be used as potent offensive weapons? What was perhaps most striking was that the hard questions about the program were not getting much of a hearing in the inner councils of the administration. By almost all accounts, support for what was to be known as the Strategic Defense Initiative, or S.D.I., became the touchstone of loyalty to President Reagan.

■

Reagan's efforts to escape the nuclear nightmare did not begin with his S.D.I. vision on March 23, 1983. A year earlier, Defense Secretary Caspar W. Weinberger approved a planning or "defensive guidance" document that sought to avoid nuclear war the old-fashioned way, by being able to win it. Under the general heading of "Wartime Strategy," the paper read: "Should deterrence fail and strategic nuclear war with the USSR occur, the United States must prevail and be able to force the Soviet Union to seek earliest termination of hostilities on terms favorable to the United States."

Among the main requirements for doing this were the following:

> Deployment plans that assure United States strategic nuclear forces can render ineffective the total Soviet military and political power structure through attacks on political/military leadership and associated control facilities, nuclear and conventional military forces, and industry critical to military

power. These plans should also provide for limiting damage to the United States and its allies to the maximum extent possible.

Forces that will maintain, throughout a protracted conflict period and afterward, the capability to inflict very high levels of damage against the industrial/economic base of the Soviet Union and her allies, so that they have a strong incentive to seek conflict termination short of an all-out attack on our cities and economic assets.

United States strategic nuclear forces and supporting C3I (command, control, communications and intelligence) capable of supporting controlled nuclear counterattacks over a protracted period while maintaining a reserve of nuclear forces sufficient for trans- and postattack on our cities and economic assets.

According to Reagan administration officials, these precepts were embodied in another secret document, National Security Decision Document 13, approved by the President. Three ideas stood out: developing the capability to strike military targets, being able to control and fight a prolonged battle, and having the power to prevail.

The idea of placing first priority on hitting military targets (enemy forces, lines of communication and air fields) rather than population centers was not new. But it had been a perennial red flag for liberal critics of nuclear strategy. To them, it smacked of a war-fighting mentality going beyond an interest in pure deterrence. As they have always seen it, a decision to blow up weapons and soldiers is easier for leaders to make than a decision to kill civilians and risk mutual destruction of population centers, and if easier, it was less desirable, because it made nuclear war more likely.

The fact is, however, that once the American strategic nuclear stockpile ran into the thousands of warheads and bombs, it ran well beyond the number needed to strike population centers. This gap became greater all the time as the United States built more nuclear weapons and discovered more Soviet military targets by spy aircraft and satellites. Also inevitably, as warheads became more accurate, more ambitious military targets were selected. Thus, the classified documents speak of attacking political power structures, communications centers and conventional military forces on the move. But these sensitive targets were first added to the list by Carter, not by Reagan. Without doubt, this advanced the war-fighting concept. There was little reason to believe the Soviet target list was any different. This thinking presented increased dangers for both sides. But it was also a fact of life that the new capabilities existed and little could be done about it now.

More troubling to liberal critics than the target lists was the administration's emphasis on flexibility, that is, having "limited nuclear options." That was the idea that the President should have choices between no response to a nuclear attack and massive retaliation. The critics feared that an approach that envisioned any action short of an all-out response made such responses more thinkable and therefore more likely. More worrisome still was the related idea of a controlled and prolonged nuclear war that could be won in some meaningful sense. Here Professor Thomas C. Schelling of Harvard made a key point: "There is an enormous difference between a doctrine that postulates the efficacy of 'fighting limited war' as a deliberate policy, and a doctrine of doing everything possible to provide opportunity, in the event the undesired and unintended nuclear war should happen, to stop it, to slow it down, to bring the destruction to a halt. The former doctrine would reflect hubris, the latter prudence. The former may reflect an obsession with victory, the latter only with tragedy."

In the Reagan administration's apparent belief in being able actually to control a nuclear war, and to fight it over a period of perhaps months—and win it—doctrine was carried beyond well-established bounds. Such a belief, critics feared, could induce some leader someday to think he could risk starting a nuclear war. For the last twenty years, administrations had used words like "preventing defeat" or "avoiding an unfavorable outcome" to describe their belief that there could be no winners in a nuclear war.

The secret documents embodying the Reagan policy ideas were leaked to The New York Times and sparked sharp debate. As a consequence, Mr. Weinberger stated that "nowhere in all of this do we mean to impy that nuclear war is winnable. This notion has no place in our strategy. We see nuclear weapons only as a way of discouraging the Soviets from thinking they could ever resort to them." The President also issued denials.

Nonetheless, the suspicion lingered that the leaders of the administration had something in mind in choosing the word "prevail." There were officials in the Reagan administration who wrote and spoke of the likelihood of nuclear war, and the need for the United States to prepare to fight, survive and win it. How widely this view was shared in the administration is not clear.

The more charitable explanation was that, to them, "prevailing" really translated into the goal of gaining strategic nuclear superiority over the Soviet Union. Many of these officials helped draft the 1980 Republican Party platform, which called for achieving overall military and technological superiority over the USSR. To many on the Reagan team, nuclear superiority was important because they believed it translatable into diplomatic power that, in the event of a crisis, can be used to coerce the other side to back down.

The idea is debatable. Soviet agreement to remove its missiles from Cuba in 1962 appears to have been the result of overwhelming and usable American conventional military superiority in the Caribbean and of President Kennedy's willingness to remove comparable American missiles from Turkey. In no other case since both sides acquired sizable nuclear capability did either side back down or make concessions in the face of a nuclear threat.

To argue that Western Europeans are drifting toward neutralism because of presumed Soviet nuclear superiority is also stretching a point. Europeans have been drifting ever since Moscow achieved nuclear parity at least a decade ago, and is mainly because of a combination of Soviet conventional superiority and lack of confidence in American diplomacy. As for the benefits of nuclear superiority in a state of emergency, former Defense Secretary James R. Schlesinger remarked in an interview, "One should not underestimate the risks leaders will take to win in a crisis." In other words, with so much nuclear punch on both sides, it is in the interests of neither to expect to win a crisis showdown.

Early Reagan administration thinking was preoccupied with the so-called window of vulnerability—a major Reagan theme in the campaign against President Carter in 1980. The charge was that Carter and his predecessors had permitted Moscow to develop a first-strike capability sufficient to "disarm" American retaliatory power. The same fear writ large caused the Carter administration to adopt Presidential Directive 59, the so-called countervailing strategy, and to press forward with weapons and programs to nullify this presumed Soviet advantage.

The Reagan administration wanted to talk about how to close the "window." Critics wanted to argue whether it was open in the first place. To critics, Soviet leaders would have to make three assumptions before launching such an attack, each of which seemed implausible. First, anything less than a perfect first strike would mean a failed first strike. Large numbers of weapons would survive to retaliate, including ICBMs capable of destroying Soviet missiles. Could Moscow assume perfection when virtually all experience in warfare showed otherwise, and when no such strike had ever been tested? Second, even assuming perfection, could Moscow further assume that its strike would kill only a few million Americans or a small enough number not to prompt an American counterstrike against populated Soviet areas? The "window" rests on the proposition that if the Soviets destroyed only strategic weapons, Washington would not respond with weapons that could only kill Russians—that would invite a Soviet strike on American cities. But if Moscow were to strike at all major American strategic bases, tens of millions of Americans would perish instantly, and many more later. Third, if Moscow still were willing to make the first two assumptions, and then attack, could it also assume that Washington would then capitulate? American armed forces would still be available, along with Allied forces, plus some reduced nuclear capability at sea and in Europe. What would Moscow have gained—and at what risk?

Even as this debate went forward, the Reagan administration accelerated weapons development and selected weapons designed to implement its war-fighting strategy. It added extra funds to Carter programs for the MX missile, Trident submarines and powerful new Trident II or D-5 missiles, and various kinds of land, sea and air-based cruise missiles. Reagan also restored the B-1 bomber to production. If the United States could not close its "window," it could open a Soviet window of vulnerability. Perhaps of equal importance, the Reagan administration gave the highest priority to what experts termed C3I—command, control and communications plus intelligence-gathering facilities such as satellites. In short, weapons were being put in place to fight a nuclear war and so were the means to control it.

Were these efforts closing the "window"? Reagan's own Commission on Strategic Forces, headed by Brent Scowcroft, reported that the window did not exist. But if it did, the Reagan programs were not closing it. If Moscow had a first-strike capacity against American missiles, the missiles were still sitting in silos, still vulnerable. So the Scowcroft Commission proposed mobile ICBMs: a small single-warhead model known as Midgetman, and a large MX on rail cars.

Mobile missiles were a way to close the window. Reagan experts, however, were cool to this from the outset. They did not like the cost. More important, they did not like the idea of Moscow's having mobiles as well. Without public opinion to worry about, Soviet leaders could move mobiles around the vastness of their country with no problem. American leaders could not. Consequently, they proposed in the nuclear arms talks to ban mobiles. They also rejected the idea of moving away from fixed ICBMs toward the deployment of more submarines. They worried that the invulnerability of submarines might not last much longer. Thus they and their President found their way back to ballistic-missile defense—to protect missiles and population.

The debate did not rest easy on President Reagan. He did not want to fight nuclear wars or even win them, or engage in the never-ending quest to close windows and gaps. He wanted a permanent and unalterable escape from the nuclear nightmare.

So he unveiled his ideas for space-based defenses in the March 1983 speech, and called on scientists to find ways to render nuclear weapons "impotent and obsolete." It was precisely the problem that Reagan's predecessors, from Lyndon B. Johnson on, had wrestled with. They had all said no to making the transition from mutual assured destruction to mutual assured defense, in which attacking missiles would be destroyed before they could reach their targets. Their objections were based largely on the grounds that such defensive systems were not feasible. Now, Reagan and many of his advisers maintained, this had changed. "Current technology," he said in unveiling his plan, "has attained a level of sophistication where it is reasonable for us to begin this effort. It will take years, probably decades, of effort on many fronts."

S.D.I. would make matters all the worse, charged a host of American scientists, arms-control specialists and the Soviet Union. Rather than a more stable and sensible peace, they argued, Reagan's vision would touch off a new and more dangerous arms race in space and succeed only in destroying prospects for arms control. Soviet officials countered that they would have to accelerate their research program and keep open the option of making more offensive nuclear warheads to overcome prospective defenses. They also expressed concern that once the research program gained momentum, future American presidents would find it difficult to stop. They argued that a system to defend populations would not work, but some tended to think it might be possible to build a limited system for the defense of missile sites. Still, most did not want to open this door either. As for feasibility and rendering nuclear weapons obsolete, former Defense Secretary Harold Brown, a nuclear physicist, spoke for scientists critical of the program when he wrote, "The combinations of limitations—scientific, technological, systems engineering costs—and especially the potential countermeasures make the prospect of a perfect or near-perfect defense negligibly low."

Lieutenant General James A. Abrahamson, Jr., the director of the Strategic Defense Initiative, disputed this: "There is very little question that we can build a very highly effective defense against ballistic missiles someday. The question is how soon and how affordable and what degree of effectiveness can initial steps allow us." As for those who disagree, he suggested that it was "because for a lifetime they have been dedicated to another idea and they are not very willing to accept a new thought process. What is really happening is that there are a large number of dedicated, talented people working on this in government and industry. And when they all have a goal to march to, and that's what the President gave us, you just cannot stop the progress they are making and that progress is what's happening."

Mr. Reagan, in effect, enlarged the notion of developing defenses to protect missile sites, inspired in part by his monthly meetings with the Joint Chiefs of Staff. His Star Wars speech was viewed by administration officials as essentially a way of telling them that this was one of his top priorities, perhaps his ultimate legacy. He made few concrete decisions about the program other than to approve large increases in spending on missile-defense research programs. His senior aides, many of whom acknowledged being taken by surprise, proceeded to fill in the blanks and push their own views, often in contradictory ways.

Reagan's aides split on what purpose S.D.I. should serve, one that is limited and achievable in the short term or a broader more ambitious one that would take a long time to realize. Specifically, they fell apart on the question of whether Star Wars deployments should be used to defend missile silos and other military targets or whether they should defend people. Administration officials were at pains to deny that they had any intent of turning Mr. Reagan's vision away from defending people and toward defending weapons. Many of them said they felt this would knock the bottom out of public support for the effort. But many legislators maintained that protecting military targets is the real goal.

Essentially, Reagan officials solved this problem by talking about missile defense as a first stage toward people defense. But the compromise has been an uneasy one. "S.D.I. is all things to all people," commented Paul C. Warnke, a director of the Arms Control and Disarmament Agency under President Carter. "To the President, it is saving peoples' lives. To Defense Secretary Weinberger, it is a technological steppingstone from missile defense to the President's larger conception of immaculate defense. To others, it is simply a means of defending missiles. To some, it is a bargaining chip in arms-control negotiations, while to others, including the President, it is untouchable."

Mr. Reagan's advisers were divided on other issues as well—on the flexibility of the system, on how to judge whether it should be deployed, on

Allied concerns, and on how to make the critical transition from a world dominated by offenses to one protected by the great defensive umbrella in space. The Reagan administration split over the feasibility and importance of S.D.I. At one end are the doctrinal purists such as Fred C. Ikle, Under Secretary of Defense for Policy, who argued: "The Strategic Defense Initiative is not an optional program, at the margin of the defense effort. It's central, at the very core of our long-term policy for reducing the risk of nuclear war." Like the technological optimists such as General Abrahamson, they believe not only that it can be done, but also that it must be done.

There are also those who would wait and see, such as Paul H. Nitze, the primary arms-control adviser to Secretary of State George P. Shultz. Mr. Nitze stated in a speech, "Quite frankly, it may prove impossible to obtain." No other official inside the administration said publicly what Richard D. DeLauer, former Under Secretary of Defense for research and engineering, did in 1983: "This is a multiple of Apollo programs," in terms of the technological advances required, and if it is deployed, Congress will be "staggered at the cost." Some officials privately shared this view, as did many outside experts.

Skeptics and critics also argued that it remained easier and cheaper to overcome defenses with offensives than to neutralize offensives with defenses. Reagan responded that the defense could prevail, as it did in World War I, when gas masks were an effective defense against chemical warfare. Others suggested that the use of poison gas was stopped when an increase in its use threatened to destroy both sides without benefit to either.

A more neutral answer came from Mr. Nitze, who said: "New defensive systems must also be cost-effective at the margin, that is, it must be cheap enough to add additional defensive capability so that the other side has no incentive to add additional offensive capability to overcome the defense. If this criterion is not met, the defensive systems could encourage a proliferation of countermeasures and additional offensive weapons to overcome deployed defenses, instead of a redirection of effort from offense to defense." But the Pentagon fought hard to eliminate the cost-effective criterion, and the matter remains unsolved.

Other problems were cited. As defenses against ballistic missiles are deployed, each side could also increase its number of aircraft and cruise missiles flying in the atmosphere to circumvent them. To this, administration officials replied: Better these slower-flying weapons, which allow time for response, than the fast-flying missiles.

Then there was the diplomatic juggling act with the Allies. "One of the worst problems we're having with the President's plan is with the Allies," a high State Department official said, "and it only looks as if we have it under control for the moment." Some Pentagon analysts argued that missile defenses were good for Western Europe and Japan. These analysts said that in the short run, protecting the United States would lend credibility to Washington's threat to use nuclear weapons to protect them. In the long run, they held out the promise of extending the protective umbrella to the Allies as well.

But the Allies did not see it this way at first, and Mr. Reagan worked out a deal with Prime Minister Margaret Thatcher of Britain to patch over the disagreements. In effect, the agreement provided that the Allies—minus France—would publicly support research, and in return the administration would consider decisions on the ABM treaty and deployment to be matters for Allied consultations and negotiations with Moscow. Also, Britain and France were concerned that an American defensive system would make the Soviet Union develop a full-scale defensive system that could negate French and British nuclear missiles. Their fear was that the Soviet network might not be good enough to block an American attack but might be good enough to neutralize the West European deterrent.

The Allies in general worried that in the short term, defensive systems to protect the superpowers would make Europe alone the likeliest nuclear battlefield. Finally, West European diplomats worried that uncertainty about American plans for defenses would complicate and perhaps undermine the chances for progress on arms control, and particularly on reducing medium-range nuclear forces in Europe.

An overarching problem remained: how to manage the transition between MAD and Star Wars. Fred Ikle contended that it would not be a destabilizing period. He said, "As a growing fraction of the Soviet missiles could no longer reach their targets, Soviet planners would face increasing uncertainties and difficulties in designing a rational first strike." Not so sanguine was Mr. Nitze, who said the transition could take decades, could be tricky and would be dangerous if Moscow developed better defenses first. "We would have to avoid a mix of offensive and defensive systems that, in a crisis, would give one side or the other incentives to strike first."

The real fear of the critics was that the side that got to the optimal mix first might reason that it could win—destroy most of the other side's forces in a first strike and blunt the retaliatory blow with defenses. This, in theory, would make nuclear war "rationally" thinkable for the first time. Mr. Reagan and others said the transition could be managed through arms-control negotiations by agreeing on what to deploy and when. He would help this along by sharing, in some fashion, the technology with Moscow. Officials and critics alike acknowledged, however, that negotiating a transition would be far more difficult than any arms-control task yet undertaken with Moscow.

In a curious way, Mr. Reagan's efforts to find an escape from a nuclear Armageddon led him to retrace the footsteps of his predecessors. He went from enhancing deterrence with more arms to wanting to improve capacity to wage nuclear war to wanting to build defenses instead of offenses to wanting arms control. Even if S.D.I. proves technically feasible in years to come, it could well be impractical and unwise without arms control. Without sharp limits on offenses, more missiles could be reckoned as likely to overcome defenses. Without carefully constructed scenarios with Moscow for cutting offensive forces while defenses were being deployed, the transitional world could prove to be the most dangerous one in the history of nuclear peace.

Seeing such complications down the road, some officials began curling back toward more modest, traditional thinking. Richard N. Perle, Assistant Secretary of Defense for Policy, said: "It is not true that we've already made the decision to abandon mutual assured deterrence or the policy that seeks to achieve security by the threat of retaliation. That will still be with us for years."

But the great debate on defenses had already been joined.

5

HOW IT
WOULD WORK

In the past, the greatest obstacle to building a defense against ballistic missiles has been the enormous destructive power of the nuclear warheads carried by the missiles. "Awesome" was the word former Secretary of Defense Harold Brown, a man of dry, understated language, used to describe this power. Noel Gayler, a retired admiral, recalled that very few military officers now on active duty have ever seen an atmospheric nuclear explosion, but anyone who has will never forget it. Now, several years after President Reagan made such a defense one of his foremost priorities, this destructive potential clearly remains the primary drawback.

The difficulties can be illustrated with a few examples. The *terminal*, or last-ditch component of a Star Wars kind of defense, would require a system of radars able to locate enemy missiles through the atmosphere and to provide initial guidance to the intercepting warheads, which would then seek out the incoming missiles and destroy them. But to be effective in actual warfare, such radar installations would have to be hardened, or reinforced, to withstand the effects of nuclear detonations. Using reinforced concrete and tubular metal shields, the United States has already learned how to "harden" missile silos to withstand 2,000 pounds of pressure per square inch—enough to ride out all but a very near miss or direct hit. In design studies and tests, promising work has been done to greatly increase such shielding. However, existing missile-defense battle-management radars—such as the Russian model near Moscow and the Perimeter Acquisition Radar built for the now deactivated American ABM defense near Grand Forks, North Dakota—are large above-ground facilities with little hardening. Even in theory, however, the best-designed radar protection can only withstand much lower pressures. This is even more dramatically reduced during periods when the radar antennas are popped up above ground level. In other words, it is difficult for many experts to see how the indispensable radar component of terminal defenses could survive more than the first salvo of Soviet missiles directed at a given field of U.S. missile silos. The initial defense would do some good, but many experts believe it would be quickly overcome by what is called a structured attack, in which Soviet planners arranged to "ladder down" the detonations of their weapons, from very high altitudes to very low ones, until eventually warheads were exploding in the missile field itself.

Another example involves an electromagnetic pulse, the very powerful burst of electrical energy caused by a high-altitude nuclear explosion. Against unshielded defensive components, an electromagnetic pulse probably would knock out the essential electronic brain, the computers and electronic circuitry, of defensive missiles and radars. Shielding is possible, and Mr. Reagan's Star Warriors are working hard on that problem and also on protecting missile-defense components from other nuclear effects such as radiation, heat and blast. But skeptics are unconvinced that even advanced technology can offset the stupendous energies created by a nuclear explosion.

One way to describe the problem of nuclear defense is to ask: How good is good enough in the case of a defense against nuclear weapons? Another way to describe the problem is to state that most senior United States officials—and, even more important, the public at large—have never really believed in or embraced as a goal something called "damage limitation," that is, the reduction or limitation of the devastation that would be incurred in a nuclear war. Soviet leaders have demonstrated that they are firm believers in damage limitation, not only in written military doctrine, but also in their substantial civil defense program and their extensive system of air defense against U.S. bombers. So have a long line of middle-level United States bureaucrats and academic analysts, exemplified by the Pentagon official who told an interviewer early in the Reagan administration that "with enough shovels" to cover wooden lids on crude pits, most of the American population would survive a nuclear strike. However, for most of the general public and for almost all senior political leaders, damage limitation has seemed both futile and even repugnant. One might indeed argue persuasively that it would be worthwhile to reduce anticipated United States casualties from a possible high of 120 million dead to a possible low of 20 million or even 10 million. But public resistance, even hostility, to civil defense programs in recent decades indicates that many people regard such reasoning as macabre. Nuclear strategists may routinely ponder the hard-to-answer question of "acceptable" losses in nuclear war, but when the figures begin to include seven or more zeros, laymen tend to take the view that there are no acceptable losses.

Nor is this attitude confined to laymen. Over a period of many years most members of the Joint Chiefs of Staff acquiesced in a decision to permit the American air defense command to wither into a vestigial state. The reasoning was that with the advent of ballistic missiles, the United States would suffer so much damage from these high-speed, prompt weapons that protection against slower-arriving bombers was not worthwhile. Whether Mr. Reagan's Strategic Defense Initiative changed Americans' belief in damage limitation, or whether Star Wars was understood by that large segment of the population that tended to support it in opinion polls as a promise of damage elimination—however difficult to fulfill—is a question that thoughtful members of Congress said they could not answer.

A starting point in the design of any weapon, from a simple rifle to a complex radar jamming set, is deciding on the detailed requirements that the weapon must fulfill. In the case of Star Wars these are complex and, in many ways, discouraging.

The flight of modern ICBMs and SLBMs is divided into four phases.

Boost phase is the period from ignition of an enemy's attacking propulsion rockets (usually several, which are called stages) to burnout, when sufficient momentum has been achieved to put the payload into an unpowered ballistic trajectory, much like that of an unpowered bullet leaving the muzzle of a rifle, up out of the atmosphere and into space. In currently operational missiles, this phase lasts from about three, though only in a few cases, to

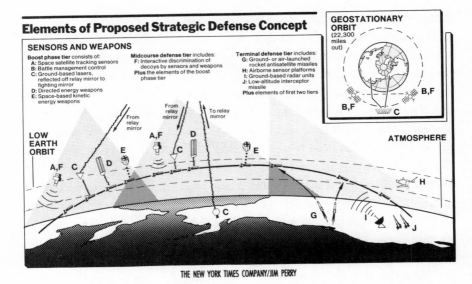

Elements of Proposed Strategic Defense Concept

GEOSTATIONARY ORBIT (22,300 miles out)

SENSORS AND WEAPONS

Boost phase tier consists of:
A: Space satellite tracking sensors
B: Battle management control
C: Ground-based lasers, reflected off relay mirror to fighting mirror
D: Directed energy weapons
E: Space-based kinetic energy weapons

Midcourse defense tier includes:
F: Interactive discrimination of decoys by sensors and weapons
Plus the elements of the boost phase tier

Terminal defense tier includes:
G: Ground- or air-launched rocket antisatellite missiles
H: Airborne sensor platforms
I: Ground-based radar units
J: Low-altitude interceptor missile
Plus elements of first two tiers

LOW EARTH ORBIT

From relay mirror

To relay mirror

ATMOSPHERE

THE NEW YORK TIMES COMPANY/JIM PERRY

about five minutes. In current designs, rocket burnout occurs just above the atmosphere.

There is wide agreement that, if it is possible to do so, the most desirable time to defend against a ballistic missile is during boost phase. One reason is that the most dangerous modern missiles carry multiple independently targetable reentry vehicles, known as MIRVs. The reentry vehicle consists of the nuclear warhead itself and a heat-resistant protective cone which can withstand the friction of reentering the atmosphere above the target. The largest Soviet missile, the SS-18, carries ten reentry vehicles. So does the new U.S. MX, which became operational in small numbers late in 1986. Other American ICBMs, the Minuteman III models, carry three warheads each. Submarine missiles have been designed to carry from eight to fourteen warheads, although they have until recently had warheads of relatively low explosive yield. If the missile can be destroyed during the boost phase and before it has dispensed its multiple reentry vehicles, commonly called RVs, a single successful shot by the defense can destroy all of the nuclear warheads. This gives the defense what Star Wars planners call maximum leverage.

Another advantage of boost-phase defense is that propulsion rockets are much softer and more fragile than reentry vehicles. Much less energy from a directed energy beam, such as a laser or atomic particle beam, is required to cause structural collapse of the thin skin or relatively weak metal beams of a rocket stage. Finally, the warheads fall back on the territory of the nation that fired them. They are unlikely to explode, but if they did, they would be less likely there to destroy the American defense system.

Post-Boost Phase. The multiple reentry vehicles are carried on a small platform called a post-boost phase vehicle, known in military jargon as a PBV, or "bus." At the moment of separation from the final propulsion rocket, a thin-skinned nose cone covering the bus and its reentry vehicles also separates and falls away. The bus contains computers and gyroscopes that provide inertial guidance meant to send each reentry vehicle to its selected target. The reentry vehicles are dispensed one at a time as the computer signals the bus that it has achieved the correct speed and position to send the warhead on its way. Post-boost phase, though shorter, also has the advantage of destroying missiles before all, or some, of the reentry vehicles have been dispensed.

Midcourse. After the reentry vehicles have been released, they coast in a high arc through space for twenty to twenty-five minutes, in the case of land-based ICBMs, and for a shorter period in the case of submarine missiles which are fired closer to the target. The bus or post-boost vehicle can be, and usually is, also designed to carry and dispense lightweight "decoys," metal chaff and other deceptive articles called penetration aids. Because there is no friction in space, these penetration aids have the same trajectory and speed in space as the much heavier reentry vehicles. This will cause a serious "discrimination" problem for those who design Star Wars. The use of decoys and other penetration aids, which would resemble the actual reentry vehicles on conventional radars, greatly increases the number of potential targets with which a ballistic-missile defense must cope, something planners call the "threat cloud."

Reentry Phase. As the cloud of objects begins to reenter the atmosphere, friction-generated heat quickly strips away and destroys the light, unprotected penetration aids. The defense can now clearly discriminate between decoys and warheads and spot the real targets. However, because of the high speed of reentry vehicles it has only seconds to react. It also has the problem that its defensive mechanisms must be fired from the ground upward through the earth's atmosphere. This is a physical impossibility for such weapons as neutral particle beams, is a potential problem for lasers and limits the speed of chemically powered interceptor rockets. Still another difficulty is that if the reentry vehicles explode in the atmosphere, they may do damage on earth and to the delicate nervous system of the defense network itself.

How can these dangerous targets be destroyed at various phases of their flight? Theoretically, there are many ways. Lasers, or beams of concentrated, coherent light, could burn holes in the skin of rocket stages or perhaps even in heat-resistant reentry nose cones. Very powerful lasers now being investigated in laboratories—such as the nuclear bomb–triggered X-ray laser or the promising free-electron laser—can deliver powerful pulses of energy that can destroy or damage material through shock.

Beams of subatomic particles created in accelerators are another directed-energy weapon possibility. However, because the earth's magnetic field will bend electrically charged particles into unpredictable paths, charged beams will be too inaccurate to be guided successfully. Neutral particle beams which have no electrical charge will follow a straight line in outer space and may prove useful someday, although they are regarded in practical terms as a fairly remote technology requiring many years of further research. When neutral particle beams strike air molecules in the atmosphere, they pick up an electrical charge and become unguidable again. For that reason neutral particle beams can only be used in space and cannot be directed successfully down through the atmosphere or up through the atmosphere from the ground.

Kinetic-energy weapons, which are also called "hit-to-kill" devices, are another possibility. As the name suggests, such nonexplosive weapons do damage through a very high speed collision with their targets. There are many plausible variations. In 1984, in a project called "Homing Overlay Experiment," the Army succeeded (after five failures) in intercepting and destroying a dummy reentry vehicle in space with a hit-to-kill device fired into space on an obsolete Minuteman I booster. The final guidance mechanism involved small infrared, heat-seeking sensors and small, adjustable guidance rockets. An umbrella-like metal net unfolded at the last moment and caught the dummy, much like a baseball in a catcher's mitt, except that both objects were destroyed. The Army Homing Overlay Experiment has since evolved into the ERIS (or exoatmospheric reentry interception system) project in the Star Wars program, a prime candidate for last-ditch defense by ground-based rockets. Kinetic-energy weapon possibilities also include small interceptor rockets fired from space satellites and projectiles fired at high velocities from electromagnetic railguns. Because some final guidance devices would probably be necessary to achieve interception, the small projectiles from such guns have been nicknamed "smart rocks."

A defensive system would require more than weapons. A vast system of sensors is needed to detect missiles and reentry vehicles in flight, track their paths and assist in guiding beam energy or projectiles to the targets. Computers and software programs of unprecedented complexity and speed must control the whole system and a high-speed, reliable communications network must tie everything together.

An already complicated problem is made more complex by the near certainty that any major nuclear attack by the Soviet Union would be a "structured" attack in which follow-up ICBMs would be arriving in waves and in which submarine-launched missiles with different flight times would be delivering their payloads. The wartime environment, therefore, in which the defense would have to function would probably involve multiple nuclear explosions at varying altitudes, even if the defensive weapons were hitting most of their targets.

As has been said, there was tension among advisers to President Reagan even before his Star Wars speech as to what the scope, size and nature of a missile defense should be. Men like General Graham, of the organization High Frontier, and Senator Wallop advocated the rapid development and deployment of a relatively crude but also more quickly available defense based on so-called off-the-shelf technology, such as chemically powered lasers and/or small interceptor rockets. However, many of the top scientists working in the national weapons laboratories and other scientists warmly or lukewarmly sympathetic to S.D.I. thought it better to try to develop more sophisticated and exotic defensive technologies, such as nonchemically powered lasers or electrical railguns that could fire the kinetic-energy weapons. Such experts felt that although such weapons as chemical lasers could be developed sooner, they would never achieve the power and lethality levels needed. Subsequent research, experts said, confirmed this impression.

To have an operational, workable missile defense requires what the experts call system architecture, a design that pulls all of the elements of a defense together and includes effective strategy, tactics and military doctrine for its use.

It is not simple to create such an architecture. A final design will depend on which of the proposed technologies and weapons prove to be possible to design and build, and on measurements of how lethal they are in practice against ballistic missiles. It will also depend on an assessment of the enemy threat, the size and nature of the missile fleet, and associated decoys that may be thrown against the defense. This is a variable. Scientists at the Sandia weapons laboratory told the staff assistants of three U.S. senators that the longer and more deeply the scientists studied the possible Soviet threat, the greater it seemed to be. Senior officials in the S.D.I. office said that if all plausible Soviet countermeasures to Star Wars were taken into account, the problem became increasingly daunting.

However, research cannot be managed properly and decisions on alternatives cannot be made intelligently without parallel work on the overall architecture of a defense. One factor is that different designs will give different levels of effectiveness—some capable of intercepting a high percentage of targets and some capable of intercepting fewer. Therefore, work on studies of system architecture began soon after the Stategic Defense Initiative Organization (known as S.D.I.O.) was created in early 1984. The research conducted since then was done primarily by private defense contractors closely supervised by high-level officials of S.D.I.O.

A generally shared assumption is that the most desirable defense would have several tiers, or multiple layers, that would permit interception of missiles and RVs in all four of the phases of ballistic-missile flight: boost, post-boost, midcourse and reentry. A multilayered defense would have many advantages. Some failure, or "leakage," is to be expected in any single tier. However, with several layers, each successive one would have to deal with a much smaller total number of surviving RVs, which would substantially enhance overall effectiveness. In 1985 the S.D.I.O. made public some of the results of its initial studies on defensive architecture. The designs ranged from a preferred, or ideal, system, consisting of seven layers meant to work during all four phases of missile flight, to a simple system of strictly ground-based interceptors, with no defensive weapons based permananently in space.

The preferred design is meant to protect a total of 3,500 major targets in the United States. The targets include missile fields, military command and control centers, other vital military facilities from bomber and submarine bases to major troop bases, and major urban population and industrial centers. Why seven layers for four flight phases? Two different groups of weapons would be used in the boost and post-boost phase, three in the mid-course phase and two in the reentry, or terminal, phase.

The preferred design postulated "tens" of large space satellites equipped with some form of directed-energy weapons, probably some form of laser, and "thousands" of smaller satellites, each carrying from one to ten kinetic-energy weapons. This cluster of weapons would be, in military argot, "dedicated" to boost phase and post–boost phase defense against missiles still rising over the Soviet Union or against the buses, loaded with warheads, flying in near space just after rocket separation. A separate cluster of dedicated weapons would operate in the midcourse phase as RVs coasted through space.

This might include "tens" of large directed-energy platforms and "thousands" of small kinetic-energy weapons on smaller satellites. It might also include two different groups of mirrors orbiting in space, designed to reflect and direct laser beams generated by ground-based lasers in the United States to targets. The ground-based lasers would first direct their beams to relay mirrors in high-altitude orbit. These mirrors would then relay beams to "fighting mirrors" at lower altitude which would focus the energy on targets.

The architecture study also contemplated the possibility of a third mid-course layer, consisting of clouds of small pellets. These clouds would not destroy, or even hinder, the flight of nuclear-armed reentry vehicles, but would be designed to strip away or slow the flight of decoys and chaff, helping to solve the problem of differentiating real from false targets that an enemy would be expected to deploy as countermeasures to thwart a defensive shield.

The terminal, or reentry, phase would be defended by two kinds of ground-based interceptor rockets. One model of rocket, the ERIS, would be used to attack "exoatmospheric" targets just outside the atmosphere. The second kind, called HEDI (for high endoatmospheric defense interceptor) would have higher flight speed and attack "endoatmospheric" targets, those at high altitude inside the earth's atmosphere.

Because a Star Wars defense must be survivable against possible enemy attack, separate groups of antisatellite weapons would be in orbit to play a role analogous to fighter escort planes for bombers. These weapons would be meant to attack and destroy any Soviet antisatellite weapons bent on destroying the United States weapon platforms. The design also envisioned an intricate system of sensors and battle-management equipment. Infrared sensor satellites would circle at very high altitudes to give early warning of enemy missile launches by detecting the great heat released by missile rockets. Tracking satellites, using various kinds of sensor technology, would follow the flight of missiles and the reentry vehicles they dispense. Star Wars designers expressed a desire for a "birth to death" tracking system to keep track of every object fired from Soviet launchers and dispensed in space—from launch to destruction. This means the tracking sensors would have to be capable not only of tracking but of making battle damage assessment as well. In short, they would be required to detect misses and hits and the destruction or neutralization of every RV (and all decoys), and then pass this information on to battle-management computers. Although much of this equipment would be in space, ground-based radars and other devices on earth would also be employed. This would permit Star Wars to allocate remaining defensive weapons efficiently against still dangerous objects.

Still other sensors would be required to perform the task of discrimination. Infrared sensors would attempt to detect the faint emissions of heat from reentry vehicles and decoys and to distinguish one from the other. Sensors have traditionally been divided into active and passive categories. A radar is an example of an active sensor because it transmits energy, in the form of electromagnetic radar waves, to an object and picks up the return radar wave bounced off the object. A passive sensor, on the other hand, picks up emissions from an object without emitting energy itself. The "fuzz-buster" radar detector, which many motorists mount in their cars to give warning of police traffic radars, is an example of a passive sensor. Infrared sensors are also passive.

As work has progressed, Star Wars officials and planners say they have, for many reasons, begun to question whether even highly refined versions of passive and active sensors can satisfactorily or wholly solve the problem of discrimination between targets and decoys. The jamming of sensors with powerful and deceptive bursts of electromagnetic energy can degrade their performance. And such sensors must work, in most cases, with computers loaded with problem-solving algorithms. A machine, after all, is only a machine. It cannot actually "see" anything, nor can it identify an object in the same way the human brain can. Instead, it is provided by weapons designers with programed specifications of electronic data. If an object gives off, or seems to give off, an electronic "signature" with certain characteristics which are translated into mathematical terms, the computer-assisted sensor will call it a deadly reentry vehicle. If the received signal is only slightly different—because of Soviet-designed deceptive measures or changes in the electronic signatures of their RVs and decoys—it could cause the sensor to reach the wrong conclusion.

David Parnas, an American computer expert who has been teaching in Canadian universities, resigned from an outside advisory panel on computing and battle management assembled by S.D.I.O. in 1985, expressing the opinion that the computing problems of ballistic-missile defense could probably never be solved. In an interview, Mr. Parnas said one of his nightmares about Star Wars is the danger posed by espionage. He explained that if Soviet agents were able to learn details of the problem-solving algorithms used in S.D.I., it might be possible for the Soviets to greatly simplify the task of baffling the sensors and thus the whole defense system.

In seeking solutions to such problems, Star Wars officials by 1986 were expressing optimism about an approach they called "interactive" sensors.

They talked about, and worked on, the possibility of employing ground-based lasers and space-based mirrors to "paint" or illuminate all of the vast cloud of RVs and decoys coasting through space in the mid-course phase. Such beams of energy, General Abrahamson said, would be able to "bump" each object with relatively low bursts of energy. The hope would be that the light, fragile decoys would be revealed as harmless decoys; they might even be bumped from trajectories in ways that could be detected by sensors. The heavier RVs would react to the probing laser beams differently. Scientists also believe that the same interactive sensors could detect the presence of nuclear warheads in the actual RVs. Officials believed that the mid-course discrimination problem was so important that in 1986 (or fiscal year 1987), substantial sums of money were shifted from research on the purely weapons uses of lasers to study ways in which lasers could be used in interactive sensing.

A successful system architecture must also take into account a number of apparently mundane and workaday problems, often neglected in the artists' sketches and animations flashed on television screens. The weapon platform satellites and the sensor satellites must have some form of electrical power. In the case of sensors or kinetic-energy rockets, this might only involve small batteries or solar collectors—but they must be very reliable and long-lived. For space-based lasers or electric railguns very powerful electrical generators would be required. Ways will have to be found to make them light enough to be lifted into orbit and still provide the power levels needed to enable weapons to generate sufficiently lethal lasers to destroy a reentry vehicle. At some point, S.D.I.O. officials will have to make desired requirements conform to engineering reality. If a workable, miniaturized laser has been developed but the lightweight generator to work it has not, compromises in the grand design will have to be made. A comparison might be made to an eighty-pound infantry rifle, which is hypothetically "feasible" but a wholly impractical military weapon.

The architecture, too, must take into account very real problems of deployment and maintenance, just like any other weapon. In the case of S.D.I., one of the main problems of this sort is space transport. The vast array of Star Wars components must be put in orbit at an "affordable" cost. Once in orbit, components must continue to give reliable service over very long periods of time. This problem offers a useful illustration of how thinking undergoes changes as officials and scientists reexamine and reconsider evidence. Early on, some thinkers in S.D.I.O. were discussing the possibility of making such components as space-based electrical generators "maintenance-free" for periods of as long as ten years. This could be dismissed as "only" an engineering problem, less glamorous than laboratory experiments with exotic new kinds of lasers. However, that kind of engineering excellence has seldom if ever been achieved, mainly because it has not been necessary. A large electrical utility company finds it easier and better to provide human mechanics to repair equipment than to try to make it that reliable. The best clue as to how formidable a problem such engineering excellence is can be seen in the S.D.I.O.'s suggestion to Congress in 1985 that it was considering routine, periodic maintenance of equipment by sending maintenance personnel into space at relatively short intervals to do such work.

The revelation of the rough details of initial architecture studies brought a mixed political and technical reaction. For one thing, in the preferred design, the so-called constellation size, the number of satellites that would have to be put into orbit totaled several thousand. This caused amused smiles and some derision among critics and opponents of Star Wars who said they doubted whether a system that large could be successfully erected and maintained. But the design was also unwelcome news to advocates of a near-term, more simple ballistic-missile defense; people who believed that technologies already understood—i.e., "on the shelf"—could be used to weld together a more rudimentary system but one that could be constructed quickly. Senator Dan Quayle, Republican of Indiana, warned General Abrahamson during a Senate hearing that it would be necessary to make a quick start on deployment of S.D.I. in order to commit the nation to ballistic missile defense. Otherwise, Mr. Quayle and other political advocates of defense argued, Congress would steadily chip away at annual appropriations for Star Wars on the grounds that it was "being researched to death" but offered no prospect of improving the strategic balance with the Soviet Union.

George Keyworth, who continued as President Reagan's White House science adviser until 1985, made an attempt to stem that tide, warning that unless a multilayer, complex defense that offered some chance of protecting a sizable part of the civilian population was selected, "the President's vision would be lost." However, a simple ground-based defense of U.S. ICBM missile fields remains a possible first step toward, or even a final design for, the Strategic Defense Initiative.

Finally, it must be said that despite the truly startling scientific and technological accomplishments that have been made, in space research and particle physics, for example, no one, in all probability, will know for years precisely how the Strategic Defense Initiative would work if a decision is ultimately made to develop and deploy it. An enormous amount of costly and complex research will continue to be necessary before any kind of safe and effective antinuclear missile shield could actually be lifted into space and put into orbit.

6

THE STRUGGLE
TO BUILD IT

Deep in the New
Mexico desert, government scientists have begun work
on a $1 billion facility that, when finished in the 1990s, will house the
biggest and most powerful laser on earth. The area is so desolate the Con-
quistadors called it Jornada del Muerto—Journey of Death. It will take 2,000
workers to build the facility, which will be two miles wide, ten miles long
and become a part of the White Sands Missile Range. The laser itself will
consume about 100 megawatts of electricity, enough power for a city of a
quarter-million people. Cooling it will require more than 450 million gallons
of water a year, no small amount in the desert. About 250 people will be
needed to run it. They will direct the formation of the laser beams in subterranean chambers. After these beams gain strength over miles of tunnels, they
are to flash upward past sagebrush and cactus, past ancient lava beds and the
San Andres Mountains, toward targets hundreds of miles away in space.

Despite the enormous difficulties and obstacles in the path of its deployment, Star Wars has become no simple fantasy or political gambit. The antimissile plan at its core is a vast scientific project the size of which is unrivaled. Defenders and detractors fought through most of the 1980s—and will no doubt continue to fight through the 1990s and perhaps for generations after that—over its feasibility. Congress may blanch over its vast budgetary implications, and governments may engage in wary diplomacy over its futuristic goals. But at laboratories and test sites around the nation, thousands of the nation's best scientists are already pushing tomorrow's technology to the limit today in the biggest research project of all time.

The sprawling laser facility in New Mexico, known officially as the Ground-Based Free-Electron Laser Technology Integration Experiment, is but one of hundreds of antimissile projects under way at universities, think tanks, government laboratories and industrial research centers across the nation. This coordinated assault is key to the antimissile challenge. At its core, it is an attempt to forge arms more powerful and precise than any others in the history of warfare. Its goal, basically a vision of the twenty-first century, is so challenging that even antimissile advocates agree there is no guarantee of success.

Since the program got started in 1983, scientists have, indeed, made remarkable headway. In June 1984 they did, after all, destroy a mock warhead in space with a "smart" projectile, in the Homing Overlay Experiment that the Air Force was so pleased with, hitting "a bullet with a bullet." In 1985 they shot laser beams through the earth's turbulent atmosphere without distortion. And in 1986 they programed a pair of satellites to play a deadly game of cat-and-mouse in space. In the future, the pace of progress will pick up as billions of dollars already invested start to produce results. But the program has also had its setbacks, its clashes, the emergence of rival ideas and sudden changes of direction. The vast research effort is clearly dynamic in the sense that the envisioned way of achieving antimissile goals is often in flux. Amid all these twists and turns, one man remained greatly influential: Edward Teller.

In awarding more than a thousand antimissile contracts, the Pentagon generally followed Teller's vision that the national laboratories pursuing futuristic goals should lead the research. Their assignments include the perfection of advanced weaponry, computers, optics, sensors, microcircuits, mirror coatings, nuclear reactors, rocket engines and futuristic industrial processes in dozens of areas. At the Livermore laboratory, federal researchers began creating a new generation of nuclear weapons. Thousands of miles away at the Brookhaven National Laboratory on Long Island, researchers began investigating the effects of nuclear radiation on semiconductor chips meant to control remote battle stations in space.

Industry set out on slightly less esoteric projects. In Orlando, Florida, the Martin Marietta Corporation has attempted to push its 1960s-vintage missile interceptors into the next century. In Bethpage, Long Island, engineers for the Grumman Corporation are studying how to build radars in space. On the West Coast, companies like Rockwell, TRW and the Boeing Corporation began building big lasers, power supplies, and sensor devices. So eager have industrial contractors been to gain Pentagon contracts that they have supplemented government spending with tens of millions of their own dollars, attempting to develop new technologies that might be incorporated in a space- and ground-based missile defense.

Early on, the national and commercial scientists found themselves fundamentally at odds, their differing views often clashing openly. They disagreed on how much sophistication was needed, and therefore on the time needed for development. Federal laboratories favored work on advanced systems whose deployment might be decades away; in contrast, most industrial contractors wanted more conventional systems deployed as soon as possible. In late 1985, the differences broke into the open. Federal antimissile scientists charged that the Star Wars program was being seriously threatened by exaggerated assertions and costly public-relations razzle-dazzle. Their complaints focused on showy tests of conventional weaponry made by private corporations. The public attack was highly unusual. Critics outside the government had long said the antimissile defense program was structured to promote the illusion of quick technical gains, no matter how great or small the actual accomplishments. But the new criticism came from within, from prominent federal scientists at the forefront of the President's program. They said their technical credibility was at stake.

███

Essentially, what distinguishes Star Wars from the earlier attempts at missile-defense systems in the 1960s and from the present Soviet ABM complex around Moscow is its greatly advanced high technology, much of which operates at the speed of light. The advantage is one of range. A single laser might be able to flash its destructive beams over many thousands of miles of space in the course of a battle at the speed of 186,000 miles per second. In contrast, it might take hundreds of rocket-powered interceptors to achieve that same breadth of destructive power.

At the moment, there are no clear winners in the race to perfect different kinds of weapons from among the possible three categories: the lasers (speed of light), particle beams (near speed of light), and computer-guided or "smart" projectiles and rockets (relatively slow). Although there are exceptions, the federal laboratories have tended to be pioneers of the high-speed weaponry. It may turn out that slow projectiles, which smash a target, are simply more feasible than their exotic brethren. In the end, the sheer complexity of laser weapons may make them unworkable for the rapid wars of the nuclear era.

The free-electron laser, or F.E.L., project in the New Mexico desert is one of the most ambitious. Pentagon officials have adopted it as one of the most promising of the efforts to harness intense beams of light for weaponry, primarily because of its flexibility and power. However, because of its great size and weight, the F.E.L. must stay on the ground. Generated on earth, the intense beam would be bounced off a series of orbiting mirrors to zap missiles over the Soviet Union, destroying them in their boost phase moments after lift-off.

All lasers work by creating quick movements among electrons, tiny particles that normally orbit around the nucleus of an atom. When jostled correctly, electrons give off waves of light and beams of radiation that move coherently in step with one another. Incredibly concentrated, this laser light can bounce off the moon or bore through metal. Unlike regular lasers, F.E.L.s use electrons that are "freed" from atomic nuclei, much like the free electrons that produce television pictures. The electrons are accelerated to close to the speed of light in huge particle accelerators and then wiggled magnetically to produce laser beams.

This freedom results in all kinds of unique qualities. Normally, a laser's wavelength is fixed by its atoms and the distance between electron orbits. But an F.E.L. can be "tuned" to any wavelength, from microwave to the ultraviolet, and researchers are vying to extend its range up the electromagnetic spectrum to include X-rays. This tunability greatly extends its range of antimissile applications, allowing it to be adjusted to the right frequency for best penetration of the earth's atmosphere. In addition, F.E.L.s can develop enormous power since they manipulate electrons more efficiently than regular lasers. Where conventional lasers often convert into laser light only a small portion of the electrical power put into them, working with an efficiency of only a few percent, F.E.L.s by 1986 had achieved efficiencies of 42 percent and were heading for 70 percent and perhaps even higher.

The vision of creating powerful bursts of laser light led the Strategic Defense Initiative Organization to embark on construction of the New Mex-

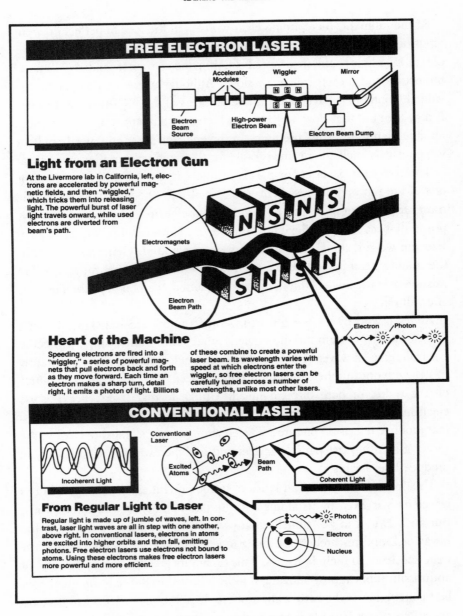

FREE ELECTRON LASER

Accelerator Modules · Wiggler · Mirror · Electron Beam Source · High-power Electron Beam · Electron Beam Dump

Light from an Electron Gun

At the Livermore lab in California, left, electrons are accelerated by powerful magnetic fields, and then "wiggled," which tricks them into releasing light. The powerful burst of laser light travels onward, while used electrons are diverted from beam's path.

Electromagnets

Electron Beam Path

Heart of the Machine

Speeding electrons are fired into a "wiggler," a series of powerful magnets that pull electrons back and forth as they move forward. Each time an electron makes a sharp turn, detail right, it emits a photon of light. Billions of these combine to create a powerful laser beam. Its wavelength varies with speed at which electrons enter the wiggler, so free electron lasers can be carefully tuned across a number of wavelengths, unlike most other lasers.

Electron · Photon

CONVENTIONAL LASER

Conventional Laser · Excited Atoms · Beam Path

Incoherent Light

Coherent Light

From Regular Light to Laser

Regular light is made up of jumble of waves, left. In contrast, laser light waves are all in step with one another, above right. In conventional lasers, electrons in atoms are excited into higher orbits and then fall, emitting photons. Free electron lasers use electrons not bound to atoms. Using these electrons makes free electron lasers more powerful and more efficient.

Photon · Electron · Nucleus

The free electron laser and the conventional laser: how they work.

DEPARTMENT OF DEFENSE

ico test facility in 1986. The task of developing the laser was divided between the Livermore weapons lab and the Los Alamos lab. "Two years ago there were a very, very few small laboratory versions of these" free-electron lasers, General Abrahamson, director of S.D.I.O., told reporters. "We have already demonstrated the most efficient laser in the world, operating at 42 percent, at the Lawrence Livermore Laboratory. And as a result of that we're ready to skip steps. We're ready to skip the intermediate steps and move directly to much larger versions."

According to Pentagon officials, a working F.E.L. would need a beam with a strength of several hundred megawatts. One of its potential problems is that its beam may be so intense that its direction by mirrors on earth may prove impossible; the mirrors might simply crack or melt. In New Mexico, scientists plan to get around this problem by sending the laser beam through a 2.6-mile-long underground vacuum tunnel so it can expand, reducing its power density and leaving its optics undamaged. But that plan might also fail, leaving Drs. Hans A. Bethe and Richard L. Garwin, both respected antimissile critics, to suggest the possible Catch 22: The F.E.L. will be ineffective if too weak and impossible to handle if too strong. "While high efficiency may be achievable," they wrote in the summer 1985 issue of *Daedalus*, the journal of the American Academy of Arts and Sciences, "it is not yet known how multimegawatt optical powers can be handled on the small mirrors that F.E.L.s will apparently use."

But if the F.E.L. could be made to work and if the nation decided to deploy antimissile weapons, the New Mexican scientists hinted at what might lie ahead. Even larger F.E.L. facilities would be needed for the actual fighting of antimissile wars. An operational system might consist of a half-dozen F.E.L. farms scattered around the United States, each containing about ten lasers similar to their $1 billion facility. And each laser would use 100 to 1,000 megawatts of electrical power. "Sometime in the next century," said Dr. Richard Briggs, F.E.L. director at Livermore, such lasers "could be used in a ballistic-missile defense if the fundamental questions are answered." Before then, he added, single F.E.L.s could be used to knock out enemy satellites, if that were somehow to become a military objective.

Further along in development and less exotic in their technical aspects are chemical lasers, which get their energy from the combustion of fuels similar to those used in rocket engines. During a firing, much of this chemical energy is lost as heat. But significant amounts can be extracted in the concentrated beams of laser light. Hidden in the rocky canyons of the Santa Susana Mountains north of Los Angeles is one of the world's biggest chemical lasers, a behemoth created by the Rockwell International Corporation, whose main enterprise is building advanced rocket engines. Code-named Sigma Tau, the laser project was begun secretly for the Air Force in 1976. Sigma Tau and its support equipment today cover several acres, looking a bit more like a small oil refinery than an antimissile weapon that could be lofted into space. A 150-ton baseplate helps steady the laser's beam. Part of Rockwell International's goal was to build lasers whose resonators, which help extract the light beams from chemical reactions, are compact cylinders instead of long, narrow tubes. The idea was to make them ultimately as small as possible, so chemical lasers could possibly fit into the cargo bay of the space shuttle, for example.

Rockwell's main rival in chemical lasers is the TRW Corporation, which is working on two large devices of the same general class as Sigma Tau. One, called Miracl, was the first laser in the Free World to produce more than a megawatt of light energy. When its output reached 2.2 megawatts in the 1980s, the Pentagon called it "the Free World's highest average-power laser." Miracl was built in the late 1970s for the Navy, and was originally meant to investigate the protection of American ships from attacks by enemy planes and missiles. Congress killed that program. But the Miracl laser was later resurrected by the Pentagon for lethality tests, and in 1984 was assembled at a top-secret, $300 million installation surrounded by barbed wire and armed guards at the White Sands Missile Range in New Mexico. Its beam was fixed, unable to be directed at moving targets, though the Pentagon's aim was to perfect a complex beam director that could direct it. The laser's delicate mirrors, dozens in all, were fashioned so that heat was removed by the circulation of 9,000 gallons of cold water. About 370 people were needed to operate the laser site. In September 1985, Miracl flashed to life in a dramatic test. About half a mile from the laser, engineers erected the second stage of an old Titan missile, its liquid fuel having been drained away. After being irradiated by the Miracl beam for "several seconds" (the Pentagon would be no more specific), the Titan casing exploded in a hail of shredded metal. The stationary casing in the desert was meant to mimic a Soviet missile in flight, according to Pentagon officials. Close-up films and photos of the exploding missile were widely distributed, and were shown repeatedly on television before the Geneva summit meeting of President Reagan and Soviet leader Gorbachev in November 1985. "This advance gives us greater confidence in our ability to focus the laser beam into a small spot at long range," General Abrahamson told the Philadelphia World Affairs Council, hailing it as one of the program's "world-class breakthroughs."

But critics outside the government said the destruction of the missile was far more showmanship than science. They noted that in space an antimissile laser would have to fire its beam thousands of miles, adding that big lasers have been used for decades to burn holes in metal over short distances. Furthermore, they said the Miracl test was misleading. "The impression was that the laser blew it apart," said John E. Pike, head of space policy for the Federation of American Scientists, a nonprofit group based in Washington that is skeptical of the antimissile plan. "But it was the gadget at the top, the cross bar that was ostensibly there for dynamic loading, with the cables pulling down, that caused it to fly to pieces. The test looked much more impressive than it was."

Such complaints were echoed by some federal scientists who were themselves working on the antimissile program and who said their scientific credibility was threatened. Dr. Roger L. Hagengruber, director of system studies at the Sandia National Laboratory in Albuquerque, New Mexico, said in an interview: "If one was going to demonstrate the lethality of microwaves, one could put a digital watch in the horn of a microwave generator, blow the watch apart, and say microwaves kill watches. For the lay public and Congress, that might be impressive. But it's actually far removed from reality, and interferes in a way with more thoughtful experiments. These demonstrations have the potential to be what we call strap-down chicken tests, where you strap the chicken down, blow it apart with a shotgun and say shotguns kill chickens. But that's quite different from trying to kill a chicken in a dense forest while it's running away from you."

Miracl was big and powerful, yet relatively old and out of date. Its only realistic application was perhaps showy tests. Meanwhile, in the hills near the famous mission at San Juan Capistrano in California, TRW engineers struggled to perfect a much smaller beam—the Alpha, a highly classified, lightweight laser designed to operate from a platform in space. Its power would be about the same as Miracl, but, unlike Miracl, Alpha might actually be good for antimissile tests if not actual wars in space.

▬

Despite the government's expenditure of billions of dollars on chemical lasers, their future became uncertain in November 1985 when General

Abrahamson announced a significant shift in the structure of the antimissile program. In a long, rambling news briefing meant to describe "incredible" advances by Star Wars researchers, he said that work on chemical lasers was being radically downgraded in favor of heat-seeking rocket interceptors and the free-electron lasers. Significantly, both these antimissile weapons would be, or could be, based on earth, which of course would be far easier to undertake and manage and would be safe from enemy attacks in space.

Still, the F.E.L.s on earth would be dependent on the huge, orbiting mirrors, and the major problems with the mirrors remained essentially un-solved. Normally, the beam of a ground-based laser is considerably distorted by the atmosphere through which it must travel. According to Dr. Gerold Yonas, the Pentagon's chief scientist for antimissile research from 1984 to 1986, progress had been made on the distortion problem. Laser beams, he said in an interview, could now be bounced off adaptive optics or "rubber mirrors" that distort the light to form an optical conjugate of the turbulence it is to meet in the atmosphere, to distort, in effect, the distortion. "As it goes through the atmosphere, this wiggly wavefront is then made smooth," he said.

On June 21, 1985, a blue-green laser beam knifed up through the darkness from a mountaintop in Hawaii and locked onto the space shuttle *Discovery* in what a Pentagon scientist called the first successful shuttle experiment of Star Wars. The test was viewed by Pentagon officials as crucial to determining whether ground lasers could be used to destroy warheads in space. Flashing up from the Air Force Optical Station on Maui, the beam of low-powered light hit an eight-inch mirror on the side of *Discovery* 220 miles overhead as the winged spacecraft traveled at more than 17,000 miles an hour, several hundred miles an hour faster than a speeding warhead. The mirror bounced the beam back to earth, sending data that enabled scientists to adjust the laser to counteract the distorting effects of the turbulent atmosphere, mean-while keeping the beam locked on the shuttle. After the test, the astronauts relayed a dramatic recorded television picture of the laser as it pulsed and flashed. Accompanying it was music from Tchaikovsky's 1812 Overture.

As is often the case in antimissile testing, this success had been preceded by failure. Two days earlier, on June 19, ground controllers inadvertently sent faulty instructions to the *Discovery* astronauts, which resulted in their pointing the mirror out to space instead of toward the incoming laser beam. So the laser beam hit the wrong side of the shuttle.

There are other problems with lasers in addition to atmospheric distortions or the excessive force that can break the needed mirrors—their bounciness, for example. If they can bounce off laser mirrors on earth, they might also bounce off highly polished enemy missiles. The vision of mirrored missiles is one of the relatively simple countermeasures that have led critics to question the general advisability of replacing offensive missile capability with missile defense. Isn't offense, or the potential for offense, always the best defense? they ask.

An altogether different type of weapon that might be able to outwit mirrored missiles is particle beams. These would accelerate a stream of tiny subatomic particles (electrons, protons or neutrons) to nearly the speed of light and fire them at enemy warheads and missiles, going easily through mirrors and light shielding to heat internal structures and destroy sensitive electronic circuits. Although relatively slow, subatomic particles pack much more punch than particles of light, which have no mass at all. The allure of particle beams, too, is that they are nearly impossible to stop, penetrating and damaging almost any warhead or missile. The key countermeasure, thick lead shielding, is far too heavy to be carried aloft by enemy missiles.

Accelerators for particle-beam weapons resemble the huge atom smashers pioneered by civilian scientists. All of them start with charged particles (electrons or protons) because these can be manipulated by magnetic and electric fields, whereas neutrons cannot. With special tricks, a beam of speeding charged particles can, just before leaving the accelerator, have their charges removed. The problem is size. Accelerators for beam weapons are currently too big to get off the ground, and their beams cannot be fired from earth: The particles are stopped by the atmosphere. At Livermore, scientists are at work on a $50 million machine called the Advanced Technology Accelerator, which stretches out hundreds of yards across the shallow, dry valley. The site was chosen so the surrounding hills could provide shielding in case of an accident.

The Sandia Laboratory in New Mexico is using particle technology developed in the search for fusion energy in an attempt to create particle beam weapons, and the Los Alamos lab in New Mexico is building a particle-beam accelerator known as White Horse. This device uses a key breakthrough, known as a Radio Frequency Quadrupole, that can accelerate a particle beam to two million electron volts, roughly what is needed for a Star Wars preaccelerator. The RFQ is the size of a desk. Its predecessors were the size of a house. The RFQ was invented by Soviet scientists and recently perfected in the West.

The Strategic Defense Initiative Office has marked the Los Alamos effort for a high-visibility $700 million test of neutral particle beams on the space shuttle in the early 1990s. Such weapons, even if initially not powerful enough to knock out enemy warheads and missiles, are intended to discriminate and track Soviet warheads from thousands of accompanying decoys. One problem with the charged particle beams (electrons or protons) is that their path in space could be deflected by the earth's magnetic field. So a proposed solution is to use only the neutral particles (neutrons), as planned for the shuttle test.

Another possible approach is to fuse lasers and charged particles together. In September 1985, Los Alamos scientists announced they had used a laser beam to guide a series of intense particle-beam pulses. The experiment, they said, suggested that beams of charged particles could be made less vulnerable to the earth's magnetic field. "The test turned out better than we dreamed," said Dr. Randy Carlson of the laboratory's dynamic testing division. The scientists filled an eleven-foot pipe with gaseous benzene and then fired a half-inch laser beam down the center. This caused positive ions to form in the beam path. Then intense pulses of negatively charged electrons, moving close to the speed of light, were fired into the laser's positively charged beam path. According to the scientists, the attraction between the electrons and the ions kept the beam tightly focused as it sped toward the target at the end of the pipe. "The guiding force is incredibly strong," Dr. Carlson said.

The slowest class of Star Wars weapons is also the nearest to being perfected. Kinetic-energy weapons work by simply flying into a target at great speed and smashing it to bits, the destructive power coming from the momentum of both target and interceptor. They are similar to the weapons proposed by General Graham's High Frontier group. On June 11, 1984, a kinetic-energy weapon on the Pacific isle of Kwajalein was lofted by a rocket into space and sent forward to search out a mock warhead. Nearing its target, the interceptor unfurled a deadly spiral of eight-foot steel arms to increase its destructive radius. Speeding at 5.5 miles per second, guided by on-board detectors, it smashed directly into the warhead. In essence, it achieved the traditional antimissile goal: A speeding bullet could hit another speeding bullet. This Homing Overlay Experiment, which came right before a critical vote in Congress on arms funding, received much publicity. Often unmentioned, however, was that three earlier HOE attempts had ended in failure, interceptors altogether missing their targets in space. The successful June 1984 interception was the final test in the HOE series. The next generation of prototype kinetic-energy weapons is the HEDI, the high endoatmospheric defense interceptor, which is to weigh less than HOE and have improved sensors.

If research proves successful, kinetic-energy weapons might be flung toward targets by electromagnetic fields rather than chemical rockets. So far, such electromagnetic railguns have been used only in laboratories on earth. But in theory, their powerful magnetic fields could be used to speed kinetic-energy weapons along metal guides and out through the frictionless void of space. At the University of Texas, an experimental railgun named Gedi sits in a high-ceiling laboratory crammed with electrical generators and equipment. It would have been named "Jedi," as in the movie *Star Wars*, but that name is protected by copyright. A few dozen feet long and less than an inch in diameter, it can fire pellets weighing eighty-five grams to high velocities. With Star Wars financing, the Texas researchers are building Gedi II in a new seven-story building. Altogether, with its special detectors and equipment to measure the speed and characteristics of projectiles, the gun will measure more than 130 feet long. "I think advances in power supplies and launchers in the next twenty-five years are going to be mind-boggling," said Dr. William Weldon, a scientist at the university's Center for Electromechanics. "The biggest worry I have is hitting multiple targets."

One of the most advanced railguns is under development near Dover, New Jersey, at the Army Armament Research and Development Center, a $1.5 billion operation with 6,000 federal civilian employees and 250 military personnel. An experiment using electromagnetic propulsion for tactical weaponry began here in the late 1970s, and an electromagnetic laboratory was later established, according to Curtis L. Dunham, the engineer in charge of the space-gun project. Manpower and federal funding increased ten times in one year in the mid-80s. The bulky prototype consists of a big electrical generator, a huge switch and a forty-foot-long rectangular metal barrel. It has attracted a steady stream of top military officers, congressional delegates and foreign visitors.

Today railguns fire small, simple projectiles. In the future, they might fire heavy, sophisticated "smart" weapons that would be able to home in on targets. Dr. Yonas, former head of Star Wars research, said in an interview that "smart rocks" the size of a loaf of bread would fly off the end of a railgun and zero in on speeding warheads, guided by tiny sensors and thrusters. "Smart rocks can seek out and kill most assuredly. There is no question of lethality. You can try to run away from them, but there's no place to hide. They just keep seeking you out." One crucial impediment in their current

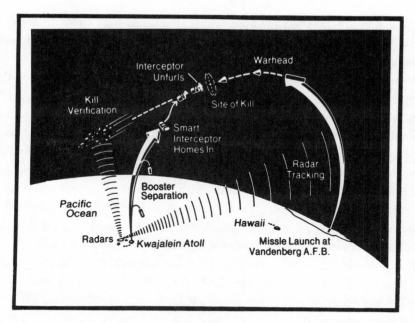

(A)

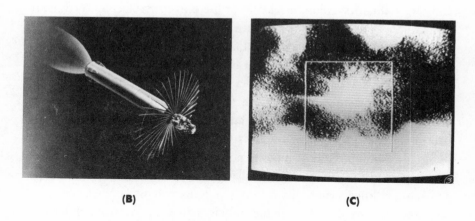

(B)　　　　　　　　　　　　　　　　**(C)**

On June 11, 1984, a nonexplosive kinetic-energy weapon on the Pacific atoll of Kwajalein was shot into space at the rate of 5.5 miles per second (A). Guided by radar-tracking devices and onboard heat sensors, it moved to within range of its target: a missile launched into space from Vandenberg Air Force Base in California, more than 5,000 miles away. The Homing Overlay Experiment (B) then unfurled its whirling arms and destroyed the warhead (C) merely by the speed and force of its impact.

DEPARTMENT OF DEFENSE PHOTOS

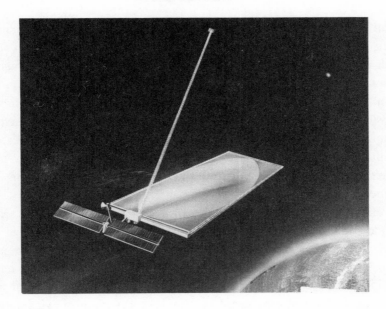

The proposed Star Wars space shield could require radar platforms the size of several football fields. GRUMMAN CORPORATION/HORIZONS MAGAZINE

state of development, however, is that "smart" weaponry is too fragile. Space-based railguns would produce magnetic fields so strong and accelerations so rapid that the weapons themselves would be destroyed as they were accelerated.

If such hurdles can be overcome, and the weapons perfected, the successful construction and deployment of space-based battle stations would require a host of other technical achievements. One is cheap electrical power. A supply under study by the General Electric Corporation is a three-ton, 300-kilowatt nuclear reactor that would take up one-third of the payload bay of the space shuttle. It is called SP-100. Since, during a battle, vast amounts of power would have to delivered very quickly, this type of orbiting nuclear reactor might be used merely to charge batteries, capacitors or other storage devices on battle stations.

Another technology that would have to be perfected is shielding. "Some of the biggest challenges we face," Dr. Yonas said, "are making weapons not only lethal but survivable—survivable in the sense that boost-phase weapons will orbit over the Soviet Union and thus be subject to attack." According to an estimate by scientists at the Livermore Laboratory, the protection of battle stations in space might call for a million tons of shielding. To obtain such vast amounts of material, mining the asteroids or the moon might be easier and more economical than shipping it from earth, according to Pentagon studies. At the Sandia lab in Albuquerque, Star Wars scientists addressing the same problem are creating a new generation of microelectronic "chips" meant to have built-in protection from the rays of enemy weapons. At the Brookhaven lab on Long Island, scientists are using their linear accelerator to irradiate such "chips" and electronic circuits to test the effectiveness of their protections.

Perhaps almost as important as space arms themselves are advanced sensors to find and track enemy missiles and warheads as they streak toward targets. The job is especially challenging for mid-course interceptions, where many decoys are likely to be mixed with real warheads. The need for a very refined sensitivity by trackers is great. At a Hughes Aircraft Company plant in El Segundo, California, engineers have completed a mock-up of a giant infrared sensor so powerful that, against the cold backdrop of space, it can detect the warmth generated by a human body from a distance of 1,000 miles. Indeed, the tracking job is so challenging that some of the biggest Star Wars contracts are aimed at the sensor problem. The Boeing Company's Airborne Optical Adjunct program, with a budget of $289 million over five years, is meant to develop a long-wave infrared sensor capable of aiding traditional radar systems in detecting warheads just as they are about to reenter the atmosphere. The plan is to test sensors atop a Boeing 767 jet. In an ambitious cat-and-mouse sensor test in September 1986, an unmanned Delta rocket carrying two satellites was fired from Florida into space. As they orbited the earth, the satellites moved about according to prearranged programs, all the while tracking each other. The experiment ended when the satellites were directed to smash together in a hail of metal. The Pentagon declared the test a complete success.

Detecting a single enemy missile approaching from the incomprehensibly vast reaches of space is only one stage of the battle; aiming a weapon at it is another. So complex is the job of trying to aim lasers accurately, or particle beams and railguns, and so big is the equipment that some planned experiments would require the huge payload bay of the space shuttle. Originally, the first big shuttle test was to have occurred in late 1986. Known as a Tracking and Pointing Experiment, it was to have aimed a laser beam at satellites and rockets. But the explosion of the *Challenger* in January 1986 threw the shuttle program into chaos, and the test was put off.

The sudden crippling of the nation's rocket power also underscored the extreme difficulty of creating an enormous battery of space vehicles to lift the antimissile system into place. Even before the shuttle disaster, Star Wars officials estimated that the deployment undertaking was so big that it might require up to 5,000 launchings of shuttles or shuttle-sized rockets.

Despite the multibillion-dollar effort to create battle stations for deployment in space and to shield them from enemy attack, some experts believe plans for space basing remain fundamentally flawed. These experts say battle stations would be relatively easy for an enemy to find, track and destroy. Space mines could disable them. Ground-based lasers and regular nuclear bombs could knock them out. In space, they note, a single nuclear weapon can destroy unshielded satellites thousands of miles away. Flashing through the void at the speed of light, the bomb's radiations set up extremely high electric fields in the metallic skin of a satellite—on the order of 100,000 to one million volts per meter—knocking out delicate electronic devices. Discovered in the 1970s, this military nightmare is known as system-generated electromagnetic pulse, or EMP.

Ironically, Dr. Edward Teller is one of the chief critics of space as a place for future weaponry. In April 1983, just after President Reagan's speech, he told Congress: "We are not talking about battle stations in space. They are much too vulnerable. We should merely try to have our eyes in space and to maintain them." To get around the vulnerability of weapons in space, Dr. Teller would keep them on the ground and shoot them into space at the last minute, just as enemy missiles started to rise from silos in the Soviet Union. Lasers, particle beams and railguns would be far too heavy for this job. Years of rocket flights would be needed to deploy them in space, not the mere seconds available to respond to a ballistic attack.

There is only one type of weapon light enough and small enough to be quickly carried aloft by a rocket—that powered by nuclear bombs. Pound for pound, nuclear reactions in a bomb pack thousands of times more punch than the reactions of batteries, chemical lasers or even nuclear reactors. Dr. Teller calls the strategy nuclear "pop up." It is so alluring (and so threatening if the Soviets achieved it first) that President Reagan directed that more than 10 percent of the S.D.I. budget be devoted to the development of advanced nuclear weapons for the job, even though he repeatedly characterized his antimissile program as nonnuclear.

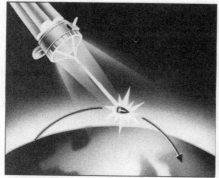

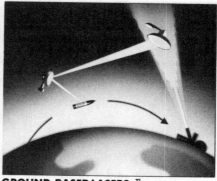

SPACE-BASED LASERS: In theory, these would combine chemicals in the manner of rocket engines to fire beams of concentrated laser energy through space. Lately, they have lost luster because of fears about the vulnerability of space-based objects.

GROUND-BASED LASERS: These devices, especially free-electron lasers, would bounce beams off orbiting "battle mirrors" toward enemy missiles. Such systems, which are cheaper because heavy lasers need not be lifted into space, are viewed as less vulnerable to attack.

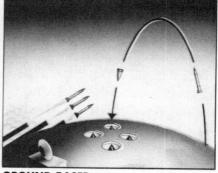

RAILGUNS: These devices, based in space, would use electromagnetic fields to accelerate and launch "smart" projectiles to home in on enemy boosters. The small projectiles are envisioned as something similar to those recently tested in American antisatellite weapons.

GROUND-BASED INTERCEPTORS: Using conventional rocket technology, these would be used to destroy enemy warheads during final phase of their flight, just before they hit targets. Such interceptors are often viewed as ideal for defending fields of American missiles.

The new exotic arms: progress and problems.   ILLUSTRATION BY JIM LUDTKE

Nuclear bombs meant to channel their power into deadly beams have been under development in the United States since 1980 and are known as third-generation weapons (the first two being the atomic and hydrogen bombs). Peter Hagelstein's nuclear X-ray laser is the best known. As with many Star Wars programs, it is wrapped in official secrecy. Yet, surprisingly, the X-ray laser has often been publicized as federal scientists leak news of advances, and others counter with news of setbacks.

The saga of the X-ray laser illustrates the general difficulty of trying to

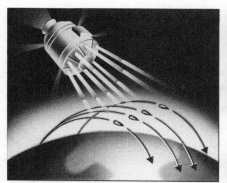

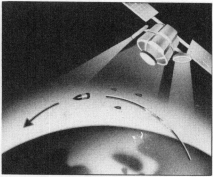

X-RAY LASERS: Powered by nuclear bombs, these would fire beams of X-rays at targets before consuming themselves in fireballs. Small and light, they could be "popped up" into space as needed. But problems in their testing have cooled enthusiasm.

SPACE SENSORS: These "eyes" would be critical for coordinating battles and knowing which missiles and warheads had slipped through the defensive shield. An emerging hurdle is seen as quick digestion of sensor data and its relay to military commanders.

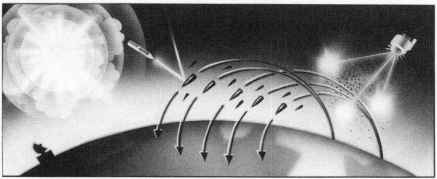

COUNTERMEASURES: An enemy could try to outwit a shield by attacking it or by complicating its job. Chaff dropped from missiles could confuse space-based radars and sensors. Decoys could complicate targeting. Missiles and warheads with mirror-like coatings could reflect laser beams.

Most challenging of all, an exploding nuclear warhead, set off accidentally by defender or intentionally by enemy, would send out electromagnetic pulses that would wreak havoc in electrical systems in space and on earth.

size up the real progress of antimissile research. In theory, the device is to channel nuclear power into laser rods that emit powerful bursts of radiation before it is consumed in a giant fireball. Over long distances in space, however, these rays would tend to spread out, gradually reducing their powers of destruction. In early 1985, an advance was made at the Livermore lab that seemed to increase the brightness and thus the power of the X-ray device by focusing its rays. And such increased brightness was crucial if the laser were to be effective, according to both its defenders and detractors. The experiment took place during a nuclear test at the nation's underground site in the Nevada desert on March 23, 1985, the second anniversary of President Reagan's proposal to make nuclear weapons obsolete. The key aspect of the test was the use of special optics to focus X-rays as they streamed out of the nuclear explosion. Many critics had viewed this task as virtually impossible, since X-rays tend to penetrate matter rather than be reflected, bent or focused by it.

In April 1985, Teller alluded to an X-ray laser breakthrough in a speech at the University of California. Then, in May, news of the laser focusing was leaked to the news media, resulting in detailed accounts of the claimed success. But anonymous rebels among the space scientists eventually objected to the claims of breakthroughs and categorical success, some risking jail sentences to give journalists top-secret details. In November, the journal *Science*, a widely respected scientific publication, reported that a key monitoring device had been miscalibrated, rendering the results of the focusing tests uncertain. Further disclosures revealed that the government intended to forge ahead with its next X-ray test, even though the design flaw had not been eliminated. On December 6, 1985, thirty members of Congress sent a letter to Defense Secretary Weinberger urging him to postpone the test, which was to cost $30 million, until the problems could be fixed. They also asked for an immediate top-secret briefing on the X-ray laser program, including the experimental flaw. Federal officials publicly confirmed that there were unresolved technical problems in the X-ray laser experiments but characterized them as minor.

Where does the X-ray laser program really stand? For those without a Q Clearance, the federal pass that allows access to secret information about the design of nuclear weapons, the question is almost impossible to answer. One hint of the size of the task is that top Los Alamos scientists in April 1986 estimated that the perfection of third-generation nuclear weapons could take hundreds of nuclear explosions beneath the Nevada desert.

The problem of separating antimissile fact from fantasy is not unique to the X-ray laser. Indeed, leading Star Wars scientists, concerned about their credibility, charged in late 1985 that President Reagan's program was being seriously threatened by exaggerated assertions, hyperbolic tests and costly public-relations razzle-dazzle, like the Miracl demonstration at White Sands. In the future, they warned, showy tests could take precedence over cautious and technically sound science, especially as budget cuts forced changes in the antimissile program. "I'm very alarmed at the degree of hype, promises and a failure to focus on what this national program really is—a research program with lots of unanswered questions," Dr. George H. Miller, head of defense programs at Livermore, said in an interview. "I'm afraid the public is losing sight of how difficult this job is." And Roger Hagengruber, the director of system studies at the Sandia National Laboratory, asked, "Will the science be negatively affected by the fact that there's so much pressure for stunts and demonstrations? Clearly the answer is yes, especially as the dollars go down. The need for progress in a program of this size is irreducible."

Lieut. Colonel Michael Havey, formerly an official on antimissile issues in the President's Office of Science and Technology Policy, said, "Salesmanship is clearly a factor. It has to be when you're dealing with people. But what's important is that we're selling a quality product. It's not been anything but honorable men trying to find the best way to convince the public at large, and Congress in particular, that we have a viable program, both technically and politically."

7

THE SOVIET
THREAT

From the start, one of
the most persistently used arguments by advocates of
the Reagan Strategic Defense Initiative was that the Soviet Union long ago
began pursuing the same goal of a massive ballistic-missile defense and was,
in fact, probably well ahead of the United States in such research and
development. Some critics believed that the argument was consistently abused
and was extended far beyond the supporting evidence. Nevertheless, such
spokesmen for the Reagan administration as Defense Secretary Weinberger
contended that the United States had to try to develop a Star Wars shield
because the Soviet Union was perilously close to having one of its own. So
to understand the American Star Wars research program, it was essential to
understand the Soviet missile defense plans, as well as they could be learned.

The administration was actually not homogeneous in its views, or wholly
consistent in assessing the evidence. When professional intelligence specialists and technocrats were speaking, the assessment of Soviet efforts in

ballistic-missile defense was usually guarded, dry and less alarming than the statements of political appointees. The professional appraisal, repeated many times in testimony to Congress and in official documents, was that the Soviet Union was approximately equal to the United States in some relevant technologies, ahead in none, and lagged badly in such fields as computers and signal processing.

In the nearly three decades that both countries have conducted research in so-called traditional systems for shooting down ballistic missiles, chemically powered, ground-based rockets armed with nuclear warheads were developed that do not require pinpoint guidance and accuracy to destroy a missile reentry vehicle. The much debated 1972 ABM Treaty, which limited the number and area coverage of antimissile weapons, unambiguously permitted limited deployment of such traditional systems. Originally, each nation was to be permitted two defensive sites of 100 interceptor rockets each, but a 1974 protocol to the treaty reduced this to one permitted site. The Soviet Union deployed sixty-four "Galosh" interceptors in the Moscow area. These weapons were designed to attack U.S. missiles outside the atmosphere with low-yield nuclear warheads. Because they would be easily spoofed by U.S. decoys and because they cannot be rapidly reloaded, U.S. targeting specialists and strategic planners never regarded the Moscow ABM defense as a serious problem: It could not, they believed, prevent a determined and successful attack on the Moscow region.

The United States built and deployed a similar, but probably more sophisticated, ABM site near Grand Forks, North Dakota. However, the site was deactivated in the mid-1970s on the grounds that even the annual maintenance and operational costs were not worth the limited protection the system gave to a nearby intercontinental missile field. In addition to building exoatmospheric rockets similar to the Soviet Galosh, the United States developed a high-speed endoatmospheric (inside the atmosphere) weapon called Sprint that would have served as a second layer of defense. It employed a smaller warhead meant to deactivate the incoming nuclear warhead by radiation, rather than by heat and blast.*

* The controversial and never deployed "neutron bomb," meant to help defend Western Europe by killing Soviet forces with radiation while reducing collateral blast damage to German towns, was only a terrestrial application of the old Sprint warhead.

Present ABM System Around Moscow

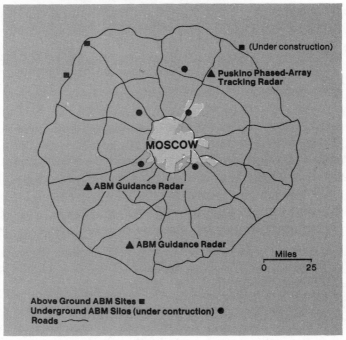

Unlike the United States, the Soviet Union has at present an antiballistic missile system in place, which rings Moscow.

THE NEW YORK TIMES COMPANY

The Soviet Union was believed in the late 1980s to be undertaking an expansion and modernization of the Moscow-area ABM site. Intelligence analysts believed the Soviets planned to increase the number of launchers to the 100 permitted by the treaty but to include high-speed endoatmospheric launchers similar to the old American Sprint. They also apparently planned to replace the Galosh with an improved interceptor. However, weapons experts believed the "new" Soviet weapons would still be comparable only to technology developed by the United States in the 1960s and deactivated

---

In both cases, the enhanced radiation warhead is simply achieved by eliminating the uranium mantle or cladding which usually encloses the plutonium trigger and heavy-water charge of an orthodox thermonuclear weapon. Although called a "hydrogen bomb," fission of the uranium outer mantle—produced by neutrons from the fusion explosion of hydrogen isotopes—provides about 45 percent of the thermal and blast energy of such an orthodox warhead. Remove the uranium mantle and you get a nearly 50 percent reduction in blast effect and a big increase in direct neutron radiation effective to a range of a few thousand yards.

at Grand Forks. Such a step is legal under the terms of the 1972 treaty. Moreover, Pentagon officials said privately that such modernization at the Moscow site would not in any significant way degrade U.S. ability to undertake a devastating retaliatory attack on the Soviet Union in case of nuclear war.

Modernizing the Moscow site was one thing. However, at what was initially a low level of urgency, some administration and Pentagon hawks argued that the Soviets might be planning to break out or "creep out" of the restrictions of the ABM Treaty and deploy the nationwide defense of their territory prohibited by the treaty. The 1986 edition of "Soviet Military Power," a Pentagon assessment published annually under Weinberger, asserted that the Soviets had developed "a rapidly deployable ABM system for which sites could be built in months rather than years." To experts, some of whom very seriously doubt the assertion, this implies that the Soviets developed transportable, if not truly mobile, radars and command and control facilities that could be installed quickly, in contrast to the prolonged construction required for modern, phased-array radars which are very large and complex physical structures. The publication went on:

> We estimate that by using these components the Soviets could by the early 1990s quickly deploy an ABM system to strengthen the defenses of Moscow and defend key targets in the Western USSR and east of the Urals. . . . Taken together, all of the Soviet Union's ABM and ABM-related activities are more significant—and more ominous—than any one considered individually. Cumulatively, they suggest that the USSR *may be* preparing to deploy rapidly an ABM defense of its national territory, contrary to the provisions of the ABM treaty.

This language was not different from that in previous editions of "Soviet Military Power," based primarily on work by Defense Intelligence Agency analysts. But in early 1987, officials of the Defense Department began to put forward an even more ominous interpretation that was vigorously contested by officials of the State Department and, reportedly, by the Central Intelligence Agency. The Pentagon made clear that it wanted the United States to declare that the Soviet Union was now actively undertaking the development of a nationwide ABM defense, not that it "may be preparing to deploy" one. The evidence for this assertion was not made public, but State Department officials told journalists that such a conclusion was not justified. The debate illustrated and underlined one of the sorest points of difference between Defense Department officials and others in the Reagan administration. Official administration policy is to "prevent further erosion" of the 1972 ABM Treaty. The adoption of the Defense Department charge that the Soviets had already begun to deploy a nationwide ABM defense would, of course, if correct, make the treaty a dead letter and justify U.S. abrogation of it, a course recommended for several years by Weinberger and some of his key assistants.

■

In June 1985, in rare public testimony about a national intelligence estimate of Soviet strategic plans and capabilities, Robert Gates, who later became deputy director of the CIA, and Lawrence K. Gershwin, national intelligence officer for strategic matters, told a Senate committee that they did not judge it likely the Soviets would in fact attempt to deploy a nationwide ABM system in the near future. But any defense based on purely traditional ABM technologies would be unlikely to fundamentally degrade U.S. offensive striking power, anyway. If a workable defense against ballistic missiles were ever to become plausible, it would probably have to be built around more promising and difficult technology. And, in fact, long before President Reagan gave his 1983 Star Wars speech, the Soviet Union as well as the United States was trodding precisely that path. What information that existed on Soviet missile defense came essentially from the Pentagon.

Lasers were clearly one key area of Soviet progress. Both nations earnestly explored the possibility of applying intense beams of coherent light—that is, light whose electromagnetic waves roll uniformly, in step as it were with the force of a marching army—to destroy an attacking missile. Laser light too weak to destroy a missile might be strong enough to dazzle or destroy a more flimsy reconnaissance satellite.

The 1986 edition of "Soviet Military Power" said the Soviet research program covered many of the same technologies involved in the American Star Wars program but represented a "far greater investment of plant space, capital and manpower. The USSR's laser program is much larger than U.S. efforts and involves over 10,000 scientists and engineers at more than a half-dozen major research and development facilities and test ranges." Much of this research, the report said, took place at the Sary-Shagan Missile Test Center in Kazakstan, where the Soviets also conduct traditional ABM research. "Soviet Military Power" estimated that there were several lasers for air defense at Sary-Shagan, lasers capable of damaging some components of satellites in orbit and a laser that could be tested for possible use against an ICBM. It contended, too, that a laser-weapons program of the magnitude of the Soviet Union's effort would cost roughly $1 billion per year in the United States.

Some interesting aspects of the Pentagon position seemed to stand out. The first was that the Pentagon does not furnish new evidence buttressing the claim that far greater investment in missile defense is being made in the Soviet Union than in the United States. Possibly that evidence could not be accumulated. The Defense Department also published a slender booklet called "Soviet Strategic Defense" in 1985. But it contained no new revelations. Second, critics argued that some of the Pentagon intelligence was based on debatable methodology. One expert, a highly regarded consultant to the Defense Department, said, "what they measure is what can be measured from space with photoreconnaissance satellites, things like floor space and the likely capacity of electrical generators. That's where you get estimates of '10,000 scientists and engineers.' I regard it as faulty and meaningless." It was also true that such statistics as the cost of $1 billion for laser research if done in the United States was based on old and controversial intelligence methods. These methods convert the actual ruble cost to the Soviet Union to estimated dollar costs in the United States without taking into account different procurement and management methods. *

The Office of Technology Assessment, an official arm of the U.S. Congress, agreed with the Pentagon that the Soviets are vigorously developing advanced technologies potentially applicable to ballistic-missile defense. However, it said, the *quality* of that work is difficult to determine, and its *significance* was therefore highly controversial: "It has been estimated that the total Soviet effort in directed-energy research is larger than that in the United States. However, in terms of basic technological capabilities, the United States clearly remains ahead of the Soviet Union in key areas required for advanced ballistic-missile defense systems."

"Soviet Military Power" also said the Soviets were conducting research on three types of gas lasers. The technology was considered promising for weapons applications, the Pentagon said, and appeared generally capable of supplying the prime power, energy storage and auxiliary components needed

---

* Under this formula, every time inflation increases in the United States, we raise the estimated annual military expenditures of the Soviet Union by an equivalent amount.

for most laser and other directed-energy weapons. Another cautionary note might be sounded again here, however, since the American managers of S.D.I. have virtually written off gas lasers for weapons use on the grounds that power levels needed to make them lethal against laser-armored reentry vehicles seem unattainable. "Unlike the United States," the publication said, "the USSR has now progressed in some cases beyond technology research. It already has ground-based lasers that have a limited capability to attack U.S. satellites . . . and could begin testing components for a large-scale development system in the early 1990s." The authors did add some cautionary notes, saying: "The remaining difficulties in fielding an operational system will require more development time. An operational ground-based laser for defense against ballistic missiles probably could not be deployed until the late 1990s or after the year 2000."

A series of studies of Soviet research programs undertaken in 1985 by the Rand Corporation, a research institution that gives analytical advice to the Air Force, cast a slightly different hue on Soviet laser development from that seen by the Pentagon. One of the Rand papers concerned free-electron lasers, which General Abrahamson identified as perhaps the most promising for antimissile defense. The Rand report said that in terms of manpower and in depth and breadth of research, the Soviet free-electron laser research was at least equal to American efforts. But the report said that American scientists had done twice as many experiments, in attempting to verifying the basic concept, and that they had obtained significantly better results.

Some of the crucial understanding of how subatomic-particle beams could be made practical as weapons or as a shield against weapons is based on Soviet research conducted ten to twenty years ago. The Pentagon called the Soviet work in this area impressive. At the same time, it suggested that any particle-beam weapon capable of destroying missile boosters or warheads probably could not be built until sometime in the next century. The use of such beams as antisatellite weapons, which have much softer targets, could come, it said, by the late 1990s.

In 1987 Secretary Weinberger and others began to argue that the United States could quickly deploy by the early 1990s a partial, "first-stage" ballistic-missile defense consisting mostly of space-based kinetic-energy rockets and ground-based interceptors also using guided kinetic-energy projectiles. But in the 1986 edition of "Soviet Military Power" there was an explicit statement that this was not a plausible course for the Soviet Union. According to the report, "Long-range, space-based kinetic-energy systems for defense against ballistic missiles probably could not be developed until the mid-1990s or even later."

Most advanced weapons programs, including ballistic-missile defense weaponry, are, or will be if they are put into place, dependent on remote sensor and computer technologies, areas in which the West has led the Soviet Union by a substantial margin. A major concern of the Reagan administration in the Star Wars research era is the fear, no doubt well-founded, that the Soviets are deeply engaged in a well-funded effort to purchase illegally U.S. high-technology computers, test and calibration equipment and sensors through third parties.

The Reagan administration often made it a point to say that the Soviet Union was making, as, historically speaking, it always had, large expenditures and efforts in the field of strategic defense. The Reagan spokesmen pointed out frequently that the Soviet Union had greatly outspent the United States in recent years in strategic defense and had even spent almost as much in that field as in the development of offensive strategic weapons.

True. But what did that really say about the Soviet Union program in ballistic-missile defense? Although the United States never really embraced the concept of damage limitation, that is, the attempt to limit the devastation in a nuclear war, the Soviet Union always endorsed the concept, even in circumstances not apparently cost-effective. For instance, the Soviets by the late 1980s were believed to have about 13,600 surface-to-air air defense missiles called SAMs and at least 1,200 interceptor aircraft dedicated to defense against intruding bombers, with an additional 2,800 fighters of the Soviet air forces that could be diverted to such defensive missions. This is in stark contrast to the United States, which, in the ballistic-missile age, virtually ended an attempt to defend the North American continent from bomber attack on the grounds that the threat from Soviet land- and sub-marine-based missiles was so great that massive bomber defense was not really worth it. Moreover, much of the massive Soviet air defense system would be effective only against high-altitude and medium-altitude aircraft.

But United States bombers have not operated at high or medium altitudes for many years and the new cruise missiles never do. Instead, these air-breathing bombers and cruise missiles would penetrate Soviet airspace at very low altitudes at which most of the Soviet air defense is helpless. This is not a recent Soviet aberration. In the late 1940s and 1950s, when effective night and all-weather fighters did not exist, the Soviets deployed thousands of day fighters for antibomber defense. All the Strategic Air Command would have had to do was to attack at night or in bad weather. Nonetheless, the Soviets clearly believed the effort was worthwhile.

Stephen M. Meyer of M.I.T., an authority on Soviet military policy and a longtime Pentagon consultant, remarked in an interview that the Soviets simply have a different philosophy than the long line of budget-conscious Pentagon officials who would and did resist deploying American systems that could not remotely achieve needed mission requirements. Meyer said, and available evidence seemed to support him, that the Soviets have a long record of deploying less-than-satisfactory weapon systems and attempting to improve them with subsequent modifications. The Soviet Union is also much slower to replace obsolete or outdated equipment. As newer, better systems come along, they have tended to keep the old weapons in the field, piling the new onto the obsolescent. Meyer also said with a smile that he believed the Soviets would be ahead of the United States in putting a laser into space. He added: "It probably won't be a useful weapon. But it will be in space and it will lase. A lot of our people in the Pentagon will go bananas."

The Soviets have also spent and done much more than the United States in the field of passive defense. They have a large civil defense program that apparently includes plans that might include large-scale evacuation of civilian populations from urban centers in times of nuclear crisis. Some strategic thinkers regard this as wasteful, believing that in an actual crisis the Soviets would never order the evacuation since it would deprive them of any shred of strategic surprise and might dangerously alarm U.S. officials. The Soviets also have an elaborate system of deep and well-hardened underground bunkers in cities and, according to the Pentagon, 1,750 alternate command and control bunkers for high party officials in outlying areas. Soviet expenditures to harden, or reinforce, ICBM silos, radars and communications facilities have also been included in the Defense Department estimates of Russian strategic defense spending.

Except for a more modest program of hardening ICBM silos and the provision of a few, probably inadequate, leadership relocation centers, the United States has never done much in the field of passive defense. The prevailing view has seemed to be that it was neither necessary nor desirable to emulate the Soviet Union in such fields. In any case, most of the items listed under strategic defense by Star Wars advocates had nothing to do with ballistic-missile defense and thus did not help sustain the argument that the United States was trailing the Soviet Union in Star Wars research.

This was not to suggest that Soviet research programs in technologies relevant to ballistic-missile defense have had no importance. Long before President Reagan inaugurated his S.D.I. program, most experts were advocating the continuation of then ongoing American research programs in such fields as directed energy and sensors. The research was highly worthwhile in itself because the experts regarded a truly workable defense against missiles as obviously attractive. Moreover, the research would be insurance, would it not, against technological surprise by Soviet scientists? Still, those experts, mostly critical of the size and nature of the Star Wars program, argued that there was more than one way to manage what they called a prudent or measured program.

In sum, though the sources of real information were few, no one doubted that the Soviet Union was engaged in a vigorous and significant research program of its own on missile defense. But there did seem to be noticeable differences between the Soviet and the American programs. The Office of Technology Assessment described the basic character of the Reagan administration program as "technology-limited." In other words, the program was theoretically to proceed as rapidly as advances in research would permit. In fact, relatively small but significant annual budget reductions by Congress added some money limits, but only against the determined resistance of the White House and the Department of Defense.

The Soviet Union, however, had not announced a test schedule, and the intrusive and capable reconnaissance satellites of the United States had by 1987 detected no large-scale organized test program. Some intelligence analysts in the Pentagon did, however, claim that the Soviet Union had excercised some surface-to-air antiaircraft missiles during test flights of ballistic missiles and that the SAM-12, a new missile, might have some capability to intercept "some" types of U.S. ballistic missiles, probably older submarine-launched reentry vehicles and some medium-range missiles.

The Soviets, of course, made a vociferous, persistent chorus of complaints about the American S.D.I. program. They originally took the position that even research should be prohibited. This was not realistic. Even American critics of Star Wars agreed that a ban on purely laboratory research could not be verified and therefore could not appropriately be prohibited by treaty.

Gradually, officials of the Soviet Union began to hint they would continue to oppose field testing in space and on the ground but might agree to "under the roof" laboratory research, and that this kind of testing continue. Most of the Soviet's own program, many experts believed, was under-the-roof research.

How long it would stay under the roof, or, indeed, how neatly it always did fit there, no one could say with any real certainty. A 1985 O.T.A. analysis made the point that the manner in which the United States pursues its Star Wars research itself could conceivably provoke undesirable responses from the Soviet Union. The American program could well encourage Soviet exploitation of ambiguities in the 1972 ABM Treaty, the Congressional investigators warned, or it could stimulate the Soviets into deploying ballistic-missile defense and enhanced offensive forces at a time more advantageous to them than to the United States. In other words, the best evidence seemed to indicate that the Soviets were plodding along on research of their own, that it probably did not measure up to that of the United States, for all practical, deployable purposes, but that careless or too-little-thought-out experimentation and experiments that raised questions about treaty compliance could run the serious risk of provoking the Soviets into reactions that would eliminate the possibility of deferring deployment of Star Wars until the best technologies are mature.

But that research proceeded apace.

8

COUNTERATTACK
IN SPACE

The most enthusias-
tic adherents of the Strategic Defense Initiative often
cite the U.S. achievement of landing a manned spacecraft on the moon less
than a decade after President Kennedy proclaimed that goal. Skeptical scientists like to respond by saying that the moon did not shoot back or move
from its predictable orbit. Although their emphasis and some of their basic
assumptions are very different, both sides are in broad agreement that the
task of building Star Wars will certainly be complicated because it must be
done in the face of unpredictable actions by a responsive adversary.

Published documents and remarks by Soviet leaders make it eminently
clear, for example, that Soviet thinkers have already begun to consider the
steps they would take if the United States continued to press ahead with
development and deployment of a ballistic-missile defense. It seemed equally
clear to most analysts that it was too early to be sure exactly what moves the
Soviet Union would make. For one thing, it could well be a decade before

113

U.S. policymakers decided the exact form and size that a Star Wars defense could, or should, take. Presumably, the Soviet planners would wish to tailor their response as precisely as possible to the perceived nature of the U.S. threat. For another thing, some possible Soviet responses require careful technological evaluation: They may be scientifically plausible but quite difficult to attain or to produce at affordable cost.

But, as with missile defense itself, many of the broad principles of overcoming or nullifying a defense must be anticipated in general terms. Possible Soviet responses to Star Wars fall into four broad categories: (1) The deployment of an advanced ballistic missile defense of their own, much larger in scale and capability than the limited ABM, or antiballistic missile, interceptors now permitted by the 1972 ABM Treaty.* (2) Direct attack on the United States missile defense system, known in military jargon as "defense suppression." (3) Countermeasures designed to permit Soviet nuclear delivery vehicles to penetrate the American defensive shield. (4) A significant increase in the numbers of Soviet long-range nuclear weapons, undertaken with an intent to saturate a U.S. defense.

But as with every other aspect of the Star Wars debate, there are technical uncertainties about the finer details of Soviet responses that must be anticipated. This is an area of debate that is also loaded with extremely important political arguments. If it is plausible that the Soviet Union can make Star Wars ineffective, or only marginally effective, then the great expense of building a defense may be rejected by future Congresses. And if deployment of Star Wars causes Soviet responses that decrease international stability, especially in times of tension and potential crisis, the project may never bear fruit. It is natural, then, that critics of S.D.I. tend to foresee Soviet responses that will be technically feasible and strategically undesirable for the United States. It is natural, too, that proponents of ballistic-missile defense predict a much more optimistic future.

S.D.I.O. director General Abrahamson, for instance, has said that the real aim of missile defense is "to modify Soviet behavior." He and other Reagan administration officials supportive of the program argue that the S.D.I. program will eventually convince Soviet leaders that offensive nuclear weapons are losing their military utility and persuade Moscow to move cooperatively with the United States through a transition to mutual defenses in which numbers of offensive weapons and their great destructive potential will gradually wither away.

---

* This possibility is discussed in greater detail in Chapter 6.

The most obvious possible response to defense is more offense.

A wide range of specialists and analysts outside of the Reagan administration have always believed that the first response to Star Wars by the Soviet Union will be an effort to increase the number of deliverable nuclear warheads in its arsenal. A 1985 report by the Congressional Office of Technology Assessment said, "An obvious, 'brute force' response to defense is to build more offense." This is also a very troubling prospect to administration officials, but they tend either to deny that it is a likely response or to argue that the Soviets can be disuaded from taking such a step. The logic for increasing offense seems simple but has some subtle twists. It is common to discuss the effectiveness of ballistic-missile defense in percentage terms, to speak of a 50 percent effective defense, say, or a 99 percent effective shield. In practical terms, however, a Star Wars defense would be a finite system and not an infinitely expandable system. Only so many space battle stations, or ground lasers, or battle management sensors would or could be deployed at any given time.

And even highly capable weapons, whether they are designed for defense or offense, have physical limitations. For instance, rocket-powered kinetic-energy weapons are one-shot devices that cannot be reused. Some directed energy or "beam" weapons could be fired many times—many experts have discussed possible retargeting times of from one second to one-tenth of a second for an antimissile laser. This is the time required for tracking and aiming sensors to swing the laser beam from one target to the next. Nevertheless, the fact remains that any deployed missile defense will only be able to engage, and, one hopes, destroy, a finite number of targets and will be designed to deal with a finite Soviet threat. If the size of the Soviet offense is significantly increased, the percentage effectiveness of the existing defense will necessarily decline.

The aim in increasing the fleet of intercontinental ballistic missiles would be to overwhelm or to saturate the defense to insure that a militarily important number of Soviet warheads would still penetrate U.S. territory. This could be done in at least two ways. The Soviet Union could increase the number of ICBMs themselves or it could increase the number of MIRVs carried by each one. The United States could, of course, respond by expanding its defense. But this might be met in turn by a further expansion of the Soviet

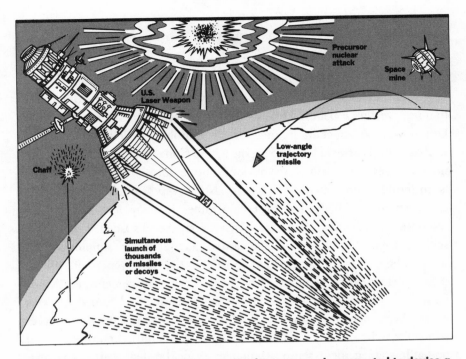

Some experts contend that Soviet strategic planners may be prompted to devise a variety of methods to counter the proposed U.S. space defense system. These would include Soviet space mines, chaff and decoys launched into space, the launching of thousands of ballistic missiles to overwhelm the defensive shield, and missiles that would dart underneath it. ILLUSTRATION BY BRAD HAMANN

offense—the kind of open-ended, ever-escalating arms race a Star Wars defense hopes to avoid.

An offensive buildup is, in fact, what the United States itself chose to do in the late 1960s in response to the Soviet Union's deployment of the small, localized antiballistic-missile system ringing Moscow, one permitted by the 1972 ABM Treaty. To deal with the possibility that even small ABM defenses might reduce the American ability to penetrate Soviet territory, the United States added MIRVs to its force of 550 Minuteman III intercontinental land missiles and to its submarine-launched missiles. The Soviets responded by MIRVing their own missiles, and outdid the United States by placing from six to ten warheads on their best ICBMs, clearly outgunning the three MIRVs on Minuteman missiles. In retrospect, many Congressmen and former policymakers see the U.S. decision to deploy MIRVs, rather than trying to reach agreement with the Soviet Union to ban the technology, as a costly mistake. It was the development of Soviet missiles with many MIRVs that aroused fears in the late 1970s and early 1980s of a "window of vulnerability" in which the land-based leg of the American strategic deterrent was seen as open to successful attack.

Indeed, an offensive buildup is also exactly what the administration threatens to do itself if the Soviet Union should break out and deploy a nationwide missile defense, which the ABM Treaty forbids. Just before President Reagan went to Geneva in November 1985 for his first summit meeting with Soviet leader Gorbachev, Defense Secretary Weinberger sent the President a letter which was leaked to the press. In that document, Weinberger said the United States should increase its own offensive striking force in circumstances in which Soviet defense merely seemed a probability, far less a certainty. "Even a probable (Soviet) territorial defense would require us to increase the number of our offensive forces and their ability to penetrate Soviet defenses to assure that our operational plans could be executed," the Weinberger memorandum said.

On the other hand, administration officials took the position from 1983 onward that the development and deployment of Star Wars would not encourage the Soviet Union to increase offensive forces. Instead, administration spokesmen have insisted that deploying S.D.I. would provide what a Pentagon statement in 1986 called "strong incentives" for both sides to *decrease* offenses and move toward mutual defense. Their argument is that Star Wars would make offensive weapons "lose their military usefulness." There has been no real attempt, nor would it be easy, to reconcile the Weinberger statement of U.S. intentions and the administration appraisal of probable Soviet response to S.D.I.

Whatever the American response would be and however uncertain a military adversary's response will always be, the Soviet Union repeatedly and clearly threatened to undertake an expansion of its offensive nuclear forces if Star Wars goes forward. At the November 1985 Geneva summit, Gorbachev warned that the Soviet response to Star Wars "will be effective, though less expensive, and quicker to produce." In an interview that fall, Marshal Sergei F. Akhromeyev, chief of the Soviet General Staff, said of S.D.I. testing: "If this process goes on we will have nothing to do but to take up retaliatory measures in the field of both offensive and defensive weapons." Only four days after President Reagan's 1983 speech, the late Yuri V. Andropov, then the Soviet leader, warned: "Should this concept be translated into reality, it would in fact open the floodgates to a runaway race of all types, both offensive and defensive."

Several military analysts have said the Soviet Union is, at the present time, better able to begin an offensive arms race than the United States. The production line for American Minuteman missiles was closed down years ago, and the production of Midgetman, the small ICBM, is not expected to begin until about 1992. The first U.S. MX missiles, with ten warheads each, began in 1986, but Congress limited production to fifty missiles and experts believe it would be very difficult to accelerate or greatly expand MX production. In contrast, the Soviet Union between 1980 and 1984 built 875 ICBMs, 950 submarine-launched missiles and 2,175 tactical range missiles—an average of 800 new ballistic missiles per year. All of its production lines are at least "warm" and some are hot.

According to Stephen Meyer of M.I.T., the Soviets probably have about 1,000 missile boosters stored but not deployed. He suggested in an interview that there might be several anti–Star Wars uses for this excess missile capacity. If armed with warheads, they would nearly double Soviet missile ICBM inventories within a short time span.* Or they could be launched, in case of war, without warheads to increase the problem faced in boost-phase defense by Star Wars.

The Soviet Union also seemed more able, especially in the short term, to increase offensive striking force through proliferation of MIRVed reentry vehicles. The Soviet SS-18 heavy missile has about eight times the "throw weight" of the American Minuteman and perhaps three times the throw weight of the MX. American spy satellites and long-range radars have never detected a test of the SS-18 with more than 10 warheads, and the United States Joint Chiefs of Staff have expressed doubt in congressional testimony that any nuclear power would increase the number of warheads on such a missile without a thorough test program. However, the Chiefs told the Senate in 1979 that the SS-18 could probably lift up to 30 RV's, instead of 10. Other experts said that it would be relatively easy to increase the payload of the missile from 10 to 14 warheads. With 308 SS-18s now deployed, such an augmentation would give the Soviets an increase of 1,232 warheads.

Because the Strategic Defense Initiative was chartered only to investigate defense against ballistic missiles, the Soviets could also be expected to accelerate an already expanded production of bombers and low-flying cruise missiles, according to military experts. Unless the United States undertook a very expensive program to improve conventional air defense against such "air-breathing" aerodynamic threats, the Soviet Union could simply fly under

---

* However, this would also require the construction of new missile silos, which would require considerable time and would probably be more expensive than the missiles themselves.

the Star Wars shield. Although described as conventional, such air defense is by no means easy. Even today, reliable radar detection of low-flying aircraft is a serious problem. If the Soviet Union emulated U.S. advances in "stealth" technology of aircraft with low observable radar and infrared signatures, it seems possible that both nations will be able to penetrate the air space of the other with significant numbers of nuclear weapons.

One of the most disturbing possible Soviet responses to Star Wars would be to seek methods to destroy it by direct attack on the components of the missile shield.

This defense-suppression system approach is different from countermeasures meant to ensure penetration of a defense. Although the two approaches are not necessarily mutually exclusive, some experts believe it is unlikely that Soviet planners would elect to undertake the massive expense of developing both weapons to destroy the defense and countermeasures to penetrate it. If the defense suppression depended on the detonation of large numbers of nuclear weapons in space or in the high atmosphere, it is not thought likely that the Soviets would bother to build as well a Star Wars system of their own, because the nuclear blasts would tend to degrade or destroy their own missile defense. Defense suppression is a disturbing possibility for several reasons. First, any attempt to defend Star Wars from a determined attack raises very serious technological problems. Second, it raises troubling political and strategic questions and the more disturbing possibility that human leaders might have to surrender some of their war-or-peace decision-making powers to electronic sensors, computers and machines.

From a technical point of view, one of the most plausible defense-suppression techniques would probably be space mines, which would consist of explosive charges carried on satellites. They could be either nuclear warheads or conventional explosives that would propel clouds of pellets or metal fragments to destroy the sensors, battle stations, laser relay and fighting mirrors and other components of an S.D.I. defense. Because there is no shock wave or blast effect from an explosion in space, the mines would have to be detonated at relatively short range, although some experts believe that in the case of nuclear weapons this could be many miles from the U.S. component.

Such space mines could theoretically be put into orbit near U.S. satellites carrying sensors and ballistic-missile defense weapons. Alternatively, they could be "parked" in orbit farther from the Star Wars components and moved within lethal range during times of crisis or as a prelude to a Soviet nuclear attack. The mines would be detonated by radio signal from the earth and could punch a hole in the defensive system through which a successful nuclear attack might be launched. Space mines would not be useful against the ground-based rocket interceptors of the terminal, or last-ditch layer of a Star Wars defense. However, other measures could be used to negate terminal defenses. And several pro–Star Wars government experts have freely conceded that any terminal defense, standing on its own, can probably be overwhelmed.

One possible defense against space mines would be for Star Wars satellites to shoot at them. But a technique called "salvage fusing," in which warheads are engineered to detonate when struck by a hostile object, could make a shoot-back defense useless. If the mines were within the lethal radius, they would destroy the satellite anyway. A purely physical defense against space mines would, therefore, be difficult to devise. Some proponents of Star Wars have suggested that U.S. defensive satellites could use small rocket motors to maneuver out of lethal range when a space mine was detected close by. But, of course, space mines themselves can be made maneuverable.

Because of the difficulty of physical defense against mines, advocates of ballistic-missile defenses have suggested that the United States could declare, and enforce, keep-out zones in space. This would require the United States to declare that no Soviet—or third nation—satellite could be placed in orbit within a given radius of an S.D.I. satellite. Alternatively, some pro–Star Wars thinkers, such as Robert Jastrow of Dartmouth College, have suggested that the United States could, and should, take the position that the near approach of any potentially hostile satellite to a component of the American defense was "an act of war" that would be met by a counterattack to destroy the space mine.

There would be some ironies if the United States should attempt to post keep-out zones. In the late 1950s and early 1960s, when the United States was developing the first reconnaissance satellites to monitor Russian military developments, American officials were worried that the Soviet Union might declare outer space over its boundaries as part of its territorial air space and attempt to exclude American spy satellites from orbits over Soviet territory. The United States was prepared then to resist this claim strenuously. The concept of keep-out zones obviously raises serious questions of international law and may conflict with the Outer Space Treaty, which seems to rest on the premise that space is international and cannot be divided by sovereign boundaries.

A drawing released by the Pentagon, said to be made from intelligence photographs, of the Soviets' mobile, ten-warhead intercontinental missile system, which the proposed Star Wars shield would block.

AP/WIDE WORLD PHOTOS

But international law aside, the concept raises more practical difficulties if, as seems likely, the Soviet leaders decline to accept it. A policy of destroying another nation's satellites may not be compatible with a ballistic-missile defense advertised as the best prevention of war. Moreover, such a system is probably not amenable to human control. Some critics argue that if mines already deployed somewhere in space are to be destroyed before they reach the lethal radius, the shoot-back weapons on Star Wars satellites will have to be programed to react automatically, without human intervention.

Still another form of direct attack on Star Wars could be antisatellite weapons, known as ASATs. The Weinberger Defense Department repeatedly charged that the Soviet Union had the world's only "operational" ASAT weapon. The United States was testing at the same time a more sophisticated ASAT, although the tests were hampered by restrictions imposed by Congress, where a powerful faction of legislators hoped to see negotiations for a treaty that would prohibit ASAT weapons.

The Soviet ASAT consisted of a conventional explosive warhead mounted on an older model of an intercontinental missile. The warhead had to be put into orbit and then shifted to the vicinity of the target. The U.S. model was a "direct ascent" ASAT carried to high altitude by an F-15 fighter plane and then into space by small rockets. It could reach its target much faster than the Soviet model and had better sensor technology. The tests of the Soviet ASAT showed mediocre results, even with radar sensors. All tests with more advanced infrared sensors failed. The American and the Russian ASAT could only reach low-orbit satellites. A former Air Force chief of staff, General Lew Allen, told the Senate that the Soviet ASAT was not a serious threat to U.S. military satellites.

Nonetheless, unless a treaty is negotiated, much more effective ASATs seem certain to be produced by the laboratories of both nations. They would pose a serious threat to any space-based ballistic-missile defense, although possibly not an insuperable threat. Colonel George Hess, the director of survivability studies in the Star Wars program, said the United States was already deeply engaged in studies of possible tactics and counter-counter-measures to protect battle stations and sensor satellites from possible ASAT attack. One obvious counter-counterdefense was proliferation—to divide a Star Wars defense system among thousands of small satellites so as to make successful attack on the system as a whole more difficult. Colonel Hess said making the Star Wars satellites highly maneuverable was also a possibility. Studies were under way, too, on how to give American satellites "shoot-back" defensive capability to protect themselves or to place anti-ASAT weapons in space patrol to play a role analogous to fighter planes escorting bombers in conventional war. And studies were begun on possible ways to provide armor or shielding for S.D.I. satellites. This would, of course, probably create weight problems and complicate the already daunting task of getting a full-scale Star Wars system into space with transport rockets. Because the closing speed between a satellite and a homing ASAT is so tremendous, there are doubts about whether that armor could protect it against a hit-to-kill kinetic-energy projectile.

In some ways, ASATs are not ideal for a surprise, preemptive attack on an S.D.I. defensive constellation in space. Even if high-speed, direct-ascent ASATs were used, it would be easy to detect the launching from Soviet territory. U.S. officials would presumably assume that war had commenced. Full strategic surprise could not be achieved in that manner. But in other ways it has been thought that they could well be particularly nasty. An ASAT devised from the nuclear bomb-pumped X-ray laser technology being researched by United States scientists might be effective, indeed. Although a laser powered by a nuclear bomb can obviously only be used once, the bundle of lasing rods it carries can theoretically attack many targets simultaneously at great range. While Americans were beginning their investigations of X-ray lasers for use as antimissile weapons, some scientists such as Kurt Gottfried, a Cornell physicist who opposes Star Wars, noted that an X-ray laser could be even more effective against satellites than against missile reentry vehicles. In fact, Gottfried said that a fundamental problem facing Star Wars designers was that any weapon capable of dealing with heat-resistant, hard RVs should be even more effective against satellites.

Other, relatively simple weapons have been discussed for attack on Star Wars. If the defense system employed relay and fighting mirrors to redirect laser beams, then clouds of pellets, gravel or any other material placed in the path of the orbiting mirrors could easily destroy the optical surfaces, unless ways could be found to shield them. Furthermore, if ground-based laser beams could theoretically destroy missiles and warheads they could certainly be used as well to attack satellites, which fly in predictable orbits.

Reconnaissance experts using information from American satellites have been obsessed for some time by a mystery site south of Dushanbe, the capital city of the Tadshik Republic in the Soviet Union, not far from the Afgan border. There under construction atop the region's tallest mountain is an elaborate complex of roads, buildings, laboratories and ten domes to hold lasers and tracking telescopes. The site, 7,600 feet above sea level, is linked by heavy power cables to the nearby Nurek hydroelectric plant, one of the largest in the Soviet Union. According to United States intelligence experts—who spoke to *The New York Times* in 1987 only after great hesitation and requests for anonymity—the domes of Dushanbe will one day house lasers that will flash their concentrated beams of light into space. The question that divided experts, however, was how powerful the lasers would be and what would be their ultimate purpose.

The view of American scientists both inside and outside the government was that the Dushanbe facility could well pose a threat to low-orbit American battle stations in space. The electric power going into the planned laser station suggested that it might, indeed, be a powerful laser. In an unusual departure, a senior Soviet scientist agreed that large lasers could threaten space-based antimissile arms. "At present we have a kind of . . . basic research in lasers, just to keep our hands in such things," Roald Z. Sagdeyev, director of the Space Research Institute of the Soviet Academy of Sciences said during a visit to the United States. But he said he believed that if there were a final American decision to proceed with S.D.I., some of those technologies "would be very helpful for countermeasures." American experts said that Dushanbe might be used to disrupt or destroy antimissile satellite systems in low orbit and to track them at high altitudes. The ultimate purpose of the mountain site will probably be unknown for years, as it is not expected to be completed before the 1990s.

The fusing of the nuclear warheads in reentry vehicles so that they would blow up when struck—a technique called salvage fusing—is another possible method of defeating or degrading the final layer of a ballistic-missile defense system. If the warheads could be so fused, they could cause considerable destruction on the ground, especially those that penetrated the atmosphere. Such damage would be greatest for RVs exploding over civilian population centers, but could be important as well in damaging ground sensors for missile silo defenses.

And, not least, even if the computing and communications functions of Star Wars are divided into semiautonomous packages, a lot of electronic data will pass to human decision makers and ground-based weapons and sensors. An attack by saboteurs, or by other means, on the ground reception and relay centers does not seem out of the question. Early in the Star Wars debate a newspaper reporter found that most of the antennas at Sunnyvale, California, which now receive a significant amount of data from existing satellites, are within eyesight and antitank rocket range of a busy California freeway.

There is no perfect distinction between defense-suppression techniques and defense penetration, that is, between attacking the defense system directly and penetrating it. A few measures overlap the boundary line.

The "eyes" of sensors mostly measure electromagnetic energy in one form or another, and they are sensitive. Sensors can be blinded or dazzled by a variety of techniques. Ground-based lasers could play such a role. The Pentagon, in fact, has for several years warned that experimental Soviet lasers at Sary-Shagan in Central Asia may be evolving to a point where they can play just such a role. Shielding of sensors might be a possible defense. Nuclear weapons deliberately detonated in space could also cause damage to or temporarily blind many sensors.

However, some countermeasures seek strictly to evade rather than to destroy a defense. One Soviet countermeasure would be to mount its nuclear weapons on "fast-burn boosters." The Fletcher Presidential Commission, which recommended proceeding with the Star Wars program, recognized and discussed this possibility in its report to President Reagan. At present,

Soviet missile rockets burn for about 300 seconds, or five minutes, and lift the postboost vehicle and its multiple reentry vehicles to an altitude of about 400 kilometers, or well beyond most of the atmosphere. Scientists are in general agreement that, by substantially increasing the size of the exhaust throat, or nozzle, of such rockets, the propulsion or burn time of missiles could be reduced to as little as fifty seconds; the rockets would still be able to place their RVs into an intercontinental ballistic trajectory from an altitude of about ninety kilometers. There is still an atmosphere at that altitude, although it is thin.

This would pose several serious problems for any defense that depended heavily on boost-phase intercept. Physicist Richard Garwin of IBM, a critic of Star Wars but also a longtime consultant to the Defense Department and one of the scientists who developed the hydrogen bomb, wrote that fast-burn boosters would prevent boost-phase interception by several of the technologies under consideration in S.D.I. experiments. Garwin and others pointed out that neutral particle beams could not successfully penetrate the atmosphere, even the thin atmosphere at high altitudes. There was also scientific doubt that the "soft" X-rays that would be produced by the proposed X-ray laser could be effective in the upper atmosphere, which would tend to absorb them. Homing kinetic kill weapons might be useless, too, against fast-burn boosters. As such a rocket began to penetrate the atmosphere, friction would heat the windows through which its infrared guidance sensors peer and blind it. Also, the flight time from launch to interception would be increased and a greater number of orbiting battle stations carrying the homing kinetic weapons would be needed to have a sufficient number of weapons in range.

Even if atmospheric heating did not blind the homing sensors, there could be other severe complications caused by fast burners. The homing sensors on kinetic kill weapons must necessarily employ long-wave infrared technology because short-wave sensors cannot detect the very faint heat emitted by a nuclear warhead (though they are useful for detecting the massive heat of a rocket engine). However, if used against RVs dispensed at relatively low altitudes by fast-burn boosters, the sensors will not see the object against the cold blackness of space but against the background of the earth, which is a massive emitter of long-wave infrared. And this could cause so much background clutter as to confuse the homing sensors. Garwin and other scientists have also noted possible problems in engagement time that fast-burn boosters would pose. With contemporary Soviet missiles, a boost-phase defense might have 200 seconds to engage and destroy the boosters (and therefore also the warheads the boosters carry). In that circumstance, a single space battle station could destroy 200 boosters before the boost phase ended. With fast-burn boosters, engagement time might be only one-fifth as long, or forty seconds, and perhaps less. Garwin calculated that this might require the United States to place five times as many space battle stations into orbit.

There are some disadvantages to the use of fast-burn boosters. They would probably reduce the total payload of a missile unless its thrust and throw weight were increased. However, one maker of U.S. missiles has calculated that the payload penalty need not be high and might be as low as 15 percent. Critics of Star Wars say this would be a small price for the Soviets to pay for frustrating boost-phase defense.

As a countermeasure, fast-burn boosters would only be effective against the boost-phase layer. During the first two years of the S.D.I. program, American officials tended in public to argue that the boost phase was vital to an effective defense. However, by 1986 Star Wars analysts themselves had begun to express doubts that boost-phase defenses could be made survivable against preemptive Soviet attack, and it was no longer clear how much, if any, an eventual defense would rest on interception in the boost phase. If boost-phase defense were abandoned, then fast-burn boosters would make no sense as a Soviet countermeasure. But the United States would lose, too, by abandoning what Reagan officials always described as the "great leverage" of being able to kill all of the objects on a missile before they go into ballistic trajectory.

At any rate, strong proponents of ballistic-missile defense asserted that fast-burn boosters were an unlikely countermeasure because the Soviets could not sufficiently modify their missile arsenal; they would have to replace it with entirely new missiles, which would be very expensive and take too long. This argument was usually made by persons such as Robert Jastrow who believed that an effective missile defense could be deployed within a few years of a decision to do so and at a relatively modest cost.* These defense advocates argued that it would cost the Soviet Union more, and take more years, to deploy fast-burn boosters than it would for the United States to erect a missile defense. However, scientists who believe that an effective missile defense could not be deployed until well into the 1990s or later and would cost several hundred billions of dollars drew a nearly opposite conclusion.

Jastrow was almost passionate in his arguments that fast-burn boosters

---

* Jastrow and some of his associates estimated that it would take seven years from decision to deployment at a cost of $121 billion.

represented no real threat to Star Wars. He said that the technology would not protect MIRVed missiles because the post-boost bus that dispenses warheads would have to rise above the atmosphere to dispense the warheads accurately, leaving it vulnerable. He also said that even if single-warhead missiles were used, "deployment in the atmosphere separates the warheads from the decoys at the outset, making the decoys useless." Jastrow also contended that atmospheric buffeting of warheads released in the upper atmosphere would degrade their accuracy, although he conceded that some of these problems could be offset by providing a separate guidance system for each warhead.*

Some other possible Soviet countermeasures might be quite difficult to employ effectively. This would be true of what are called simulation decoys, or decoys that would simulate the electromagnetic signatures of actual reentry vehicles. Because decoys are much lighter than RVs, emit less heat and could be moved more easily by pulses of laser energy from so-called interactive sensors, it is believed that very sensitive and capable U.S. sensors could discriminate between decoys and RVs. Moreover, real RVs undergo certain motion adjustments as they are deployed which sensors should be able to detect. And RVs contain radioactive materials that could be detected by sensors using neutral particle-beam technology. There is, however, a way around this difficulty for Soviet planners. It is called antisimulation. In simple terms, it means making reentry vehicles look like decoys rather than attempting to make decoys look like RVs. There are many plausible ways to do this. One would be to equip all decoys and RVs with balloons made of plastic, Mylar and aluminum that would envelop the objects as they were dispensed from the post-boost vehicle, or bus. Such shiny balloons would totally defeat conventional radars, which would be unable to "see through" the aluminized skin to detect which balloons contained decoys.

The long-wave infrared, heat-seeking sensors meant to identify RVs by the somewhat stronger, if faint, heat RVs emit might also be baffled if the skin of the balloons were superinsulated to contain the small heat emission. And attaching small motion motors to decoys and RVs might make it possible to make all of the balloon-encased objects move in the same way. It is even considered theoretically feasible to equip decoys with small radiation equipment to mimic the radiation emissions of an actual warhead.

In 1986, General Abrahamson told Congress several times that the technology to intercept reentry vehicles had already been proved, and that the

---

* Letter to the authors, December 22, 1986.

major problem remaining was to learn to produce interceptors at an acceptable cost. He was, he said in an interview, referring to the Army's Homing Overlay Experiment (HOE) that had failed five times before it was successfully performed in June 1984. However, several weapons engineers later told the writers of this book that the kind of antisimulation balloons discussed above would easily defeat the sensors used in HOE.

Another countermeasure that would probably defeat these sensors is tethered decoys. In this technique, a cluster of decoys would be dispensed on a sort of rope attached to the real reentry vehicle. Since the projectile used in a kinetic-energy weapon is small and depends on actual impact to destroy the target, there is almost no margin for error. Approaching a cluster of superinsulated Mylar balloons, the sensor might have great difficulty in selecting the actual target. Garwin also described the possibility of an antisimulation technique that might defeat beam sensors designed to "weigh" decoys and RVs by bumping them with pulses of energy. Such sensors would be designed to differentiate between the reactive motion of the heavy RVs and the light decoys. However, according to Richard Garwin, it should be possible for the Soviets to mount small motors and electronic equipment on RVs to make them move like decoys when the sensor beams touch them. *

Ablative coatings are another possible countermeasure. Although they would be useless against hit-to-kill kinetic-energy weapons, they could be effective against laser weapons. Such protective coatings vaporize when struck by a laser beam, dissipating much of the heat and keeping the underlying material relatively cool. This is far from a merely theoretical possibility. General Abrahamson told the Senate in 1986 that the S.D.I.O. was studying the concept of what he called "laser armor," and added that if the United States could develop laser armor the Soviets presumably could do the same thing. He added that if a final Star Wars design provided a level of laser energy that was insufficient to destroy armored missiles coated with ablative materials, a costly mistake would have been made. One Senate staff member remarked privately that this was a classic understatement, given possible Star Wars costs.

The case of ablative coatings illustrates the tremendously complex guessing game that a strategic transition to ballistic-missile defense would involve. Each side would make estimates, probably conservative, about its own devices and imagine the worst about the opponent's potential. Both would know

---

* For more about this, see Garwin's chapter in the book *Empty Promise: The Growing Case Against Star Wars* (Boston: Beacon Press, 1986).

that if the estimates were in serious error, a whole class of weapons or sensors—perhaps the entire system—might prove useless in battle. One strategist remarked that something called "the intelligence time cycle" would be as important as technology itself. The side with the most timely and accurate information about the other side's gimmickry would have a major advantage.

A number of specialists have expressed the belief that the most likely course of action by the Soviet Union would be to undertake a combination of responses that would include both expansion of the offensive arsenal and the employment of penetration-aid countermeasures meant to make it more difficult for the United States to destroy an individual missile or an individual reentry vehicle. There was an interesting and possibly significant development in December 1986 when the Soviets published for the first time an apparently authoritative book on the responses and countermeasures they said they believed would render Star Wars ineffective.

The 147-page book, entitled "Weaponry in Space: The Dilemma of Security," mostly discussed the same catalogue of possible responses to Star Wars that U.S. critics of the S.D.I. program had been discussing for years. U.S. scientists drew the conclusion that the Soviets were considering adapting, or redesigning, the Galosh ABM rockets now deployed around Moscow to serve as high-velocity, direct-ascent ASAT weapons. The Soviet book also discussed such measures as space mines and nuclear explosions in the high atmosphere to blind sensors.

Although the Soviet publication did not explicitly reveal Soviet intentions, some American scientists were struck by the emphasis the book seemed to give to direct attack—to the defense-suppression techniques, one of the most disturbing of all possible responses.

9

EUROPE'S DILEMMA

On August 1985, on the fortieth anniversary of the dropping of the atomic bomb on Hiroshima, *The Economist*, the prestigious British journal, reminded its readers that after four decades the world had come to believe that the only defense against nuclear slaughter was to threaten nuclear slaughter. But it said President Reagan changed all that with his March 1983 speech. Not that *The Economist*, which consistently argued the case for the European advocates of Star Wars, accepted the President's premise that a missile shield would make nuclear weapons impotent and obsolete. Indeed, most European proponents of Star Wars were at first either genuinely frightened, angered, annoyed or skeptical. Actually, in the weeks that followed, most did not take it seriously. But now, two years later, these Europeans, for the most part political conservatives or members of the military, were accepting the idea of a small portion of the Star Wars plan, one offering a limited defense. The possibility of stopping quite a lot of Soviet warheads, as the editors put it, was seen as significant and reassuring.

The reasoning was this: A limited defensive system would make it almost impossible for the Russians to risk a first strike against America. If the United States had this protection and the Soviet Union did not, then Europeans would look up at an American nuclear umbrella and see it as a good deal less threadbare. Of course, the United States would have to be able to protect its own silos and control centers from surprise attack. But that could be done. Simple arithmetic: If the Americans erected, say, three relatively effective layers of defense, the number of warheads Russia would need would rise logarithmically.

The European Star Warriors initially argued that the nations that could afford Star Wars defenses—the United States, the Soviet Union, possibly Japan and the countries of Western Europe—could afford in future years to be significantly less concerned about a nuclear attack than they had been for decades. They could spend less money and energy on their own arsenals and devote more, instead, to disarmament. The world, in short, would be an easier place in which to live. But even these Europeans foresaw the catch awaiting them. The overriding question was, as it would no doubt remain for years to come: Could the many Star Wars technologies be researched, manufactured, tested and deployed at a price any nation could afford? Europe's missile-defense advocates at first took it more or less on faith that this incredibly complex military technology could eventually be made to work at an affordable cost, as for centuries military technology that was regarded in its time as too complicated and expensive, from the Gatling gun to the atomic bomb, has had a way of being made to work. Thus, they argued, since nuclear weapons would always have great usefulness as a deterrent to aggression, and since a nuclear-missile defense system would enhance such deterrence by blunting an aggressive enemy's missile attack, the American investment in time and money would certainly be well worth it to the Europeans.

Though they were angered by the unilateral nature of President Reagan's Star Wars plan, European governments eventually began to fall in line. The reasoning at first centered ostensibly on a set of assumptions based on Europe's proximity to the Soviet Union and the configuration of Allied medium-range missiles on European soil. If the Russians attacked a nation of Western Europe, American Pershing 2 and cruise missiles based in Europe or long-range intercontinental ballistic missiles based on American soil would strike

Soviet missile silos. The Soviets could strike back at American silos, but S.D.I. would protect enough of them so that they could retaliate and wipe out Soviet silos. If the Soviets struck at European or American cities, the protected American arsenal would obliterate the Soviet cities. Thus, anti-missile defenses discourage not only a first Soviet strike but also a second one. A first strike by the West now becomes conceivable, and that translates into strength and safety. Once the Soviets developed a missile defense system of their own, of course, the Europeans would find themselves back where they started: feeling the force of the American deterrent against a Soviet invasion beginning to fade. And several European government officials, Helmut Kohl, chancellor of West Germany, among them, suggested that Europe would eventually have to develop Star Wars capability of its own. But in the meantime, they seemed to be agreeing that they would have greater protection for their countries by going along with the Reagan plan at far less cost to themselves. On December 22, 1984, Margaret Thatcher met with President Reagan at Camp David, where she said later they agreed on four specific points involving arms control and Star Wars: "that the Western goal should not be to achieve superiority but rather to maintain balance; second, that S.D.I. deployments would have to be a matter of East-West negotiations; third, that the overall aim would be to enhance, not undermine, deterrence; and fourth, that negotiations should aim at international security and reduced levels of offensive systems on both sides."

Though European leaders were officially coming to accept the notion of space-based defense, boiling underneath was a growing concern over potential military and political dangers to Europe, if not, indeed, to the world. It was far from clear to the many European thinkers, policymakers, military experts and government officials who spoke in dozens of *New York Times* interviews by science reporter William J. Broad and foreign correspondent Judith Miller, among others, that Star Wars would make their nations safer.

To understand this current of European unease over a plan aimed, after all, at blocking Russian missiles, it is necessary to bear in mind that the Soviet military problem for Europe is hardly restricted to missiles. Thousands of bombers, all capable of carrying nuclear weapons, and tens of thousands of tanks are a real threat as well. For a variety of reasons, the Europeans find themselves in a different position from either the United States or the Soviet Union. Forty years of nuclear deterrence have kept those tanks and bombers from crossing Western European boundaries and meant forty years of peace.

Possessing nuclear weapons has put France on a kind of parity with the two superpowers. The weapons have given the French—and the British, for that matter—a special status. But would not a Soviet defensive system reduce the importance and effectiveness of the British-French nuclear arsenal? In fact, in response to improved missile defenses around Moscow, France in the mid-1980s began to increase the number of warheads carried by its submarines, changing from single to multiple warheads on missiles. The British, too, began adding to their arsenal, and by the 1990s, those two nations plan to have 1,200 warheads. France's independent nuclear *force de frapper* has provided it unusual political unity within France and made it what Hugh De Santis, a senior associate at the Carnegie Endowment for International Peace, has called "the last champion of mutual assured destruction." But it is not only the French. As Colonel Jonathan Alford of the Institute for Strategic Studies in London put it: "The Europeans actually tend to like nuclear weapons. They don't say we want more and more of them, but they say it is nuclear weapons on the whole, their existence, the fear they induce, which has made it impossible to contemplate war."

But it was to the French that the Reagan plan to make nuclear weapons obsolete was especially unsettling. A senior official at Élysée Palace said of Star Wars: "This idea absolutely stood the classical concept of nuclear deterrence on its head." He pointed out that Europe only decided to deploy intermediate-range American Pershing 2 and cruise missiles after bruising political battles with powerful opposition groups and antimissile public campaigns in every affected country. The French had been in the forefront of the campaign to get Europe to accept nuclear missiles as necessary pillars of its own security. "Then the American President came along and told us it was possible to get rid of the weapons by replacing nuclear deterrence with a new defensive nuclear system—very dangerous." Another French ministry official agreed: "When we heard the Reagan speech, we were frightened." But then he added in defense of existing European nuclear stockpiles, "We believe it will always be possible to penetrate Soviet defense systems, although perhaps with high costs, mostly by the multiplication of warheads." He said, too, that the lightness of the new generation of warheads will allow them to carry more decoys to aid in the penetration of the Soviet defenses. So status aside, if the Europeans had begun to believe, as they clearly did, that their own nuclear arsenal played and will continue to play a crucial role in securing their own peace, then why should they want to diminish this international position for a plan they were not at all certain would work for anyone?

For the United States, space weapons were initially intended in particular to counter Soviet SS-19 missiles, with a range of about 7,000 miles. According to Pentagon officials, the space defense might also destroy SS-20s, with a 3,000-mile range. But if the missile shield did block missiles headed for America from such distances, the Western Europeans had good cause to doubt whether it would work for them. Their proximity to the Warsaw Pact nations, not only to the East German tanks but also to Russian short- and medium-range missiles, has made them vulnerable to attacks that could sneak right underneath the space shield. Star Wars is aimed at interconti- nental ballistic missiles, strategic or long-range rockets that leave the at- mosphere within a matter of some ninety seconds, travel in space halfway around the earth and reenter the atmosphere above the intended target. The time, money and effort extended to block ICBMs would have little direct bearing on European safety. European strategists pointed out that Soviet SS-22 and SS-23 missiles with ranges of 500 and 300 miles respectively would easily slip under the proposed shield, and so, of course, would the seventy-mile SS-21s. But if the American-Soviet efforts begun in earnest in late 1987 to ban medium- and short-range missiles in Europe were eventually to prove successful, this fear would be lessened.

Many Europeans suggested that a missile shield effective for the United States as a defense against missiles fired long-range from the Soviet Union would actually place the nations of Western Europe in greater jeopardy rather than less. "No matter how good the system, we will be more exposed," said Colonel Alford of the Institute for Strategic Studies. The French Foreign Ministry held much the same opinion of S.D.I.: "We don't believe for a moment that it will be useful," said one official. For one thing, effective nuclear defense would force military focus back on conventional weaponry, a distinct Soviet advantage over Europe. But beyond that, there was the question of whether the United States would really risk full-scale nuclear war to block a conventional Soviet attack on Europe, if America finally found itself secure from first-strike nuclear attack. Or would the United States risk full-scale nuclear war in response to a quick, short-range nuclear-missile attack on Western Europe? Was S.D.I. really a signal that the United States was abandoning its commitment to stretch its nuclear guarantee to Europe? Was a Fortress America mentality building to the cold exclusion of Western Europe?

There was the thought, too, that Star Wars by its own nature, Europe or no Europe, could well increase the threat of global nuclear war, rather than lessen it. Its potential as a battery of space weapons that could be turned from defensive to offensive uses was an element of that concern. The Soviet countermeasures—expanding the stockpile of Soviet missiles, adding 1,000

An anti–Star Wars demonstration in London's Grosvenor Square in June, 1986.
© JOHN CHAPMAN/SELECT, LONDON

warheads, say, to overwhelm the shield—was another element. Was Star Wars, in short, really an escalation of the arms race in the guise of a lofty olive branch? Would years of required research and testing not undermine two decades of arms-control progress? Could S.D.I. be reconciled with American adherence to the Limited Test Ban Treaty, the Outer Space Treaty or the ABM Treaty? And would Soviet attempts at countermeasures unravel SALT accords?

There was the nagging thought, echoing that of critics in the United States, that the whole thing was grand fantasy on a very high plane, that in all probability it would not work. The destruction after launching of the shuttle *Challenger* in January 1986 and the explosion of three other American rockets being launched at about the same time did little to allay that fear. If four rockets in a row could blow up, how do you launch 5,000 of them safely and on time? Some 5,000 rockets sent into space at a rate of two a day for five years would be needed to lift an effective antimissile shield into space. Technology, it was clear from the rocket failures in 1986, not only in the American space program, but also in Ariane, the European program, is not foolproof, and flaws in equipment aimed at blocking nuclear weapons could hardly be more costly. But even if the shield's working parts were perfected, there was no certainty that it would work as an instrument of preventive warfare. The basic difficulty was seen as resting in the notion that, in the end, the best military defense is almost always a strong offense.

Also troublesome was the fact that the cost-effectiveness ratio historically at work in the best of military history's weapons decisions would seem at first glance to rule out a missile shield. The idea was described in the United States by Paul Nitze, arms control adviser to Secretary of State Shultz and a voice of caution on Star Wars, and was repeated privately by government officials abroad: If it would be cheaper to build new offensive weapons to counter defensive weapons than it is to build the defensive weapons in the first place, why then you simply do not build the defensive weapons. And it seemed clear that the costs of erecting a huge, complicated, expensive, sensitive system tens of thousands of miles above the earth would far outstrip the conceivably low costs of rendering it useless, perhaps with simple chaff or antisatellite weapons or the pulse of a single nuclear weapon exploded strategically in space near the Star Wars computers.

Finally, a peculiarly European argument against the Star Wars program was that the scale of the proposal was so great and unwieldy, the consequences of mismanagement so catastrophic, that it should not be left to the Americans. This notion was expressed privately in interviews. Though few would say so publicly at the time, several European officials believed that the U.S. bombing of Libya on April 15, 1986, whether a response to past Libyan terrorism or a defensive action against future terrorism, was a highly inappropriate use of advanced technology. It was seen as an act of undeclared war, one state against another, for acts of terrorism carried out by individuals: Could acts by individual terrorists approved of or even supported by governments be properly classified as the hostile acts of a nation that justify acts of war? The U.S. Air Force strike against Colonel Muammar al-Qaddafi, in which one of his children was killed and eight others along with his wife were hospitalized with various injuries, was likened by one official to a city government's bombing one of its neighborhood apartment buildings where a mugger might be spending the night. And one nation's unprovoked bombing of another was regarded by many European foreign policy makers as not only inappropriate but also threatening to the foundations of international order and peace. The relevance of this behavior to Star Wars seemed to crystallize for the Europeans in the months that followed. Seymour M. Hersh concluded in an article in *The New York Times Magazine* the following winter that the nine supersonic Air Force F-111s, equipped with advanced laser-guidance systems, that struck Libya did so on an unprecedented peacetime mission: The goal, authorized by the White House, was the assassination of Colonel Qaddafi. The European concern was this: If America can be expected to use some of its deadly modern technology inappropriately and unilaterally (and ineffectively, as it turned out) with or without Europe's approval, that is one thing. If it were inappropriately and unilaterally to unleash the potentially cataclysmic forces inherent in twenty-first-century Star Wars technology, that is quite another. One European government official said privately soon after the attack on Libya that in his opinion more than half the officials of the governments of Europe were opposed to Star Wars in concept, though they would not fight their own government's cooperation in it. The subsequent disclosures that while the Reagan administration was making this attempt to eliminate one source of Middle East terrorism it was trading arms to another, Iran, only made the Europeans all the more uneasy.

But supposing the two superpowers did decide to deploy antiballistic-missile systems. The difficulties in some ways would only seem worse to European cities as it approached reality. Each side must go through a potentially dangerous transition, when the Soviet Union and the United States would begin to abandon the decades-old policies of deterrence. With inevitable suspicion, with, paradoxically, some degree of mandatory trust, each side would begin to lessen its dependency on nuclear weapons. Each would begin to render them "impotent and obsolete," as President Reagan said initially he hoped they would become with a virtually impenetrable missile shield. Or, as the administration later said it intended at least for an interim period, each side would attempt, in a sense, the opposite. Each would begin a process of rendering nuclear weapons more powerful and more relevant to world war or peace than ever, enhancing their ultimate power by blunting any first nuclear strike. As Hugh De Santis wrote in March 1986 in an article entitled "S.D.I. and the European Allies: Riding the Tiger," for *Arms Control Today,* a publication of the Arms Control Association: "Given the fundamental mistrust between the United States and the Soviet Union, the Allies are unable to comprehend how or why either superpower could engage in the cooperative transition from offensive to defensive forms of deterrence without raising the risk that one side might unleash a preemptive strike against the other." If the transition did erupt, Europe would be the battleground, some thought.

As it turned out, however, the most serious European opposition to the American proposal was more a matter of procedure and national effrontery than theory or global strategy. On March 28, 1985, Defense Secretary Weinberger formally invited the Allies to join in the Star Wars research program. But he gave them a deadline of thirty days to respond. Weinberger's approach was roundly attacked in Europe as a form of loyalty test.

But in the months that followed, the Reagan administration changed its political strategy. It dropped the deadline idea, deemphasized the long-range goal of rendering nuclear weaponry obsolete and stressed both the research aspect of the Star Wars program and the business, financial and technological benefits that could accrue to Europe by joining in. General Abrahamson and other administration spokesmen crisscrossed the Continent on a sales mission. The idea was to promote missile-defense development as the modern-day equivalent of the Manhattan Project that produced the atomic bomb and the nuclear era, with attendant consequences of enormous significance for both civilian and military history. The general's pitch was essentially the same one he made to congressional critics in the United States in testimony reprinted in the U.S. Information Agency's *Wireless File*. The publication goes to senior foreign officials, prominent foreign journalists and other opinion-makers. What he said then was this:

According to Abrahamson, the driving force behind Star Wars was still President Reagan's vision of nuclear ballistic missiles made, to the great relief of all mankind, obsolete. But he said, too, "I stress that S.D.I. is a research program, not a weapons development program. Its aim is not to seek superiority, but to maintain the strategic balance and thereby assure stable deterrence." His final, and perhaps most alluring, argument to American congressmen and European statesmen alike was that the technological spin-offs would be considerable: "All facets of our economy and society" would benefit, he said, and to that end he had formed an Office of Education and Civil Applications within the S.D.I. organization at the Pentagon. Its purpose, the general said, was to develop the widest possible use of Star Wars–related technologies—consistent with security considerations—for civilian use.

The argument was sorely tempting but the dilemma for Europe was as acute as ever. As sketched by Chancellor Kohl in a speech to NATO legislators in May 1985: "S.D.I. means opportunity and risk." Or, more bluntly put: cash versus risk. All things being equal, no government, no industry and none of its workers would choose to be left out of a $70 billion research project that ranked in technological ambition and potential for industrial production alongside the pyramids and the Great Wall of China.

By the fall of 1985, the European press reported that defense contractors—in West Germany and Britain, especially—were applying high pressure on their governments to get into the game. Why should they lose out on patent rights, or fail to reap the benefits of technological innovation and potentially lucrative contracts? Some of these contractors made their own contacts with American S.D.I. officials in Europe. Jean-Luc Lagardere, chairman of Matra, the French optic microelectronics and software firm, told his European industrial colleagues at one point that they should form a Star Wars club to meet and talk with the Pentagon. France's state-owned Aerospatiale, after a slow start, became actively engaged in lobbying for Star Wars contracts.

Money was clearly the chief motivating factor for the Europeans. Giovanni Agnelli, chairman of FIAT, told a Brussels audience: "Europeans have seen American genius bring about industrial and technological changes which a half century ago seemed mere fantasy." If S.D.I. is at the cutting edge of the new industrial revolution, "it is vital that European industry not be left behind." The technological advantages that might result from such a vast military research project as Star Wars were tempting. By the so-called spinoff theory, peaceful applications spin off from the research and development of weapons of war. Extruded aluminum spun out of the extruded aluminum fuselages of World War II airplanes to become Head skis and Prince tennis rackets. And, of course, there was Teflon, constantly cited as a lovely down-to-earth by-product of the Apollo moon program. "But wasn't the moon a long way to go for a nonsticky frying pan," said one British official, who was quietly pessimistic about the value of missile defense to Europe. Others, too, discounted the spinoff argument on the same ground: The cost of World War II weapons development, or the cost of flying to the moon, or erecting a space shield, was or would be much too great to be compensated for in any meaningful way by the peaceful by-products. The by-product, in other words, is far too small to justify the goal. Direct investment, metallurgical research and careful, calculated development would have been a far more efficient way of developing extruded aluminum than waging World War II.

The brain-drain issue also became a factor in Europe. Industrialists, intellectuals and statesmen feared that the talent Europe needed for development of other important technological projects, such as civilian applications of advance computing techniques, would be drawn away to the United States for work on Star Wars. They feared, too, that Europeans would be drawn in for work in Europe, but that the countries of Europe would ultimately be denied the technological benefits on the grounds of American national security. Indeed, Britain held up any agreement with the United States out of just this concern. When the terms of a tentative agreement were put before the Cabinet in London, Leon Brittan, Trade and Industry Minister, was said to have been so angered that he himself nearly flew into orbit. Brittan and officials in his department apparently believed the offered terms contained insufficient guarantees that the United States would not impose excessive restrictions on the use of results obtained by British researchers at work on S.D.I.

Also reflecting the talent-drain concern, a group of computer professors from Imperial College in London had written to Margaret Thatcher early in 1985, arguing that Britain's participation in S.D.I. would divert scarce analytical resources from more pressing industrial problems. Brian Oakley, of Britain's Department of Trade and Industry, told David Dickson of the American journal *Science* in an interview: "The issue of intellectual property rights must be decided in a way which allows the people collaborating in this work to use the result for other purposes, either for the defense of Europe or for civilian usage."

The British government was not only concerned about precisely how it would be able to use Star Wars technology it helped to develop but also how big a slice of the project and its profits it would share in. The British surprised the Pentagon in July by demanding a firm $1.5 billion commitment. The demand was eventually rejected. Washington is said to have told the British that congressional procedures make such commitments impossible. Michael Heseltine, British Defense Minister, conceded after a meeting in Brussels with Caspar Weinberger that he was not going to get the commitment he had been asking for. Anyway, the $1.5 billion had been mentioned just "to indicate the ambitions which we had in mind," Heseltine said. A compromise was worked out in which British scientists and technology firms would be able to bid on eighteen areas of research, in open competition with American firms, and the total value of the proposed contracts was said to be estimated at about $1.5 billion.

The British eventually came to believe that a satisfactory compromise had been worked out. Security restrictions on the use of research results would not be excessive, they concluded. Shortly thereafter they signed on to the American plan. The Netherlands, Canada, West Germany and most of the other nations of Europe, officially and directly, or unofficially and indirectly, followed suit. Thus, essentially with the lure of the dollar supplied by an enormous Pentagon budget, Star Wars was gaining powerful political and psychological momentum.

Now there came the promise of valuable technological help as well. An important door to the French electronics and aerospace industry was opened when their government, which remained opposed to S.D.I. politically, altered its opposition to private participation. The government's change of heart was signaled in January 1986 when Paul Guiles, Defense Minister, said publicly for the first time that he was in favor of French industrial participation. The *Financial Times* of London quoted one French official as saying, "As long as the U.S. is looking at S.D.I. as a research program and not as a political means of getting European companies to prostitute themselves for President Reagan" the lack of active French government participation should not be a problem. Guiles had previously been hostile to S.D.I. and French businessmen, eager to increase commercial ties to the United States, had been making quiet visits to the Élysée Palace to register their protests. The Pentagon was delighted with the new French interest. It had had previously successful dealings with French industry, which helped it develop a mobile battlefield communications system. Other companies in Europe as well as those in France, and, of course, the United States, helped in a decisive way to keep the Star Wars momentum going. And the Europeans did bring along their own aerospace and electronics expertise.

Late in 1985, the West German minister of defense brought up the idea that Europe really ought to have its own Star Wars capability, an idea that seemed especially salient to some Europeans in the months that followed, during the crisis in the United States shuttle and rocket programs. British, French and Dutch military officials registered strong interest. The West German Defense Ministry, and indeed, some American defense-community leaders, argued that a mini–Star Wars shield over Europe, protecting it against Soviet short- and medium-range missiles, could be erected easier and earlier than the vast shield that would be put up over the United States and Europe. Moreover, such a European Defense Initiative would offer specific protection against an especially worrisome threat to Europe, and, at the same time, would help diffuse opposition to S.D.I., of which it would become a component part.

The critics of an all-encompassing, globe-girdling shield protecting the Western world were equally skeptical about a mini–Star Wars plan for Europe. The forces of NATO, which have a major problem with the new Russian radar-jamming technology, were at risk of shooting down as many as 50 percent of their own planes even in conventional air-battle conditions. Would they not be better advised to devote time and money and energy in turning their Mark I aircraft identification system, for example, into the proposed Mark II or Mark III, than in missile defense, the critics argued?

American military leaders themselves are not eager for a European Defense Initiative. General Bernard Rogers, commander of U.S. forces in Europe, told a Senate committee that greater priority should be given a weapon "accurate enough to attack Soviet ballistic-missile sites before they are launched." John Pike and Daniel Charles, members of the Federation of American Scientists, argue that General Rogers's thinking is representative of the true American military aim: to develop the capability of staging a preemptive first strike at Soviet nuclear missile sites, that such a goal could drastically increase East-West tensions and that the debate over Star Wars thus tends to obscure a potentially more important issue.

Nor did the Pentagon's head of S.D.I., General Abrahamson, favor mini–Star Wars for Europe, to the extent that it was intended—as some in Europe, indeed, intended it—as a steppingstone toward European independence from the United States. "It's a mistake to talk about defense of Europe only," he said in an interview with the *Los Angeles Times*. "The security of the United States and its allies, in Europe and in the Pacific, is all tied together, and the solution should be, too."

Nevertheless, the first major Star Wars contract awarded to Europe—a $14.3 million contract to Britain in June 1986—apparently included $10 million for research into the development of a European defense system. The $10 million is to be passed along to British firms to develop defenses against short- and medium-range missiles. The $4.3 million was awarded directly to a private firm for research on a particle-beam weapon, a device that would fire subatomic particles in space at high speed to destroy attacking missiles. Messerschmitt of West Germany was the big early winner, receiving a $38.8 million contract for infrared devices designed to sort nuclear missiles from decoys.

The European contracts were not being obtained without some pain, however. In July 1986, the research director of the Siemens electrical group, Karl-Heinz Beckurts, was driving his dark blue, four-door BMW to work at 7:30 A.M. in Strasslach, Bavaria, fifteen miles south of Munich. Suddenly an explosion rang out and what witnesses described as a ninety-foot gusher of flame shot up from his car, which was thrown off the road with its doors, trunk, hood and interior torn apart. Beckurts, a nuclear physicist who had advised the West German government in Star Wars negotiations with the United States, was killed instantly. Although the company had no direct involvement in Star Wars, so far as was publicly known, a seven-page letter, signed by the Red Army Faction, was found near the wreckage. Beckurts was murdered, it said, because he supported the United States space-based missile program. Later the same day, a group police linked to the Red Army Faction claimed responsibility for bombing an annex of the Paris police headquarters, killing a policeman and wounding twenty-two people. Within two weeks, a research institute and an aerospace firm, both in West Germany, were also bombed as part of what federal officials said was a coordinated attack on Star Wars–related organizations and companies.

Despite the terrorism, the intense industrial maneuvering persisted. At least twenty-seven contract awards were made by the Pentagon within the year to companies in Britain, West Germany, France and Italy. Outside of Europe, Japan and Israel agreed to participate in relatively small ways. Other award winners included Germany's Carl Zeiss optical company, which manufactures sophisticated mirrors, and several units of the Ferranti electronics group and the General Electric Company, both in Britain. Britain's contracts totaled about $24 million in 1986 and West Germany's about $45 million, according to the S.D.I. office at the Pentagon. Another $14 million was awarded to fifty-one American and Allied firms in December 1986 for research and development on a smaller "theater," or short- to medium-range missile shield of the type especially important to Europe. The awards were far from the $1 billion to $2 billion the British had talked about carving out of the American initiative support, perhaps as a reward for their early support. But they were a start.

It is probably true that the Allies' critical assessment of the technical feasibility and strategic implications of S.D.I. changed very little even as the business communities embraced it and the governments gave their official support. But the Allied resistance to S.D.I. softened not only in the interests of technology to be learned and money to be made or in the interests of surface harmony among the nations of the West. The resumption of the arms-control dialogue between Washington and Moscow was also a factor. And so was what one Pentagon official called "more sophisticated rhetoric" about Star Wars goals. Despite the technical and military objections, Europeans began to accept S.D.I. on more substantive grounds once they became convinced that it did not mean the end of deterrence. "The Reagan administration's increased emphasis on terminal hard-point defense made S.D.I. more palatable," Hugh De Santis said, because "it does not alter the mutual hostage relationship or assured retaliation; and it is less likely to erode arms-control agreements."

Then came Reykjavik. Now there was a dilemma within the dilemma for Western Europe. At his summit meeting with Soviet leader Gorbachev in Iceland in October 1986, President Reagan put forth the goal of eliminating all American and Soviet ballistic missiles—that is, those that fly into space before returning to earth to strike their targets—without the framework of an arms-control accord. The President's plan would be carried out in two steps over the course of a decade. The foreign ministers of Europe promptly began a steady assault on the positions entertained by Mr. Reagan and Mr. Gorbachev. In November Margaret Thatcher met with the American President in Camp David, Maryland, and made known her government's reservations about abolishing ballistic missiles. And the next month in Brussels, Britain prevented the defense ministers of the North Atlantic Treaty Organization from endorsing that objective. Britain and other Allies had anxieties about being weakened by the elimination of ballistic missiles, according to Lord Carrington, who attended the meeting. Under the Reykjavik formulation, a 50 percent reduction in strategic—that is, long-range—weapons would take place within five years. Those would include weapons dropped from long-range bombers, for example, or land-based or submarine-launched long-range ballistic missiles that fly into space and reenter the atmosphere. Then within the next five years all the Soviet and American ballistic missiles would be eliminated.

The NATO foreign ministers said they welcomed the Reykjavik proposal for a 50 percent strategic reduction. The Allies said, for example, that they fully supported the elimination of American and Soviet medium-range missiles deployed on the Continent. Despite West German reservations about Soviet short-range weapons in Central Europe, Hans-Dietrich Genscher, the Foreign Minister, fully supported the removal of all American Pershing 2 and cruise missiles in a trade-off for elimination of Soviet SS-20s.

But the French foreign minister, Jean-Bernard Raimond, attacked the second phase as utopian. "We find—and this is what the French and British say—that the second period of five years devalues the first, which we consider a considerable gain." Again, for all the reasons that had become abundantly clear since the Star Wars speech of 1983, the French and English simply did not want their nuclear strike forces eliminated. It seemed to them that it would lessen the power that a nuclear force would give them. The Warsaw Pact's superior conventional force loomed in particular as a factor in their thinking.

The foil at Reykjavik, of course, was Star Wars. The President insisted that his plan proceed to the testing of defensive weapons in space, and Mr. Gorbachev insisted that it not. Now suddenly the Europeans found a new, in a sense, tactical or, at least, pragmatic reason for favoring the American Star Wars plan: As long as the Americans pushed it, it would appear that the Soviets would balk at eliminating all ballistic missiles. In an interview after Reykjavik, Admiral Sir James Eberle of the British Royal Navy expressed the view of many European government and military officials. The admiral, who was NATO Commander-in-Chief for the eastern Atlantic fleet and retired from the active list of the Royal Navy in 1983, spoke about the American Star Wars plan and strategic negotiations in general:

My own feelings lie at neither extreme of the wide variety of views that exist on S.D.I. I think they lie rather near the norm, though as a man with a military background, I probably take a stronger position about its practical impact as a weapon of war than others. That is what we're talking about if it is put in place in any effective way. The President's dream was a very good piece of domestic politics, but it was not so good from the European perspective. It has led us to a situation which I believe is the opposite of what the President intends. The world where we are rid of nuclear weapons is less stable, and deterrence is undermined by the President's action. And we Europeans have mixed feeling about Reykjavik. Europeans now ask, are those guarantees that we have been operating under really worth anything? Should we believe in these guarantees? Perhaps Henry Kissinger is right. He has been saying for years that we Europeans are crazy to believe that Americans would use nuclear weapons in this way. And, indeed, now Reagan was saying at Reykjavik that he was prepared to give up all strategic ballistic missiles. While from the U.S. interest this might be a sensible thing to do, it certainly isn't from the European view. Even if the Europeans don't support the U.S. side, then there is liable to be an agreement with ballistic missiles—except for S.D.I. And so the Europeans say, "Thank goodness for S.D.I." It was the one thing that stopped the President. I think that on reflection that is the general European view.

On S.D.I. itself, it is in some senses still highly objectionable. Europeans would greatly welcome a 50-50 reduction, and I think that it stopped that. So Europeans have been ambivalent, and this has helped shake them out of it, I suspect. They had wanted their noses in the trough. They had wanted to take advantage of the technology and economic and industrial development that might go along with it, though there was disappointment at the conditions and the way the contracts were handled in Europe. One of the reasons that Europe was interested, too, was to prevent a brain drain. They did not want the best technological brains going away to America. And there are still fundamental suspicions about S.D.I. The problem of Reykjavik was: How to reconcile President Reagan's dream and Mr. Gorbachev's fear?

The fear that America is taking the high ground is a real one. If you have boost-phase interception, what about pre-boost interception? Pre-boost is preemption, of course. And there is the idea that once high technology is developed by the United States, it can be used unilaterally, without consultation with the Allies. No one really believes that Star Wars can work in any sensible way. More can always be done in antimissile development. Technology has moved ahead from where we were in the 1970s. But can S.D.I. work? Nobody believes a word of it. Europeans do not believe that if we could get rid of all ballistic missiles we would be safer. S.D.I. is really an example of the President's dreaming being out of touch with reality. S.D.I. is not going to die while he is in office. But after that, we'll say: S.D.I. is dead. Long long live ABM research!

The British admiral concluded by saying that antiballistic research itself should be stopped at the point in the future when—if—some kind of international agreement were to be reached that would make the research no longer sensible. He reflected much of the initial European unease over whether Star Wars would make the world safer. In the meantime, pure and applied research continued on all manner of exotic technology and weaponry, including the next generation of supercomputers and the software to run them, research carried on in the Soviet Union, Europe, Japan and Israel, as well as the United States.

10

A WAR RUN
BY COMPUTERS

Three years after President Reagan announced his vision for a defensive
shield against nuclear missiles, military planners encountered an unforeseen
technical obstacle. This was the prodigious difficulty of developing computer
software, the complex instructions written by humans, that would tell a maze
of computers how to manage the course of a battle in the vastness of space.
While most of the initial technical debate over the feasibility of the President's
program had focused on its exotic weapons and sensors, it had become clear
by 1986 that any large-scale cluster of space-defense technology would have
to be organized and shaped in accordance with the limitations of the software.

The problem, which appeared to be the worst technical barrier across the
Star Wars path, rose only gradually to become a matter of high concern.
Although a handful of computer experts had recognized the difficulty from
the start, the significance of the problem escaped virtually everyone else.
Critics of Star Wars cited virtually every other conceivable technical diffi-

culty. Military leaders largely ignored the software in their statements. Even the congressional Office of Technology Assessment, in a September 1985 report called "Ballistic Missile Defense Technologies" that was intended to present an encyclopedic review of the issues, devoted only a few of its 325 pages to the issue. "When we were writing our report, we didn't think of software being such a big deal," Peter Sharfman, manager of international security studies for the O.T.A., said. "It wasn't until later that it dawned on a lot of people what a big problem the software was."

But the software problem was deemed so serious by the following year that the initial plans proposed by ten industrial teams about how to build a defensive system in space had to be invalidated. As a consequence, the issue stimulated a sharp increase in funding for the battle-management aspects of the Star Wars program, from roughly $90 million in the fiscal year ending September 30, 1986, to perhaps double that projected for the succeeding year. "It's the biggest technical problem for the entire program," said Lieut. Colonel David R. Audley of the Air Force, assistant director of battle management for S.D.I.O.

The stakes in solving the problem and developing reliable software are high. The software is indispensable. Star Wars simply will not work without it. If a particular sensor proves faulty or undesignable, military technologists can always substitute another. Should space lasers or particle-beam weapons prove too difficult to perfect, then perhaps kinetic-energy devices will do the job instead. But there is no substitute for the software. Any strategic defense will absolutely require it to manage the battle. "We truly believe that the battle-management area, and particularly the software, is the long pole in the tent," said Colonel Audley.

Yet the field as a whole is progressing very slowly, and, to make matters worse, according to the Pentagon's own consultants, the Defense Department and its major aerospace contractors are decades behind the software leaders in the computer field. The only solace, many experts say, is that the Soviet Union lags far behind the West in computer expertise. That may be one reason, some of these experts suggest, that the Soviet officials appear so anxious about the American Strategic Defense Initiative.

One aspect of the problem is that nobody yet knows what an effective antimissile shield would really look like. At its simplest, it might be ground-based rockets poised to intercept Soviet missiles as they plunged from the sky toward military targets in this country. At its most elaborate, it might consist of thousands of lasers, beam weapons and "smart" rocks, along with hundreds of thousands of sensors and other battle stations deployed in space, on the ground and in the air, ready to intercept Soviet missiles at all points along their flight paths.

The nightmare envisioned by some experts is that bugs, or undetected flaws, in the software might cause all or part of the system to malfunction in a crisis. Just as the first launching of the space shuttle was halted in 1981 because problems in the software programs caused its computers to fall out of synchronization, so might a strategic defense shut down unexpectedly when first called upon to block a fleet of Soviet missiles streaking toward American soil.

The consequences of even the minutest of software errors can mean total failure of a mission. The space agency lost a Mariner probe to Venus because a programmer put a period in the software where there should have been a comma, making it a good candidate for the most expensive typographical error of all time. Similarly, the Gemini V spacecraft splashed down 100 miles off target because a programmer ignored factoring into the program the motion of the earth around the sun. As we mentioned earlier, the Star Wars program itself suffered an embarrassing failure because of a mismatch between what the software program required and what normal human thought processes delivered. In the June 1985 laser-shuttle experiment, Pentagon scientists tried reflecting a laser beam off an orbiting space shuttle after firing the beam from a mountain in Hawaii. For the experiment to work, the shuttle crew had to aim its mirror toward the mountain. Ground controllers sent them the height of the mountain in feet, and the crew duly entered the data into the computer. But the computer program was written to interpret the information in nautical miles. So instead of pointing the mirror downward, to a mountaintop 10,000 feet above sea level, the shuttle flipped over and pointed the mirror up, to a spot 10,000 nautical miles above the earth. The computer, of course, worked fine. It did just what it was told to do. Here was a case of what old computer hands call GIGO—garbage in, garbage out: Tell the computer to do the wrong thing and it will do the wrong thing. The scientists tried the experiment again later, and this time it worked. "Sure enough, they got it right the second time," says Dr. David Redell, a software expert for the Digital Equipment Corp. and a critic of Star Wars. "But in a deployed SDI system it wouldn't do much good to get it right the second time."

Other experts worry that software flaws might cause a highly automated

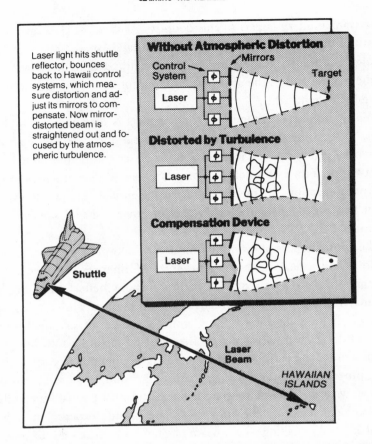

Laser light hits shuttle reflector, bounces back to Hawaii control systems, which measure distortion and adjust its mirrors to compensate. Now mirror-distorted beam is straightened out and focused by the atmospheric turbulence.

Without Atmospheric Distortion
Control System — Mirrors — Target
Laser

Distorted by Turbulence
Laser

Compensation Device
Laser

Shuttle

Laser Beam

HAWAIIAN ISLANDS

On June 21, 1985, a blue-green laser knifed up through the darkness from a Hawaii mountaintop and locked onto the space shuttle *Discovery*—the first successful shuttle experiment of Star Wars. Earlier, however, ground controllers inadvertently sent faulty computer instructions to the *Discovery* astronauts.

THE NEW YORK TIMES COMPANY

Star Wars system to fire mistakenly at a harmless target, at a peaceful Soviet space rocket, perhaps, or communications satellites, perhaps triggering a crisis that could escalate to nuclear holocaust. There is also an emerging fear that the computer programs would be vulnerable to sabotage, espionage and even hostile takeovers by Soviet masterminds, who might penetrate the software electronically, take control of it and turn the system to their own uses. Any large-scale defensive system would be so widely dispersed, with software sitting unattended on isolated stations in space, that the usual techniques for protecting highly classified material by locking it up and guarding it would not be possible. "If there's anything that the S.D.I. will revolu-

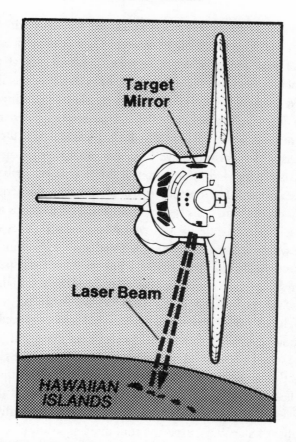

As a result, the side of the shuttle containing the target mirror, which was to have sent the light beam back to Hawaii, was facing away from Earth; the laser could not hit the target, and the experiment failed. Critics seized upon the computer-program failure as just one of many SDI pitfalls.

THE NEW YORK TIMES COMPANY

tionize, I think it will be in the area of computer security," Colonel Audley said. "That's going to be a nut we have to crack."

Regardless of how Star Wars is organized, computers and the software programs to run them would be needed at virtually all stages, including space platforms, weapons, sensors, ground stations and airplane units. These would not, for the most part, be giant mainframe computers, but rather arrays of tiny electronic chips wired together to perform high-speed calculations where needed in the system. Such computers would aim the sensors in the general direction from which an attack might emerge. They would process the enormous flood of data generated by these sensors, pouring in at the rate of millions of data elements per second, to look for evidence of missiles in flight against a background of normal signals. They would try to distinguish actual missiles from decoys, and would calculate the trajectories for enemy missiles that must be destroyed. They would aim defensive weapons at the oncoming missiles, assess which missiles have been destroyed, and re-aim. Finally, they would pass on needed information to the next layers or battle groups in the defense system. The computers would also scan the sensor data for signs of attack on the Star Wars system itself, firing off weapons to beat back any such attack. Some battle stations would be expected to respond within minutes; the whole engagement would last perhaps a half hour.

The computer hardware —the physical equipment needed to perform these feats, the tiny chips and arrays capable of performing the high-speed calculations—is not yet in hand. But experts believe it can be, an optimism based on developments in the last two decades that have produced generation after generation of smaller, faster and cheaper computers. "If jet airplanes had made the same progress that computers have made over the past decade," says Dr. Charles A. Seitz, professor of computer science at the California Institute of Technology and a Star Wars consultant, "I could fly from Los Angeles to New York in five minutes for a quarter." Virtually everyone, including critics of Star Wars, expects a continued rapid advance in hardware capabilities as computer experts explore a range of new approaches for transmitting signals more rapidly within and between computers.

The next great advance in hardware may come in parallel processing or multiprocessing, the technique that enables a computer to blast around the bottleneck that currently builds up because most computers are forced to perform calculations linearly, in sequence, with final calculations having to wait until the first are performed. With multiprocessing, arrays of tiny computers are hooked together to perform many calculations simultaneously, allowing an enormous increase in the speed of solving a problem. The idea is to turn small microprocessors into machines that can perform rapidly, removing some of the need for larger hardware. And there is general optimism that, in terms of sheer calculating speed, suitable technology will become available.

The hardware will have to meet two particularly demanding requirements. The computers based in space will have to operate reliably for a decade or more without maintenance, far beyond the length of time that current computers of any significance can operate unattended. The computers on the space shuttle, for example, are designed to operate for only a month before failing. The hardware would also have to be tough enough to survive battle damage. The neutron flux emitted by a nuclear explosion 600 miles away could penetrate and erase the memory of a space-based computer, and force it to start calculating the whereabouts of Soviet missiles all over again. Such vulnerability to battle damage must, everyone agrees, be minimized.

The details of developing the software to operate the whole system are far more daunting. The computer hardware, like the lasers, or the infrared sensors, will operate to accord with physical laws, whose implications can be discovered, treated mathematically and tested experimentally. In contrast, the software is intellectually derived, more like a book than a device. It can seldom be analyzed mathematically or tested thoroughly. Moreover, there appear to be strict limits on the complexity that the human brain, or even a large team of human brains, can handle in developing software. As in any intellectual endeavor, there is a high potential for human error to creep in. Large software programs are typically written by thousands of designers and engineers who first try to determine what situations the software must respond to, then write detailed instructions in computer language to specify what calculations should be performed and what orders issued by the computers under various circumstances.

The techniques for doing this remain more art than science. There are almost no basic laws and few analytical procedures for designing large systems. Large programs are simply written and then tested by trial and error. The process is subjective, labor-intensive and prone to error. Large software programs may take years, even decades, to develop accurately. But after years of operation, undetected flaws may still sometimes emerge. The software whose failure forced postponement of the first shuttle flight, for example, had been tested for more than 30,000 hours.

Few experts expect any major advances in software engineering in time to benefit the Star Wars program. A panel of experts convened by S.D.I.O. last year, the so-called Eastport study group, surveyed the prospects for applying artificial intelligence, automatic programming and new verification techniques to the development of better software. It concluded in December 1985 that there is no magic bullet to aim at the software problem and that progress will probably continue to be slow. "We do not say that software is advancing very fast," the group's chairman, Dr. Danny Cohen, director of the systems division at the University of Southern California's information sciences institute, commented later. "It's probably one of the slowest advancing technologies in the entire computing area." Dr. Seitz, who was part of the Eastport group, agreed: "We can't expect to make rapid progress in software because it's basically an intellectual exercise. It's like asking Hemingway to write fifty books in a lifetime. There's only so much in each of us."

The world has never experienced an all-out nuclear attack, yet the designers of the software must anticipate the weapons and decoys that will be fired, the tactics that will be used and what effect an all-out nuclear attack would have on the sensors and weapons of the Star Wars system itself. The task has been likened to that of developing a computer program for processing tax returns in some distant year, when one does not know for certain what the tax laws will be. But the size and complexity of the proposed strategic defense alone make the task especially difficult. The Navy's new Aegis air defense system for protecting ships at sea against attacking missiles, for example, is designed to track only several hundred targets at a time and is experiencing difficulties following that relatively small number of targets. Star Wars might have to handle 30,000 to 300,000 missiles and decoys, according to official estimates.

The task will require software programs containing 6 million to 25 million lines of code or computer instructions, according to official estimates, or up to even 100 million lines, according to a widely cited conjecture. These figures cannot be judged as beyond the realm of possibility. The nation's telecommunications network, for example, uses over 40 million lines of software code, of which only about 1.3 million run the electronic switching system that routes calls. The size of the software greatly increases the chances of error, computer experts say, because large programs have more places for bugs to lurk undetected, and more opportunity for one part of the program to work in opposition to another. "In software, usually we find that the worst thing that can happen is size," says Dr. Cohen. "It is a terrible liability."

The likelihood of error would be further increased because the software would have to be continually brought up to date, to provide defenses against new Soviet weapons or tactics and to incorporate new American weapons or sensors as they are developed. Anytime a change is made in complicated software, there is a risk that it will introduce new errors. Managers of the Star Wars program are hoping to design a so-called open system that would allow the rapid insertion of new components as they are developed. But as the Eastport panel said, designing open systems is still very much a research topic, not a proven technique.

Testing how well the system works may prove especially troublesome. Software designers will be forced to rely on partial tests and on computer simulations of all-out nuclear attack. But it may take years before any real conclusions can be drawn about how to test the system, in the view of Harold Brown, the former Secretary of Defense, perhaps the most technically sophisticated man to hold that job in recent decades.

Experts agree that the Star Wars system would not require software that is flawless or error-free, a feat regarded as impossible in any event in such a large program. Dr. James C. Fletcher, who headed the federal government's first major review of the technical feasibility of Star Wars before he returned to NASA to become its administrator for the second time, after the *Challenger* disaster, once implied the opposite, that the computer software would have to be perfect. An article under his name, published in a policy journal of the National Academy of Sciences, asserted that Star Wars would require "an enormous and error-free program, on the order of ten million lines of code." But in a debate later, Air Force Major Peter Worden, a special assistant in the Strategic Defense Initiative Office, confessed that he had written those lines and had afterward been taken to task by software engineers who suggested that he must have been "drunk or crazy" to do so. "I have to admit" it was "probably both," Major Worden said. "It is obvious that you don't need error-free code."

Nevertheless, he and other experts are quick to acknowledge that the system would need software that contains no catastrophic errors, and that can recover from minor errors and continue to function. That, in itself, is a formidable task lying beyond present capabilities.

As a result of the software problem, officials of the Reagan administration's Strategic Defense Initiative were forced in 1986 into the first major revision of their thinking. They abandoned their original expectations for a tightly integrated earth, atmosphere and space defense, and began moving instead toward a concept of loosely coupled clusters of battle stations that would operate with considerable autonomy.

The cluster plan was a sharp departure from that outline set forth for the government as part of the Defensive Technologies Study, headed by Dr. Fletcher, in 1984. The battle-management section of that panel's report said

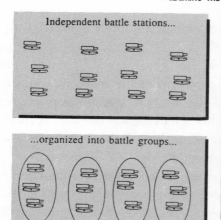

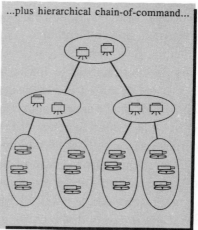

Originally, Star Wars designers envisaged giant supercomputers that would direct a global protective shield. In time, however, they perceived this as too comprehensive an assignment. They broke down the computer organization into smaller, semi-

that developing and maintaining software to manage a Star Wars defensive battle would be so complex that no one individual would have a complete understanding of the system. The only way to perform the job effectively, it warned, would be to design the software as an integral part of the whole system from the start, not as something to be added on at the end, after all the sensors and weapons have been developed, the usual approach of Pentagon contractors. The report implied that components would have to be tightly linked and coordinated so that they could help each other identify targets and inform one another which missiles were still on the way and which had been destroyed. The report envisioned a master track file, under computer control, that would provide "birth to death" tracking of all potentially threatening objects. That idealized model soon became an unofficial guide for ten manufacturing teams that later submitted proposals to the government in the first phase of developing an overall architecture of Star Wars defense. The teams generally produced tightly coordinated systems that called for close integration of all the weapons and sensors under computer command. But they paid scant attention to how the computers might do the job.

"We were getting very uneasy about the direction of the Phase I architecture work," Colonel Audley, S.D.I.O.'s director of battle management, recalls. "It didn't look right. But we weren't smart enough to figure out what was wrong and how to make it right."

So in 1985 the S.D.I.O. called in the nine-member Eastport study group, headed by Dr. Cohen. It concluded in a report dated December 1985 that

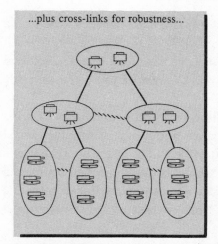
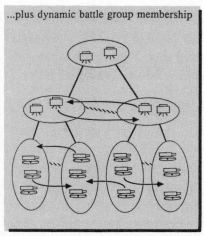

Independent battle stations that would be part of larger groups under an overall chain of command. Each battle group and command station would be cross-linked for added robustness. THE NEW YORK TIMES COMPANY/DAVID REDELL

the computing capabilities could be developed, but only if there were a revolution in the way that the Defense Department and its contractors went about their business. The panel warned that software technology was already bumping up against inflexible limits in complexity and reliability. The only way the software task could be made doable, it said, was by designing the architecture of the whole system to accommodate the limitations of the software. The panel's judgment was that the model described in the Fletcher report and initially proposed by the aerospace companies would demand too much sophistication from the software and would not allow for adequate testing. Dr. Cohen later said that although the Fletcher report was held "as a bible" by everyone in the Star Wars program, it actually described "a very dumb system—no one in his right mind would advocate building such a system."

The Eastport panel also complained that the contractors had built their systems around sensors and weapons and had paid only lip service to the software needed to control the whole system, treating it as something that could be easily and hastily added. In the future, the panel said, the key factor in designing the system should be the need to reduce the complexity faced by the software. "The most important point is that in evaluating any architecture for S.D.I. one must consider both the ability to make the required software work, and the ability to test it." The panel called the issue "so important that S.D.I.O. must be prepared to make a variety of trade-offs among all elements of a strategic defense system to make the software and the testing tractable." The key was that developers should give up the notion of a tightly coupled monolithic system capable of coordinated action on a grand scale and should think instead of loosely coupled battle groups, each operating with substantial autonomy, independent of the rest. The software would be written in smaller units that would be less complex and more easily tested.

Some panelists suggested that a realistic test might be conducted by firing actual missiles at a cluster of battle stations as they passed over the United States, to see if the stations could destroy them. The behavior of the whole defensive system, composed of many such clusters, might then be inferred from the performance of a single cluster, just as military leaders infer that the entire ICBM force will perform adequately because individual missiles have been fired successfully in tests.

The use of a more loosely coordinated architecture would offer fewer chances for sensors and weapons to exchange information about targets and decoys and would probably eliminate "birth to death" tracking, in which centralized computer files follow enemy missiles from the moment they are detected seconds after launching through their entire flight path and back down to earth. As a result, the individual weapons and sensors would have to be even more effective than previously expected, because they would have to perform more of the calculations on their own.

The Eastport panel's advice was taken to heart by Star Wars officials. General Abrahamson promptly endorsed its spirit and content and called for its rapid implementation. Similarly, Colonel Audley said that the development of software should definitely be the driving force in shaping the architecture of the whole Star Wars system. But he acknowledged that such a turnabout would not be easy: "We have so little successful history of having done the software right first and letting the hardware follow behind. And every time you turn around in this program, someone has a hardware solution. You've got to keep chasing them off."

Five of the ten manufacturing teams subsequently prepared new proposals for how to structure the system in Phase II of the program's architecture studies. Although those made a greater attempt to focus on software, Audley said he was still not satisfied that they had begun thinking all the way through the problem. And other analysts also expressed the concern that the Phase II studies were superficial.

The software issue sparked an acrimonious and widening debate among computer experts, with acknowledged giants of the field taking opposing sides in the debate. Those who believed the development of software for Star Wars feasible or at least worth further study included Frederick P. Brooks, Jr., professor of computer science at the University of North Carolina, who built the software for the IBM 360 family of computers; Victor Vyssotsky, executive director for information sciences research at AT&T Bell Laboratories, who has helped develop large software programs for the telephone system and for a previous missile defense; Solomon J. Buchsbaum, executive vice president of Bell Labs, who is a key government adviser on technical issues; John McCarthy, professor of computer science at Stanford University, who developed LISP, a major programming language for artificial intelligence research; and the two panels of computer experts convened by the Defense Department.

The most outspoken of the optimists included Dr. Seitz, of the California Institute of Technology; Richard Lipton, professor of computer science at Princeton University; and Dr. Cohen, of the University of Southern California. "It's feasible, but only if the Defense Department changes its ways," said Dr. Seitz. "I don't think there's any question that it can be done. That's the weight of the most experienced opinion on this issue." Dr. Brooks told a Senate committee: "I see nothing that means that we could not build the kind of software system that Star Wars requires with the software engineering technology that we have today. I would not be so bold as to assert that the S.D.I. software can surely be built. What I would say unequivocally is that it is much too soon for gloom. I think it could conceivably be done." Dr. Cohen assured the same committee that "the computing requirements for the battle management of the strategic defense system can be met."

The optimists generally believe that the computing job can be broken up into doable parts and that the software for these various parts can be tested thoroughly enough to provide reasonable confidence that the entire system would work. They also claim that there have already been past successes in developing large software systems, including the air traffic control system that directs airplanes safely around the country with only occasional near misses, and the telephone switching system that routes telephone calls around bottlenecks, providing generally reliable service even when storms knock out the telephones over large areas.

Perhaps the most vigorous endorsement has come from Solomon Buchsbaum of Bell Labs, who also heads the White House Science Council and

David L. Parnas, who sounded an early warning about the colossal computer problems associated with operation of a complicated nuclear defense system in outer space. © IRA WYMAN

serves as an adviser on Star Wars. "Can such a large, robust and resilient system be designed—and not only designed, but built, tested, deployed, operated and further evolved and improved?" he asked in Senate testimony. "I believe the answer is yes."

"I see no reason to believe that the job is impossible," said Dr. Vyssotsky, the top expert in complex software at AT&T. "It's clearly a very large, very challenging, very difficult job. But how large and how difficult remains to be seen. At this point in time, the job is not terribly precisely defined."

However, those who believe the likelihood of success is very small include such eminent computer experts as Herbert Simon, the only computer scientist to win a Nobel Prize; John Backus, the inventor of FORTRAN, a major computer programing language; David L. Parnas, who was called in by the Defense Department to review the software problem because he was considered one of the world's leading authorities; several experts working for the Digital Equipment Corp., a major computer manufacturer, including James J. Horning, Greg Nelson and David Redell, who have issued lengthy critiques; and Robert Taylor, head of Digital's systems research center, who formerly headed computer research programs for the Defense Advanced Research Projects Agency, the Pentagon's chief supporter of breakthrough computer research.

"I think it's pretty clear that it can't be done," Dr. Taylor said in an interview. "The goals of the S.D.I. put demands on software that are just absurd in terms of the state of our knowledge." The critics generally argue that all large software programs contain undetected bugs that could cause catastrophic failure and also, perhaps most important, that it will be impossible to test and debug the software since there are no practice nuclear wars. "I haven't been claiming that we can't build this system," Dr. Redell told a congressional audience. "It's possible that it could collapse and fail to produce a deployable system. But I don't think that's the most likely outcome. I think the most likely outcome would be that a system would be produced in which we really wouldn't be able to have confidence because the thing really can't be subjected to full-scale operational use and testing. . . . Its software would inevitably contain lurking errors that would reveal themselves only when we actually needed the system during a real nuclear war."

The skeptics also point to a rich history of past software failures that have plagued the space program, military weapons, automated banking systems and the Internal Revenue Service, among others. "I believe that the software will be very unlikely to work and that we would find it impossible to rely on it in any way," says Dr. Parnas, perhaps the most authoritative and visible critic of the Star Wars computer capabilities. "Our experience with military software systems is that they don't work at all in the first few battles. The S.D.I. is not something we can use in Grenada or Lebanon or Nicaragua to see if it works."

Perhaps the most distinguished of the skeptics is Dr. Simon, a professor of psychology and computer science at Carnegie-Mellon University in Pittsburgh. In an interview, Dr. Simon said that he is very dubious that software reliable enough to operate a Star Wars defense could be built. "We're talking about a system of immense complexity that can't afford to make mistakes. It has to have high accuracy in identifying targets and doing something about them, and it all has to be done under extreme time pressure. It's a very difficult task." Unreliable software, he said, would "scare the bejeezus" out of him.

Another prominent skeptic, Dr. Backus, a leader in developing computer programs, considered it "impossible to produce a completely reliable battle program. Many other programing professionals take this same view." Should both the United States and the Soviet Union deploy full-scale defenses, he said, "a single error in either their program or ours could cause an unprovoked attack and initiate a devastating computer-controlled war." Anthony Ralston, professor of computer science at the State University of New York in Buffalo and a past president of the Association for Computing Machinery, the leading professional society for computer experts, warned: "No regimen of testing or simulation and no application of program verification techniques is even on the horizon that would not leave such a vast program with many bugs."

The skeptics appear to outnumber the optimists, in part because critics of the Star Wars program have been more vigorous in enlisting allies than have supporters of the program. Some fourteen computer specialists at AT&T facilities have signed a letter warning that the Star Wars system might contain 10,000 errors in its software, some of which might cripple the system. Some thirty other computer experts, including fourteen who chair university computer departments and several who have won top computer awards, had signed a petition by September 1985 calling Star Wars technically infeasible in this century "with known or anticipated techniques," no matter how much money is spent on it. The petition, which was being circulated slowly by the Computer Scientists for Professional Responsibility, a group dedicated to reducing the dangers of war, also warns that the extreme time pressure on the system would "force a high degree of automation" that would delegate many decisions to unpredictable software programs, with the result that "errors, malfunctions and unanticipated developments may produce results with disastrous consequences."

■

The two sides in the Star Wars debate often appear to be talking past each other. Those who say that the software cannot be developed are usually talking about the software needed to provide a near-perfect defense for the entire population. Those who say that the software may be feasible are often thinking about a less comprehensive defense that could tolerate more software errors. And the sharp split in professional opinion may be partly due to ideology or philosophy, some participants say, with those who tend to be hawkish on military matters supporting the feasibility of software for Star Wars and those who tend to be dovish declaring the software impossible. But there are many exceptions to that theory, so a deeper explanation must be sought.

Another theory, put forth by Michael Dertouzos, director of the laboratory for computer science at the Massachusetts Institute of Technology, traces the sharp disagreements to the lack of scientific precision in the field of software development. "If I were to ask one hundred civil engineers, 'Can you build a ten-mile-long wooden bridge?' they would almost all agree," Dr. Dertouzos told an M.I.T. debate. "They would give me a consistent answer, because their field is draped by physical laws of conservation, by properties of materials, and by analytical procedures that can be brought to bear on new problems. Not so with one hundred computer scientists," he continued. "If I were to ask them, you would find a clean split down the middle. I believe that this is the nature of our field. We have no basic laws other than one. We have no analytical procedures that we can bring to bear on problems of the future. We must try things before we can actually say whether they can work."

The Defense Department and its major contractors are particularly weak in software development, in the opinion of computer experts. The Eastport group complained that many of the Pentagon's biggest software development contractors are literally decades behind the state of the art—an art that is only a few decades old. James J. Horning, a software expert called in to consult with the Eastport panel, later revealed that its members treated the software work of the Air Force contemptuously and, he said, they considered the Army's work beneath contempt. The Star Wars technical officials are themselves cautious about the prospects. They are not about to concede defeat. "I just flat reject the idea that this is impossible," General Abrahamson told Congress. But neither are they promising victory. "We're not gung-ho optimists," said Colonel Audley. "It appears as though there are some ap-proaches that look feasible. But the key word is 'appears.' We don't know yet."

Meanwhile, as he spoke, the research program was plunging ahead. Even as it did, Colonel Audley said he remained convinced that the Pentagon probably had not yet discovered the toughest problem in developing anti-missile weaponry.

THE DARK SIDE
OF STAR WARS

Not long after President Reagan gave his Star Wars speech, his science adviser, George A. Keyworth II, paid a visit to members of the editorial board of *The New York Times*. He was asked during the meeting whether the President's proposed new defensive space weapons could not be used offensively as well as defensively. He did not directly answer, saying simply that they were designed for defense. But later, in the tenth-floor hallway outside the elevator bank, he was asked again whether a weapon accurate and powerful enough to seek out and destroy an attacking intercontinental ballistic missile could not be used as well in active offense. Wasn't Star Wars really an attempt to claim the heavens as a military outpost? "I guess you'll just have to take it on faith," he said quietly.

In the series of six articles on Star Wars in March 1985 which ultimately led to the publication of this book, *The Times* brought the offensive question into the open. Though some experts interviewed on the subject disagreed, many others, both supporters and critics of the President's program, contended that the weapons envisioned for use as a defensive shield against ballistic-missile attack could, indeed, be used offensively with devastating effect.

Since then, though controversy has burned laser-hot in some technical papers and scientific journals, the possible offensive uses of the proposed system have generally received only passing attention in the public debate over missile defense. But the ambiguity between defensive and offensive weapons is beginning to cause concern among some of the scientists who are strong proponents of a better defense, as well as those who oppose the general goals of the Strategic Defense Initiative. Star Wars might not use weapons of mass destruction, like the current nuclear arsenals, that could obliterate tens of millions of people, the experts agree, although the X-ray laser would use a nuclear explosion in space to trigger an array of defense laser beams that would in turn be directed at approaching missiles. But these same authorities, in government, industry and the universities, say the proposed defensive system, if it is actually built and deployed at full strength, could serve several major offensive functions:

■   It could be used as a defensive adjunct to an offensive nuclear attack, allowing nuclear-armed missiles to be launched in an offensive strike while the defense is held in reserve to cope with any retaliatory strike.

■   It could attack and destroy enemy space satellites, which are generally far easier targets than the ballistic missiles the system would be designed to intercept. Satellites have become an increasingly important part of the military systems of the United States and the Soviet Union.

■   It could be used in lightning-fast strikes from space against relatively "soft" ground targets, such as airplanes, oil tankers, power plants and grain fields, causing instantaneous fires and damage that, in the words of John D. G. Rather, a laser expert and Star Wars proponent, could "take an industrialized country back to an eighteenth-century level in thirty minutes."

■   There is even mild concern among some military experts that the system might ultimately prove able to destroy the concrete-and-steel silos that protect missiles underground, thus providing a first-strike weapon that could disable an opponent's missiles before they could be fired. Most experts consider this possibility extremely remote, however.

The proposed defensive system could also unleash fast offensive strikes from space that could, in the words of one scientist, "Take an industrialized country back to an eighteenth-century level in thirty minutes."
ILLUSTRATION BY ROBERT NEUBACKER

The offensive uses would not be unique to the kind of weapons that are being explored in the U.S. defense program. If the Soviet Union should deploy a similar defensive shield, it, too, would almost certainly have the same offensive potential. "I've been thoroughly aware of the problem for years," said Dr. Rather, vice president of the Kaman Aerospace Corporation, who has often testified in Congress in favor of a defensive system. Anything that involves large amounts of energy can be used for good or evil purposes. A system of space battle stations designed to stop a nuclear attack also may have the potential to attack selected targets in space, in the atmosphere or down on the surface of the earth. He said the possible misuse of a defensive system for war-making purposes is something that has to be thoroughly studied and dealt with before such a shield is deployed.

By February 1987, concern had mounted to the point where the American Association for the Advancement of Science held a symposium on the topic at its annual meeting in Chicago. One panelist, Peter D. Zimmerman, a physicist and senior associate at the Carnegie Endowment for International Peace, warned that the weapons produced for Star Wars "will also serve as strategic arms, almost perfectly suited to strikes against population centers, or as instruments of coercion and destruction." Various speakers suggested that lasers or homing rockets developed for a Star Wars defense might well be adapted for offensive attacks on airplanes, storage tanks, refineries, ships, radars, communications centers, airfields, cities, troop concentrations and possibly even individual national leaders or "hardened" missile silos. "For certain ground targets," Dr. Zimmerman said, "it's the best offensive weapon."

But Edward Teller has described it as "unequivocally defensive and not offensive." Teller said he hoped new weapons could be designed strong enough to destroy what he called the vulnerable, flimsy structure of a missile in the boost phase. But he said such weapons would almost certainly be "completely helpless against silos" and would probably have great difficulty finding and tracking ground targets, which could be more readily destroyed by existing weapons. "To use this expensive system to accomplish something as pedestrian as that, something that could be accomplished much more easily by methods already available, what kind of sense is that?"

At this point, of course, no one yet knows whether an effective defense can be built or what it would look like. The Strategic Defense Initiative remains a research program designed to investigate a range of possibilities. Depending on which weapons are ultimately selected and where they are based, the S.D.I. system could possess a range of potential offensive uses.

The most obvious one would appear to be as a potential adjunct to a nuclear attack. Some arms-control strategists fear that a nation that possessed a defensive shield, however imperfect, might be tempted to launch a first nuclear strike against its enemy, secure in the knowledge that the shield could knock down a ragged and uncoordinated retaliatory strike. American officials stress that the United States, even with a defensive shield in place, would have no intention of launching an unprovoked attack on the Soviet Union. But Mr. Reagan did acknowledge in his 1983 speech that defensive systems could raise fears of an attack. "If paired with offensive systems," he said, "they can be viewed as fostering an aggressive policy, and no one wants that."

In an October 31, 1985, interview with Soviet journalists, Mr. Reagan further acknowledged that "if someone was developing such a defensive system and going to couple it with their own nuclear weapons—yes, that could put them in a position where they might be more likely to dare a first strike." That is precisely what Soviet leaders accused the United States of planning. In a nationally televised speech on June 26, 1985, Soviet leader Gorbachev called Star Wars a "program to create offensive space weapons" so as to secure strategic superiority for the United States. "Talk of its supposed defensive nature is, of course, a fairy tale for the gullible. The idea is to attempt to paralyze the Soviet Union's strategic arms and guarantee the opportunity of an unpunished nuclear strike against our country. This is the essence of the matter, and one which we cannot fail to take into account."

Beyond acting as an adjunct to an offensive attack, virtually any system that could be used to shoot down ballistic missiles in flight could also be used, probably more effectively, to shoot down enemy satellites in space. "Whatever weapons are useful in an antiballistic missile role are even more useful in an antisatellite role," said Wolfgang K. H. Panofsky, director of the Stanford Linear Accelerator Center at Stanford University, an expert on beam weapons and a critic of the President's program. And a workshop of experts brought together by the congressional Office of Technology Assessment concluded that any effective defense against ballistic missiles "is an even more effective antisatellite weapon" because "satellites are much easier to destroy" than missile warheads. They are more fragile, far fewer in number and are situated above the distorting and blunting effects of the atmosphere that make it difficult to hit missiles in the initial stages of their flights. Moreover, satellites follow predictable orbits for months or years and can thus be easily targeted at leisure, whereas ballistic missiles would no doubt be launched without warning and would have to be destroyed in minutes.

As an example of the close correspondence among different weapons technologies, the Union of Concerned Scientists points out that the anti-satellite weapon now being developed in the United States exploits homing-vehicle technologies that were originally developed by the Army for use against ballistic missiles. Many scientists believe the more futuristic technologies under consideration, such as lasers and particle beams, would probably be able to destroy satellites long before they could destroy missiles. Indeed, George Keyworth proposed in October 1983 that one of the earliest goals of the new defensive program might be to demonstrate a laser effective not against missiles, but rather "powerful enough to act as an antisatellite weapon" at ranges as great as 22,000 miles.

The X-ray laser, powered by a nuclear explosion in space, could well become a premier antisatellite weapon, according to top Pentagon officials, who add that it would thus become usable in knocking out Soviet space battle stations of the future or any other Soviet satellite deemed worthy of destruction. Scientists at the nation's atomic weapons laboratories have acknowledged the devastating offensive potential of the X-ray laser when used against enemy satellites. "If the laser works as predicted, it could be overwhelming as an offensive weapon," Paul Brown, associate director for arms control at the Livermore Laboratory, told *Science* magazine. "It could wipe out all the other guy's lasers and satellites." Curtis Hines, a systems analysis manager at Sandia National Laboratory in New Mexico, said the X-ray laser "surely looks as if it is a better" antisatellite weapon than strategic defense weapon. "It would be just devastating to a constellation of satellites." Similarly, Hugh DeWitt, a staff physicist at the Livermore Laboratory, described the X-ray laser as "a marvelous antisatellite weapon. So, what's happening is that the X-ray laser is, in my opinion, becoming much more of a possible offensive weapon than it is a defensive weapon."

The likelihood that many of the weapons being developed for strategic defense might prove even better at destroying satellites raised questions as to whether a Star Wars system based in space could itself survive an enemy attack. Former Defense Secretary Harold Brown told the Senate subcommittee on defense appropriations: "It is easier to destroy the space-based components of a strategic defense system than it is to destroy the ballistic missiles. That raises a real question about technological feasibility of space-based S.D.I. systems." Suppose both the Soviet Union and the United States have a strategic defense system, he said, "each of which is aimed at destroying the other's ballistic-missile system. It will do a better job against the other's defensive system. That raises a problem of survivability. It raises a problem of stability. And, in my judgment, it raises the question of technological feasibility. Is something technologically feasible under those circumstances?"

General Abrahamson, S.D.I.O. director, told the subcommittee that the Pentagon did, indeed, have great concerns about Soviet work on the X-ray laser and other advanced nuclear concepts that might threaten the survivability of a Star Wars defense. "It could come as a countermeasure to be used against various space assets of our S.D.I. system," he said. "That is one of the main reasons why we are so very concerned with the technical progress that could be made."

John Tirman, executive director of the Winston Foundation for World Peace in Boston, a strong critic of Star Wars, warned that satellites can be attacked not only by X-ray lasers but also by smart rocks, space mines, nuclear explosives and other weapons developed primarily for ballistic-missile defense missions. Although the Star Wars program is exploring ways to harden or protect its own satellites against attack, Mr. Tirman wrote in the May 1986 issue of the *Bulletin of the Atomic Scientists,* "There appears to be no foolproof way of confidently and economically protecting the battle stations, sensors and computers that must be deployed in space." Thus "S.D.I. is sowing the seeds of its own destruction." Worse, he added, Star Wars research is "exposing current satellites to unprecedented risks." The competition between the United States and the Soviet Union to develop strategic defenses "will heighten the vulnerability of satellites used now for early warning of nuclear attack and military command, control, communications and intelligence. This vulnerability, moreover, will occur well before the advent of space-based defense itself; whether or not Star Wars and its Soviet version reach a deployable stage, shorter term emergence of highly capable ASATs (antisatellite weapons) is a virtual certainty."

■

Although there is little dispute among experts that a defensive system has offensive potential against targets in space, there is vehement disagreement over whether the system would make a feasible and likely weapon against targets on the ground or in the lower atmosphere.

Attacking such targets would not be easy. Many of the technologies under investigation for ballistic-missile defense have limited abilities to penetrate the atmosphere. Particle beams, for example, dissipate when they collide with other particles in the atmosphere. The X-ray beams emitted by one class of laser weapons are unable to reach very far toward earth. And many of the high-speed projectiles that might be used to destroy missiles by the impact of collision would probably burn up in the atmosphere long before reaching the ground. But the proposed defensive system, if it works well, will have to have some weapons able to hit ballistic missiles shortly after launch, when they are still in the atmosphere. American military officials are also hoping to find weapons that can disable low-flying cruise missiles and bombers. Nobody knows if they will be successful. But if they can do that, many experts say, it should not be much more difficult to increase the range slightly and shift the aim to hit ground targets.

In principle, at least three of the weapons systems under investigation could ultimately be able to reach the ground from outer space:

■ High-speed projectiles, if made large enough and durable enough, could presumably be sent to collide with surface targets, smashing them to bits by the force of impact.

■ Chemical rockets armed with tough, heavy warheads or conventional explosives, if aimed precisely enough, could also rain down on surface targets.

■ Optical lasers, which focus narrow beams of intense, hot light on their targets, should be able ultimately to burn targets on the ground. The free-electron laser and the excimer laser, for example, will almost certainly be able to cut through the atmosphere. Under one proposed basing plan, the laser would sit on the ground and fire its beam up through the atmosphere to mirrors based in space, which would redirect the beam back down toward ballistic missiles taking off. Some experts believe that such lasers could provide an awesome instrument for surgically precise attacks against "soft" targets.

Dr. Rather wrote in 1982 that the country in sole possession of space lasers would be the country with the biggest stick in history—having nothing less than "the capability for unilateral control of outer space and consequent domination of the earth." He said such lasers could potentially "deliver devastating nonnuclear strikes to high-value targets anywhere on the earth's surface, in the air or in space at the speed of light, from ranges of thousands of miles, with no collateral damage to adjacent civilian populations." Key targets, he suggested, might include oil tankers on the high seas, oil tanks on land, key power transformers, military vehicles and even troops, who might be blinded by laser light.

Others have suggested that fires might be started in grain fields and storage bins, thus starving a country into submission, or that flammable structures might be torched the length and breadth of a country to spread havoc. In an interview, Dr. Rather said any defensive laser system hot enough and fast enough to destroy 1,400 ballistic missiles in a few minutes as they are boosted from the earth could almost certainly be designed to "burn down through the atmosphere and easily kill an airplane or cruise missile or surface target, because these are essentially sitting ducks."

Physicist Richard Garwin, who opposes the proposed defensive system, agreed that lasers of sufficient power could presumably "shoot down airplanes or set millions of fires simultaneously all over the Soviet Union." And Henry

W. Kendall, chairman of the Union of Concerned Scientists, which opposes the Star Wars proposal, mused at a breakfast meeting with reporters that lasers might also be used for "selective assassination," perhaps picking off a whole row of top Kremlin officials watching the annual May Day military parade.

An eight-page analysis of the potentially destructive offensive threat posed by lasers, based either in space or on the ground, was prepared in May 1985 by Albert L. Latter and Ernest A. Martinelli, two nuclear physicists at R&D Associates, a respected military analysis organization in Marina del Rey, California. They concluded that the lasers could be employed in a manner not contemplated by the S.D.I.O. Specifically, they could be targeted against the same entities they were designed to protect: cities. The authors cited rough calculations indicating that in a matter of hours a laser defense system powerful enough to cope with the ballistic-missile threat could also destroy the enemy's major cities by fire: "The attack would proceed city-by-city, the attack time for each city being only a matter of minutes. Not nuclear destruction, but Armageddon all the same." These authors concluded that lasers could conceivably ignite some 100 million fires that would coalesce into raging fire storms and consume whole cities, killing up to 100 million people. "Would the cities burn to the ground? We think the answer is almost certainly yes." The perceived attack could be carefully planned in advance so as to hit the most combustible targets and avoid having smoke obscure any targets not yet hit. "Fires engulfing a million people would be started in a few minutes, leaving little time or avenue for people to escape or do any serious fire-fighting. From such a near-simultaneous high density of ignition points a fire storm would almost certainly develop."

It was the authors' view that such a weapon in the hands of the Soviet Union would put the entire United States at risk. "Space-based or ground-based, a Soviet laser weapon system powerful enough to defend against the U.S. ballistic-missile threat can incinerate our cities without warning on a time scale of minutes per city; minutes to hours for the whole country. To deter such an attack, the U.S. could only threaten to retaliate." In other words, even ground-based lasers being contemplated for strategic defense might well play a valuable offensive role against Soviet conventional forces, ports, airfields and a variety of other military installations. "For those who have advocated limited nuclear options against the Soviet Union itself, limited laser options would produce less collateral damage and be just as effective otherwise."

The study by R&D Associates drew a sharp, skeptical rebuttal from a team

Star Wars protesters at Cape Canaveral gathered for the launching of the shuttle *Discovery* in January 1985.
UPI/BETTMANN NEWSPHOTOS

of six experts from the Defense Nuclear Agency and one of its contractors. In a six-page critique, dated August 7, 1985, the team charged that the study was marred by numerous technical errors and incorrect assumptions that caused the potential destruction from lasers to be greatly overestimated. The government's team estimated that the lasers likely to be deployed for strategic defense could start only 264 fires, not 100 million, and that fire storms were not likely to form in modern cities with tall buildings built of steel, concrete and brick. The 264 fires would be dispersed over some 100 to 200 cities in the United States or the Soviet Union, the government team said, and they would be small and easily extinguished.

Drs. Latter and Martinelli, after reviewing the government's critique, stuck by their original conclusion. "We find the criticism of our paper incorrect and will let stand our principal conclusion that Soviet S. D. I. systems based on visible light lasers can be used to threaten U.S. cities," they said in a six-page rebuttal of the rebuttal.

An even more catastrophic threat from lasers was defined by Caroline L. Herzenberg, a physicist at the government's Argonne National Laboratory, near Chicago. Like R&D Associates, Dr. Herzenberg concluded that lasers "have the potential of initiating massive urban fires and even of destroying the enemy's major cities by fire in a matter of hours." She estimated that a single laser battle station would have the capability of igniting fires at more than 10,000 separate locations in a city within minutes, thus "destroying a city by incendiary attack." A large constellation of laser battle stations could attack "substantially all of the major cities of either superpower." But beyond the destruction of urban areas, Dr. Herzenberg speculated that smoke from the fires might cause a climatic disaster that would harm large parts of the globe. "Such mass fires might be expected to generate smoke in amounts comparable to the amounts generated in some major nuclear exchange scenarios," she wrote in the January 1986 issue of *Physics and Society*, a magazine published by the American Physical Society. This could cause a "climatic catastrophe" similar to the so-called "nuclear winter" that some scientists have predicted might ensue from the fires ignited in a large-scale nuclear exchange, she suggested. After a nuclear war, it is hypothesized, smoke generated by extensive fires would remain in the atmosphere for extended periods, blocking sunlight and causing a disastrous drop in average temperatures that would disrupt agriculture and other human activities.

A more surgically precise use of lasers was suggested at a symposium sponsored by the American Association for the Advancement of Science in February 1987. Harvey L. Lynch, a physicist at the Center for International Security and Arms Control at Stanford University, noted that lasers could focus light with an intensity 400 times that of the noonday sun on a very small area, enabling attacks on political leaders or other high-value targets. Dr. Zimmerman carried the argument further, suggesting that, in a future attack on Libya, the abortive bombing raid on Muammar al-Qaddafi's tent might be replaced with a laser attack that could hit the tent directly, with few or no other casualties.

Although lasers attracted most of the initial concern about offensive uses, the AAAS symposium focused equal attention on kinetic-energy weapons, particularly chemical rockets, which may well be the first Star Wars weapons actually deployed in space. Thousands of these homing rockets may be deployed on airborne battle stations, ready to speed toward Soviet intercontinental missiles to destroy them with the force of impact. Dr. Zimmerman suggested that, without enormous difficulty, these rockets "can be redesigned and rejiggered for offensive" strikes, primarily by increasing the weight of the warhead and increasing the accuracy of the guidance system so that the rockets could land within a few yards of ground targets. Such weapons would have "real capabilities" against soft ground targets and airplanes, he suggested.

■

Any meaningful destruction of ground targets by lasers would not be easy. Scientists are still a long way from creating lasers powerful enough to serve as weapons. And detecting targets that move, like planes and cruise missiles, could be extremely difficult, especially if the new "stealth" technologies are used to hide the target from radar and other sensors. Moreover, any large-scale attack on cities and other targets would have to be carried out in good weather because clouds, smoke, fog, rain and snow can block the laser light from reaching its target. "Major cloud formations over the East Coast of the U.S. could protect our largest population centers for days at a time," the Defense Nuclear Agency team argued. Even if attacks on ground targets became technically feasible, many experts doubt that they would make much practical or military sense. Joseph A. Mangano, former deputy director of beam-weapons research at the Defense Department's Advanced Research Projects Agency, scoffed at space lasers as an efficient way to destroy ground targets. "One fire truck could hold off a space laser for a long time" by simply spraying water on the hot spot, he said. "It would be much more cost-effective to send a bomb."

Dr. John Rather countered that if a laser system was already built and deployed for defensive purposes, then the added cost of using it for offensive purposes might not be great. "It might be the most cost-effective weapon," he said. Moreover, if it was urgent to destroy many targets almost instantaneously, he said, then laser weapons would be the best choice for the job.

The Defense Nuclear Agency team questioned whether a country would really want to use its space weapons for offensive purposes. The team noted that if an attacking nation used its lasers to destroy an enemy's cities and 100 million people, it would still find itself facing some 100 million survivors and a vast arsenal of nuclear missiles, which would continue to exist unless eliminated by arms control agreements. Those missiles, based in concrete-and-steel silos underground or on submarines, would easily escape destruction by the laser-ignited fires. And the attacking nation might well have depleted its supply of laser fuel in the mass attack on cities, leaving none for defense against the nuclear missiles sure to be launched against it in retaliation. "To build an S.D.I. system to protect your people and then to use it in such a manner as to lose the protection seems to be the very height of folly," the team said.

The most devastating offensive use of space weapons from a military standpoint would be for a first strike against hardened military targets, particularly the concrete-and-steel silos that house missiles on the ground. Most experts believe that this task would be formidably difficult, even impossible. The silos of both superpowers are built to withstand the enormous pressure and heat of a nearby hydrogen bomb explosion. Although a laser beam could, in principle, deposit a lot of energy on a silo, much as a magnifying glass can concentrate sunlight on a small spot, most experts doubt that laser light could cut through a silo cover or weld it shut.

"There is no prospect that a laser could take out a silo, none whatever," said Dr. Kendall. "Silos are designed to withstand nuclear bursts a few thousand feet away. No little itty-bitty laser is going to do anything to a silo designed for that." And others suggest that it would be very easy to protect silos from laser attack—simply by covering them with mirrors or other materials to deflect, or absorb, the laser light.

A more formidable threat to silos might be kinetic-energy weapons that rely on high-speed impact to smash their targets. In principle, a suitably shaped piece of tungsten, uranium or other heavy metal could be fired from space at a silo or other hard target, possibly causing more damage than anything else except a direct nuclear hit. If the launching platform was in low earth orbit, the chunk of metal would reach its target faster than an intercontinental missile.

Robert English, a former Defense Department policy analyst who is now with the Committee for National Security, a Washington-based educational group concerned with foreign and military policy, has argued that space-based satellites "could launch high-velocity, super-accurate, nonnuclear warheads at targets on Earth, destroying the adversary's land-based missiles in a matter of minutes." He suggested that a fleet of satellites in low orbit, 100 miles or less above the earth, could fire rockets at missile silos or military command centers using highly precise guidance technology to score direct hits. Perhaps the most threatening Star Wars attack, he wrote, would use a combination of lasers, nuclear explosions and missiles launched from space against a wide range of targets. "In a matter of minutes, the victim of such an attack might find the bulk of his ICBM and bomber force gone and his command systems in disarray." In an interview, however, he acknowledged that it would be hard to test and deploy, undetected, a space-based rocket that could destroy missile silos. "It's also hard to envision a scenario in which it's sensible to do something like that. But not impossible."

American experts have studied the threat of offensive weapons in space for years and have always concluded that intercontinental missiles launched from earth would be more accurate and more reliable than anything dropped from space. Moreover, the kind of high-speed projectile useful against hard stationary ground targets would probably differ considerably from the projectiles that will be designed to intercept fast-moving missiles and warheads. Although the overwhelming majority of experts consider the possibility of an attack from space against missile silos to be extremely remote and easy to defend against, the Air Force Ballistic Missile Office at Norton Air Force Base in California is taking no chances: It solicited proposals for a study to determine whether space weapons or other nonnuclear weapons might, in fact, be able to disable a missile in a hard silo.

The two superpowers have expressed sharply different views of the offensive potential in Star Wars. Soviet political leaders and scientists have charged that the system will employ "space strike weapons" that could destroy a wide range of targets. A 1985 Soviet publication entitled "Star Wars: Delusions and Dangers" said that the supposedly defensive weapons could "deliver a strike from outer space at earth, air and sea targets," including missiles at launch sites, command, control and communications centers, power stations, airfields and various moving targets. And Mr. Gorbachev himself, after his summit meeting with President Reagan in November 1985, asserted: "The U.S. President states that the S.D.I. is a shield. I hope that we have convincingly shown that it is a space weapon which can be used against missiles, against satellites, and against targets on earth. It is a new type of weapon. A new sphere of the arms race is thereby opened."

The Reagan administration stressed from the start that its Star Wars program had no aggressive goals and is not trying to design weapons for offensive purposes, but simply for defense. President Reagan, after the November 1985 summit, acknowledged that "Mr. Gorbachev insisted that we might use a strategic defense system to put offensive weapons into space." But he added: "I made it clear that S.D.I. has nothing to do with offensive weapons; that, instead, we are investigating nonnuclear defense systems that would only threaten offensive missiles, not people." When asked at a press conference in September 1985 about the possibility that weapons developed for missile defense might ultimately be used offensively, Mr. Reagan replied: "I'm not a scientist enough to know about what that would take, to make them that way. That isn't what we are researching on or what we're trying to accomplish."

At congressional hearings in 1986, General Abrahamson said that anyone who examined the Star Wars program closely could see that it is not developing its weapons in such a way that they could be used for offensive warfare. He told the Senate subcommittee on defense appropriations on March 5, 1986, that lasers can indeed fire their beams up through the atmosphere and thus, logically, such beams could be made to travel back down. "However, we are not spending money on trying to figure out how to get down to the surface of the earth with the intensities that you might be able to hurt anybody. It would be military nonsense to take a laser and try to destroy a city by marching up and down the different avenues in that city. Furthermore, lasers cannot penetrate the clouds, although the Soviets are working intensively on that and we are examining it." Moreover, he said, most of the buildings in Moscow and Washington are "huge stone piles" that could not be penetrated by lasers.

General Abrahamson acknowledged that a space-based kinetic kill vehicle, or rocket, could be built in such a way that it could hit the earth. But this would require significant weight and a large thermal shield to avoid burning up in the atmosphere on the way down, he said, whereas the Star Wars program is seeking small and light rockets that would have the very high speeds needed to intercept ballistic missiles. "If it is light, as it gets down deep into the atmosphere, it heats up and burns up," General Abrahamson told the House defense appropriations subcommittee on May 1, 1986. "So it is a pure defensive weapon."

An independent analyst, Peter Sharfman of the congressional Office of Technology Assessment, told a House armed services subcommittee on March 11, 1986, that if defensive systems deployed in space became very large, they would create "an infrastructure that could eventually be the basis for developing offensive weapons based in space." But Dr. Sharfman, whose organization had conducted detailed, critical analyses of the Star Wars program, said that "to our knowledge, there are no such offensive weapons presently in development, and it would be many a long year before one would move from defensive weapons in space to any other kind of weapons in space."

Supporters of the Strategic Defense Initiative, skeptical that it could be used to ignite a nation's cities, stress that whatever offensive uses it may have are nothing like the enormous destructive power of nuclear weapons. "These are not weapons of mass destruction which can take out a city and two or three million lives in ten microseconds," said Lieut. Colonel Michael Havey, formerly of the White House Office of Science and Technology Policy. "The S.D.I. weapons are precision weapons that destroy only precise targets. They would not make good first-strike weapons because they could not take out the other side's cities, factories and people fast enough. These are weapons which kill weapons."

Dr. Teller said: "We are talking about defensive weapons, instruments of very high accuracy, which are directed against the instruments of attack only after they have been launched, not while they are in their silos. That is the only distinction I want to emphasize."

One strong supporter of strategic defense expressed an uneasy suspicion, however, that the weapons might find offensive uses—and that the Soviet Union had already found them. Richard Perle, an Assistant Secretary of Defense, suggested that such discoveries may have been a key reason for the Soviet opposition to S.D.I. at the October 1986 meeting between Mikhail Gorbachev and President Reagan in Reykjavik. At a Pentagon press conference on October 14, 1986, Mr. Perle offered the opinion that the Russians, after years of their own research, have "come to some conclusions about the potential for strategic defense" and "have also discovered the potential for offensive uses of space that we haven't yet discovered." Soviet leaders "seem concerned that we might somehow, in the course of the S.D.I. program, stumble upon offensive technologies, and they're trying to stop that," he said. "And my guess is that they have already stumbled upon such technologies." It is hard to imagine the researchers in either country not continuing to ponder the offensive possibilities, even if it is for just that reason—to see whether a potential enemy might do so, too.

12

THE THREAT
TO SCIENCE

For better or worse, Star Wars has brought dramatic change to the structure of science, altering, perhaps irrevocably, the way research is conducted in America. Debate has flared over whether these changes are good or bad, whether they strengthen or seriously distort the process of research and the realization of its goals. At stake, according to both defenders and detractors of Star Wars, are not only military aims but also the future vitality of the scientific enterprise in America and thus, in the long run, the nation's ability to compete in the international race for all kinds of new technologies, both civilian and military. Recent changes in the structure of science have already included a rapid increase in military research at universities, a drop in the number of open scientific meetings, a decline in international scientific exchanges, and a general tightening of restrictions on scientific freedom of speech and publication.

Angry detractors and eager defenders of Star Wars are speaking out on

A Miracl chemical laser flashed across the desert at White Sands Missile Range in New Mexico, striking the casing of a stationary Titan rocket and causing it to explode in a hail of shredded metal. Critics called the missile's destruction more showmanship than science; "the impression was the laser blew it apart," said one. "But it was the gadget at the top, the crossbar that was ostensibly there for loading, with the cables pulling down, that caused it to fly to pieces. The test looked much more impressive than it really was." UPI/BETTMANN NEWSPHOTOS

such issues in articles, talks and petitions. Indeed, fears about the impact of Star Wars on the science establishment have helped fuel one of the most extensive scientific boycotts of the nuclear era. In 1985 a group of scientists and engineers called on university colleagues to refuse to participate in the antimissile project. A year later, more than 3,700 faculty members had joined the boycott, including Nobel laureates and majorities in the top 100 physics and engineering departments around the nation.

The wide repercussions of Star Wars on the scientific enterprise stem from the research program's large budget, from its military character, and from its unique charter. For ranks of eager scientists, the goal is to search for insights, discoveries and principles that can be turned into new arms, the investigation having virtually no boundaries. This open-ended study contrasts sharply with the only historical precedents for extraordinarily large federal science programs, the Manhattan A-bomb project and the Apollo moon program. These had narrow goals involving nuclear fission and rocketry. In contrast, virtually no area of modern science or engineering has been eliminated from the Star Wars quest. "There is no parallel from the rich and diverse menu of the past," said Harvey Brooks, professor of technology and public policy at Harvard University. The sheer size and diversity of Star Wars research, he added, gives it the potential to touch nearly every aspect of the nation's scientific life.

At the forefront of the Star Wars quest is the Innovative Science and Technology Program of the Strategic Defense Initiative, run by Dr. James A. Ionson, an astrophysicist. Its goal, he says, is "to get the most brilliant minds in our country involved in this program," adding that the effort will involve "many, many Manhattan projects." Dr. Ionson's program, which aims for a budget of $600 million over five years, has targeted the best and the brightest at dozens of the nation's top science schools, including the California Institute of Technology, Cornell University, the University of Illinois and the Massachusetts Institute of Technology.

Chief among the fears of some prominent academics is that the surge of Star Wars funds will shift research attention away from other vital campus projects. "The infusion of such a large amount of money can distort activities within the university," said Marvin L. Goldberger, president of the California Institute of Technology. "It can draw people into research areas they might not otherwise pursue." Others fear the innovation program has been simply a tool to garner political support for the Star Wars program. Paul E. Gray, president of the Massachusetts Institute of Technology, charged that the involvement of some M.I.T. professors in the research, though limited, was being cited by the Reagan administration in a "manipulative effort to garner implicit institutional endorsement" of the antimissile project.

Worst of all, academics say, Star Wars is a threat to scientific discourse. They fear that antimissile work on campus—no matter how fundamental, no matter how theoretical, no matter how carefully structured to probe basic science rather than military arts—will ultimately be classified by the Pentagon as secret, thus threatening traditional rights to publish research findings and exchange those findings with colleagues around the world. "It may be unclassified right now," said Dr. Dorothy Nelkin, a professor of science, technology and society at Cornell University. "But when the work becomes interesting, I can't imagine classification won't be imposed. And then it is too late for the institutions to back out."

In defense, antimissile advocates say any harm to the structure of science is minor and eventually will be overshadowed by economic benefits to society:

Star Wars will produce not only weapons but spinoff discoveries that significantly enrich many civilian and military endeavors, leaving the nation better off in the long run. Some increased secrecy, advocates say, is necessary to stem the flow of Western expertise to the Soviet bloc. But Pentagon officials insist that little work is subject to publication controls and that sensitive projects will be quickly moved off-campus. "Of course there are technologies in S.D.I. that are vital to our national interests and are classified top secret," General Abrahamson said in an interview. "However, you'd be amazed how much of our work is nonclassified or only moderately classified. Our secrecy classification system, like the proposed missile defense itself, is organized in layers, and our policy is to permit the maximum freedom of communication consistent with the national interest. That policy shouldn't pose a real problem for anyone."

Indeed, in 1985 the White House moved to calm academic fears by announcing that the government would endeavor to place no limits on the publication of unclassified scientific research. The announcement said the President had approved a new national policy calling for the results of fundamental research to remain unrestricted to the maximum extent possible.

Despite the high-level assurances, Star Wars has, in several instances, brought on a deep academic chill. One celebrated case that stretched from 1984 to 1986 involved Dr. Andrew M. Sessler, a theoretical physicist at the University of California's Lawrence Berkeley Laboratory. In November 1984, Dr. Sessler and his colleagues announced the creation of a free-electron laser amplifier that increased energy levels 250,000 percent over current models, producing very powerful microwaves. The breakthrough was widely noted in the press. "This is the first operation of a pure free-electron laser as a high-gain microwave amplifier," Dr. Sessler said. Despite the 1984 announcement, publication of his detailed results was delayed for more than a year because a small part of the project had been financed by the Star Wars Innovative Science and Technology Program, which wanted details of the breakthrough kept secret. Beginning in March 1985, Dr. Sessler was told to refrain from publication because it would aid the Soviet Union. The ban was finally dropped and publication permitted in May 1986 after much controversy and protest, including high-level criticism of the ban by Dr. Sessler's main sponsor, the U.S. Department of Energy.

To those unfamiliar with life in scientific laboratories, the fuss over Star

Wars and the structure of science might seem a tempest in a test tube. So what if papers are kept secret? The work would still benefit the Star Wars program.

The trouble with this view is that it neglects the social nature of science. The myth of the lonely scientist culminating his work late at night with cries of "Eureka!" is wildly at odds with the reality of most scientific advance. At its heart, scientific discovery is a group effort in which many individuals supply pieces of a puzzle. Without constant interaction—through exchange of published papers, and, just as important, through formal and informal talks at scientific meetings—little progress can be made. It is no accident that Sir Isaac Newton, father of the scientific revolution, was president of the Royal Society of London, the most prestigious scientific group of its day. The group effort is especially important in the modern age of large, complex, highly technical and expensive research projects. In trying to harness nuclear fusion for peaceful power, for example, hundreds of scientists from many nations have been exchanging data for decades and will probably have to continue to do so for several more if they are to succeed.

Secrecy also makes science less rewarding. Scientists, like other professionals, strive not only for results but also for the approbation of their peers. Classification robs them of credit and recognition. Such factors help explain why top scientists, given a choice between military and civilian research, frequently take civilian jobs even if it means a smaller salary. For most, the freedom of research and publication in industry and academia are too attractive to ignore.

This urge for open discourse explains why scientists got so upset when Star Wars officials blocked the publication of unclassified papers, stopped the presentation of reports at scientific meetings, demanded the creation of special closed sessions at meetings from which foreigners are excluded and told universities to bar foreign scientists from access to certain sensitive but unclassified research materials. In September 1985, the leaders of twelve of the nation's largest scientific and engineering societies banded together to charge the Pentagon with quietly creating a new kind of classification system for such materials. The societies vowed to stop sponsoring restricted sessions at their meetings.

Understandably, the deepest restriction imposed by Star Wars has been in limiting exchanges of information and ideas between scientists from the United States and the Soviet Union. These meetings between East and West, which had occurred for decades, revolved around nonmilitary matters in so-called pure, or theoretical, science. But as Star Wars picked up speed, debate intensified over whether the exchanges should be sharply curtailed, and many Russians were eventually banned from meeting with their American colleagues. In explaining such moves, Pentagon officials said they feared the transfer of basic research that would aid arms advances. They noted that many of these Russian and American scientists work in military laboratories and that their meetings occurred as both nations searched for powerful space weapons, the perfection of which in many cases depended on developments in basic theory. Clearly, the Pentagon also feared the loss of state secrets.

The exchange prohibitions were imposed despite the fact that over the decades American and Russian arms scientists have forged curiously deep relationships. The situation was summed up by Theodore B. Taylor, formerly an atomic physicist at the Los Alamos National Laboratory. "On one level here are two countries facing each other—and it's terrible. But on another, here are two sets of scientists sharing a sense that they're both working on weapons for the same reason, to aid deterrence or whatever. And they feel friendly and hand-picked—almost mystically picked. There's a sense of camaraderie. It's curious. It's a matter of shared excitement."

Indeed, the loudest protests over limits to meetings with Soviet scientists have come not from academics but from American arms researchers in federal laboratories who say they profit from the Russian contacts. "Technology transfer is a two-way street; we bring back as many good ideas as we leave," said Dr. William A. Barletta, a beam-weapons official at the Livermore laboratory. "Aside from blueprints for nuclear weapons, nothing should be classified. If you have a free country and a vigorous country, the price of secrecy is too much to pay." Exchanges between East and West probably add to stability, in the view of Dr. Marshall N. Rosenbluth, the director of the Institute for Fusion Studies at the University of Texas and formerly a physicist at Los Alamos. "The more interaction there is," he said, "the less paranoia, and the Russians certainly have shown a good deal of that. But with S.D.I. becoming a big thing, it's harder for people to make contacts."

The Pentagon position, however, is that many Soviet scientists are, in the end, spies. In May 1985, Richard N. Perle, then Assistant Secretary of Defense for international security policy, told a news seminar that he believed that Soviet scientists visiting the United States were usually either full-fledged intelligence agents or legitimate scientists on spy missions. There are, he said, dramatic examples not only of Soviet intelligence officers but also of Soviets deeply immersed in the development of some "very menacing defense technologies who have come to this country for two and three weeks at a time and had access to the American community of scholars and engineers." He refused to provide specific examples.

Curiously, a cooling of scientific relations between East and West has apparently been encouraged by the Soviet Union as well. Russian scientists recently withdrew a paper on microwave generation scheduled to be presented at an international conference in Europe. "The Soviets decided it was classified," said Dr. Barletta of Livermore. Beams of microwaves are being studied in both East and West as a way of trying to destroy the delicate electronics of missiles and warheads.

Over the decades, Soviet and American exchanges had progressed to the point that, by the 1970s, scientists from East and West were cooperating on projects that bordered on classified areas, and sometimes even crossed into forbidden zones. Consider, for example, the nuclear fusion experiments, which attempt to harness miniature hydrogen bombs for the production of electrical power. The tiny fusion reactions are meant to heat water to turn generators. In 1976, American censors tried to classify retroactively a lecture on controlled fusion given at an American nuclear weapons laboratory by Dr. L. I. Rudakov, a visiting physicist from a major Soviet science center in Moscow. According to American arms experts, he had discussed details that were considered "sensitive." In the 1970s, during the heyday of détente, arms scientists of East and West widened their collaborations to include projects in such areas as mathematics, plasma physics, lasers and particle accelerators.

Dr. Arthur H. Guenther, the chief scientist of the Air Force Weapons Laboratory in Albuquerque, New Mexico, reflected on the scientists involved in such exchanges. "There's no question that it's a community made up of people with similar backgrounds and similar interests," he said. "It's also a community in which one is continuously on guard because the areas about which you're talking are sensitive." In 1985, Dr. Guenther was able to visit Russia to meet with Dr. Nikolai G. Basov and Dr. Aleksandr M. Prokhorov, physicists who in 1964 shared the Nobel Prize for their pioneering work in the development of lasers.

The Star Wars chill eventually eliminated nearly all formal meetings between scientists of East and West. An important area of reduced contact was research on antimatter particles, which are identical to regular particles of matter in mass and spin but have the opposite electric charge. They are also extremely rare. The military interest in them stemmed from the great energy released when particles of antimatter collide with those of matter. In the fission and fusion reactions of A-bombs and H-bombs, only a tiny fraction of matter is turned into energy, from which these nuclear weapons nonetheless get their spectacular power. But reactions between matter and antimatter produce a complete liberation of energy. It is the only known place in nature where Einstein's law on the equivalence of energy and matter (energy equals mass times the speed of light squared) works in full force.

Antimatter weapons for the destruction of enemy missiles and warheads were one of the possibilities cited by an early Star Wars inquiry. The Pentagon study was completed in October 1983 and headed by former NASA administrator Dr. James C. Fletcher. "Antimatter beams could provide an effective and highly lethal kill mechanism," the Fletcher report said.

In the more recent past, Russians and Americans united to explore antimatter not for military reasons but because the odd particles are also perfect for the study of particle physics, which seeks to understand the basic forces that shape the atom. In such peaceful experiments, a few bits of matter and antimatter are introduced into atom smashers that stretch for miles and accelerated to nearly the speed of light before being slammed together in a burst of energy. The bits of debris give clues not only to the nature of matter and antimatter but to the fundamental building blocks of the universe. Dr. Andre Gsponer, director of the Geneva-based Independent Scientific Research Institute, has written extensively on how American and Soviet arms researchers quietly worked on antimatter projects at CERN, the 6,000-person European Laboratory for Particle Physics, just outside Geneva. The laboratory has long enjoyed a reputation for pushing back the frontiers of peaceful physics.

There was no conspiracy between East and West to make weapons, said Dr. Gsponer, who once worked at the laboratory. He said there was a lot of goodwill to study, to understand, to push the technologies to the limit, and that this was exactly what the military wanted. CERN has the world's most powerful machine for producing antimatter particles. Dr. Gsponer said weapons scientists of East and West had long worked there on antimatter projects and that they also meet at international conferences to discuss their peace-related research findings with other scientists. In January 1985 at Tignes-Savoie, France, he said, a large meeting on the CERN antimatter machine was held and attended by Soviet and American scientists, some of the Americans coming from the Los Alamos weapons laboratory.

But all that changed. The Star Wars program, searching every nook and cranny for exclusive breakthroughs, exerted its influence to halt such information exchanges. An example occured at a meeting in Madrid, Spain, in

July 1986, entitled "International Conference on Emerging Nuclear Energy Systems." Among the papers set to be presented at a session on "Antimatter Energy Concepts" were those by several scientists from Los Alamos, including W. Saylor, S. Howe, D. Holtkamp, and M. Hynes. According to Dr. Gsponer, who was also scheduled to present a paper, all the Los Alamos reports were withdrawn ten days before the conference, with the result that the antimatter session was canceled altogether. "Interestingly," Dr. Gsponer said shortly after the incident, "all the people from Los Alamos are either working at CERN on the low-energy antiproton ring or are associated with a crucial antimatter experiment to be performed in some months at CERN." Dr. Gsponer also noted that other sensitive papers were withdrawn from the Spain conference, which was attended by scientists from twenty-six countries. He said cancellations by Americans outnumbered those by Russians.

Restrictions on Star Wars scientists in some cases have stretched beyond stopping contact with foreign scientists and Soviet colleagues to include prohibitions on talking to American reporters and news organizations as well. In January 1986, Major General George K. Withers, Jr., Deputy Assistant Secretary for applications at the federal Department of Energy, wrote a stern letter to the director of the Livermore weapons lab, saying Star Wars was off-limits to the media. "We do not believe that discussion of nuclear directed-energy weapons concepts during media interviews is in the best interest of the Department of Energy, the Lawrence Livermore National Laboratory, or the Strategic Defense Initiative program," General Withers wrote, the letter having been leaked to the press by a Livermore employee. "Involvement by the D.O.E. and the nuclear weapons laboratories in the S.D.I. program has received more media attention than we believe is prudent," he continued. "Even unclassified interviews which focus on nonnuclear programs can inadvertently lead to questions and responses which highlight the laboratory's nuclear S.D.I. role. For that reason, we believe a general lowering of the D.O.E. program's visibility is appropriate." The nuclear aspects of the Star Wars program, under exploration at Livermore, are especially sensitive in part, no doubt, because President Reagan repeatedly stressed that his intention was to make the antimissile program nonnuclear.

Dr. Robert W. Seidel, a science historian at the University of California at Berkeley, said increasing restrictions on American scientists may only serve to drive the best ones away from weapons research. Freedom of speech, he said, is a crucial factor in "the caliber of people you can recruit." One episode of threatened repression particularly raised the ire of arms scientists. In an April 1986 interview with the journal *Science*, Dr. Donald A. Hicks, the Pentagon's Under Secretary of Defense for research and engineering, lashed out at Star Wars critics and threatened to cut off funding of arms researchers who criticized the antimissile program. On the issue of free speech, he said the critics were "free to keep their mouths shut" and that he was "free not to give the money" for research to scientists who vocally opposed the antimissile program. "I have a tough time with disloyalty," he said. The war of words escalated and, after attacks on Hicks, he retracted his comments. He left the Pentagon in late 1986.

A more subtle challenge to the way Star Wars scientists work and express themselves was the pressure they are put under to come up with positive results and positive comments about their work, no matter what the reality. Many Star Wars researchers say such pressure is especially great because an American President staked his reputation on the outcome of their work. At worst, they said, this can lead to outright lies and the fabrication of results. However, many of the nation's top arms researchers rejected such compromises, saying in comments to the press that their scientific credibility was at stake.

Because of the vows of objectivity and the necessity that truth stand at the center of the scientific enterprise, some academic critics feared that continuing pressures to exaggerate Star Wars results had resulted in a significant shift of talent away from the antimissile program, and that it would continue to do so. "Can such intellectual integrity as still exists in the U.S. government bureaucracy and in industrial leadership survive the pressures of the constant need for selling the program to the American public and to our allies?" asked Harvey Brooks of Harvard University. He discussed the question in the fall 1986 issue of *International Security*, in an article entitled "The Strategic Defense Initiative as Science Policy."

Advocates of Star Wars, while sometimes acknowledging strains induced by the antimissile program, say any harm will be outweighed in the long run by benefits. Their main argument is that the massive Star Wars investment in national security will also produce a host of spinoff discoveries to enrich civilian life and industry. To help achieve this goal both for Star Wars and other federal research projects, the Reagan administration took a series of policy initiatives to allow individual federal scientists to sell their rights to unclassified discoveries. The hope was that productivity would skyrocket.

But critics said serious conflicts of interest can arise when federal scientists seek private gain from publicly financed research, with the resulting threat of distorted judgments and skewed aims. Dr. Hugh DeWitt of the Livermore laboratory said: "You're being asked to serve two masters. The temptation is to conduct your research in such a way that it satisfies monetary goals."

In response, Dr. Jack B. Marling, a Livermore physicist who has sold the rights of his federal laser invention to a private concern, said serving two masters was not the right way to look at federal scientists who are engaged in commercial ventures. "They're really serving one master, the human race," he said. "It doesn't matter whether they're working for the government, the private sector or both. The ultimate beneficiary will be the people, one way or another."

The spinoff debate is complicated by two trends. The first is the widening search for all kinds of industrial applications for research made at the nation's federal laboratories—a network of 755 facilities that spend about $15 billion a year. Instead of retaining all rights to inventions, as it did in the past, the Reagan administration encouraged federal scientists to sell patents to industry, to accept private funds for research projects, to work with industry scientists in exchange programs and to found business ventures. The second trend involves the increasingly expansive search for technologies and ideas related to the antimissile quest. Since Reagan's 1983 speech, federal laboratories have taken the lead in pursuing not only exotic weapons but also advanced computers, optics, sensors, microcircuits, mirror coatings, nuclear reactors, rocket engines and industrial processes in dozens of areas.

In September 1985, S.D.I.O. director General Abrahamson created a new office to encourage civilian spinoffs from the military program. That October he told a congressional committee that missile-defense scientists have a "splendid opportunity to capitalize on the results of the research of the S.D.I. and apply it across all facets of our economy and society."

Although commercialization of antimissile research is still in its infancy, federal scientists in some cases have already made financial gains. One center for such spinoffs is the Livermore lab in California, which employs some 8,000 workers. According to Livermore scientists, a key antimissile technology with potential for spinoffs is a supercomputer known as S-1. In April 1983, shortly after the celebrated speech, Dr. Edward Teller told Congress that the Livermore's S-1 supercomputer project was a key to creating a defense against enemy missiles. "By using these upcoming supercomputers," he said, "we can make decisions in proper time so that we can orchestrate our defenses, and we can make sure that we do the best possible job in shielding ourselves from any strategic attack." In addition to its antimissile role, Livermore scientists said, S-1 technology has wide commercial applications. In one S-1 technique, a laser is to etch the circuitry of a room-sized supercomputer onto a fist-sized wafer of silicon. According to S-1 project scientists who are pioneering the process, American companies are negotiating with Livermore researchers for the rights to commercial application. "The big companies realize they're going to have to go this way or be out of the business in ten years," said Dr. Bruce M. McWilliams, who heads Livermore's wafer work. He added that he and other members of his Livermore team had patented parts of the laser process.

Antimissile critics say such commercialization has serious pitfalls. "Federal servants are paid to be impartial," said Dr. Charles Schwartz, a physicist at the University of California at Berkeley. "If there are financial interests or conflicts, it raises questions of whether it's really disinterested advice." And many top-level federal advisory committees evaluating the merits of Star Wars are made up of scientists from the government's weapon labs.

A hidden danger in the pursuit of spinoffs is that evaluating them and their commercial feasibility is clearly a much easier job than that of weighing the merits of a complex system of space-based antimissile defenses. Commercial spinoffs either work or fail, depending on the judgment of the marketplace. But short of actual war, a missile defense system is too complex ever to be thoroughly tested. Unlike a commercial product, its ultimate utility can never be reliably known. The result is that the judgment of a federal researcher might be skewed. Potential windfall profits might color, perhaps unconsciously, personal judgments about antimissile feasibility. "Who's to say whether this stuff works?" asked John Pike, head of space policy at the Federation of American Scientists. "With a vaccine it's really clear. But with Star Wars there's not much opportunity for consumer feedback. You have to take somebody's word on it."

A final objection of the critics is that public monitoring of conflicts of interest under the new policy may be difficult or nearly impossible because of antiquated laws and regulations. A federal researcher who sells the rights of an invention, for instance, might have no requirement to reveal publicly whether he also owns stock in the recipient company. "No one objects to technology transfer in principle," said Albert H. Meyerhoff, an attorney at the Natural Resources Defense Council, a private group generally critical of the antimissile program. "But you want it in a way that protects the public trust. At a minimum there should be full disclosure of any financial benefits accruing to government scientists from the for-profit use of their work products." He added: "In general you're playing with fire when you mix the goals of the private sector, which is for profit, with the goals of the public sector, which should be devoted to finding new knowledge and benefiting society as a whole."

No matter what the merits of the overall dispute, the changes being wrought by Star Wars in the structure of American science have clearly helped prompt widespread scientific boycotts that are rare in the annals of science. In September 1985, scientists opposed to Star Wars sponsored a rally in Cambridge, Massachusetts, home of Harvard University and M.I.T., to announce formally the start of an unusual campaign among the nation's scientists. The message was simple: Take no funds for antimissile research. According to the organizers, the message spread to thirty-nine campuses, gathering signatures from about a thousand of the tens of thousands of professors and graduate students in physics, chemistry, engineering and the computer sciences.

Lieut. Colonel Lee DeLorme, a spokesman for the S.D.I.O., said at the time that the military did not expect the pledge to have any effect on the program. "We are presently considering over 2,600 applications from individual researchers and universities to participate in the S.D.I. program," he said. Nevertheless, Professor Zellman Warhaft, a Cornell University engineer, said that the campaign was a watershed in the history of modern arms research. Scientists and engineers, he told a crowded news conference on the M.I.T. campus, had never before organized so widely to boycott the development of a specific weapon. At Cornell, in Ithaca, New York, Dr. Warhaft said, more than 500 faculty members and graduate students in the hard sciences, or about half of Cornell's total in these fields, had signed the pledge "neither to solicit nor accept" government funds for antimissile research.

Philip Morrison, Institute Professor of Physics at M.I.T. and a prominent supporter of the campaign, recalled only two earlier periods in which significant numbers of scientists publicly avoided weapons research: the late 1940s, in opposition to nuclear bombs, and the late 1960s, in opposition both to the antiballistic missile system and also to the idea of constructing an electronic "wall" between North and South Vietnam. But several other scientists said that no earlier research boycott had been so national in scope or so pointed as signing a simple pledge not to work on a weapon. One of the main points in the four-paragraph pledge, distributed in September 1985, was that S.D.I. funding would restrict academic freedom and blur the distinction between classified and unclassified research. While the pledge charged that Star Wars threatens the traditional structure of science, its main criticism was aimed at President Reagan's vision: "Antiballistic missile defense of sufficient reliability to defend the population of the United States against a Soviet attack is not technically feasible," it said. "A system of more limited capability will only serve to escalate the nuclear arms race by encouraging the development of both additional offensive overkill and an all-out competition in antiballistic weapons. The program is a step toward the type of weapons and strategy likely to trigger a nuclear holocaust."

13

THE FATE
OF ARMS CONTROL

Hofdi House in Rey-
kjavik, Iceland, was said to be haunted. And the re-
sults of the get-together there between Soviet leader Gorbachev and President
Reagan in the fall of 1986 certainly haunted the two leaders and the world
for months thereafter. The Soviet-American meeting was supposed to be a
ritualistic affair, a run-up to a full summit in the United States later that
year. The leaders of the two nations had been sparring for months—ever
since they met in Geneva the year before. The new Soviet boss contended
that there must be substantial progress toward agreement on arms control
before another summit meeting. Reagan, entering his sixth year in office,
recalled that in Geneva no such precondition had been set. As often happened
when pressures mounted, however, they found some common ground. They
agreed to put aside the major issues of disagreement for the moment, such
as reductions in strategic forces and the future of space-based defenses. In-

Soviet leader Mikhail Gorbachev and President Ronald Reagan face to face before their farewell at the disappointing arms talks in Reykjavik, October 12, 1986. (Man at center is an interpreter.) Star Wars was a chief stumbling block.
AP/WIDE WORLD PHOTOS

stead, they would concentrate on lesser concerns, nuclear testing and medium-range missiles in Eurasia.

The arrangement was simple and promising. But success was not to be. Each leader had surprises in store for the other across the table at Hofdi House. Reagan and Gorbachev each proposed, on October 11 and 12, the most far-reaching schemes for vastly reducing nuclear weapons. Each in fact proposed virtually to rid the world of these devastating weapons. But even as they began to approach each other regarding offensive forces, both stumbled once again over what to do about Reagan's Strategic Defense Initiative. Gorbachev made all that he had conceded on offensive forces dependent on confining Star Wars tests to the laboratory. And Reagan said no.

The President, looking uncharacteristically grim, saw the General Secretary to his limousine. Then they and their aides began sharing with the world conflicting tales of what had transpired. On one point, however, they were agreed: Reagan's insistence on keeping Star Wars and Gorbachev's on killing it had blocked an accord.

From that March day when Mr. Reagan first unveiled his vision of space-based defenses to make nuclear weapons "impotent and obsolete," experts had no doubt that the course of arms-control negotiations would be fundamentally changed. Reagan administration officials maintained S.D.I. would make everything better: better because the two superpowers would switch from offenses to defenses, from the specter of annihilation to genuine safety; and better because Soviet fears of American technology in this most futuristic of technologies might induce concessions on offensive nuclear forces. As the Reykjavik story unfolded, it seemed that Moscow was in fact prepared to go quite far toward Washington's position on medium-range and strategic offensive arms if Reagan would pull in the reins on Star Wars.

Thus, space-based defenses moved to the center of negotiations. The overriding questions became whether the President of the United States was prepared to curtail his dream of defenses in return for real cuts in nuclear forces now, to sacrifice a distant future for a somewhat more secure present. The practical question became whether he would use Star Wars as a bargaining chip and trade it in for Soviet compromises on offense, or cling to his vision and become the only President in the last twenty-five years not to conclude an arms limitation pact with Moscow.

███

It was not the first time strategic defenses had been at center stage. Nearly two decades earlier, during the Nixon administration, they were also the heart of the matter. Only then it was the United States that sought to strictly limit defenses and the Soviet Union that struggled to let them be developed. The wheel had turned full circle. Up to the early 1970s, Soviet leaders saw nothing wrong in wanting to protect their homeland. Indeed, such was the principal duty of the state. But Richard Nixon and Henry Kissinger, his principal national security adviser, saw dangers in defenses. Not that they themselves were untempted by defenses. They were, and they began to promote the so-called Safeguard system to defend American missiles in their silos.

The prevailing view among American strategic experts then held that an offense-only world was stable. Neither side could strike first and avoid devastating retaliation. Experts generally believed that a situation where one or both sides had defenses could set up a strike-and-defend posture. This might make nuclear war thinkable for the first time. Of at least equal concern to the experts and Nixon was congressional opposition to defenses. To a near majority of legislators, the system was far too costly and of uncertain effectiveness. So with questions about the strategic value of defenses and with the ever-present risk that Congress would kill the program unilaterally, Nixon put defenses on the bargaining block with Moscow.

In the arms talks then under way, the Nixon administration proposed to limit offensive forces only if defenses were limited. Moscow resisted for more than two years, then relented. In the Soviet capital in May 1972, Mr. Nixon and Soviet leader Leonid I. Brezhnev signed two pacts: a five-year agreement to freeze the number of strategic nuclear missile launchers on both sides (but not to limit the multiplication of warheads atop these missiles, or to limit bombers), and an antiballistic missile (or ABM) treaty of indefinite duration.

The ABM Treaty restricted each side to no more than two missile defense sites with a small number of interceptor missiles. (This was later reduced to one site for each side.) It also mandated that radars could be deployed only on the periphery of both countries and only face outward. No large early-warning radars were permitted inside the countries where they could become the hub of a nationwide defensive system. Strict limits were placed on development and testing of new defensive systems—or so it seemed at a time when defenses meant shooting down one missile with another without the futuristic possibilities that would present themselves fifteen years later. The treaty closed the doors to Star Wars—or so it seemed.

At the conclusion of the negotiations, which collectively were known as SALT I (for Strategic Arms Limitation Talks—First Round), one important element was left hanging. The U.S. side declared unilaterally that it would reconsider continuing limits on defenses without substantial cuts in offensive forces in the coming five years. The five-year limit on offensive arms expired in 1977, at the beginning of the Carter administration. But it wasn't until June 1979 that the superpowers gathered the momentum to sign the SALT II Treaty. It called for small reductions in missile launchers and, for the first time, set limits on the growth of missile warheads. Defenses were mentioned in passing as a subject the parties would discuss afterwards.

SALT II was never ratified. Soviet invasion of Afghanistan made Senate approval very difficult and President Carter decided to hold off pressing the Senate until his second term. But he never had one. Ronald Reagan, not Jimmy Carter, came into the White House in 1981, and with a very different attitude toward arms control. The leaders of the Reagan administration essentially saw arms control as a trick designed to lull the American people into a false sense of security. The American people, they thought, equated arms control with détente and peace. They feared the American people would view arms pacts as an incentive to lower both their guard and military spending. Thus, the new administration would pursue only what they called "real" arms control. In practice, this meant no arms control, and that could not last—political pressures mounted in Europe and the United States to resume talks.

The driving factor was the impending deployment of American medium-range missiles in Europe. The notion was that these missiles would counterbalance the new Soviet medium-range SS-20s. But the political reality was that European public opinion would not countenance the deployment unless it was accompanied by a good-faith effort to eliminate the SS-20 threat through negotiations. Mr. Reagan obliged with his so-called zero-zero option plan in December 1981. If the Soviets would destroy their existing medium-range missiles, the United States would forgo its planned deployments in return. No one in the administration dreamed Moscow would entertain the idea for a moment. It was a ploy, and a good one. Soviet leaders responded predictably with promises to lower their number of SS-20s to a level equal to British and French nuclear forces, but only on condition that no new U.S. missiles be dispatched to Europe. Stalemate.

Moscow made circumstances somewhat more difficult for Reagan by demanding that the consummation of talks on medium-range forces be linked to the resumption of talks on strategic forces and a new treaty in this area as well. Mr. Reagan tried to regain the initiative here with a proposal in June 1982. Its essence was a call for deep cuts in strategic missiles, on the order of 50 percent, and even deeper reductions in Soviet heavy SS-18 and somewhat lighter SS-19 missiles. Moscow saw this as an effort to limit its strength in ICBMs with no comparable limits in areas of American advantage, such as SLBMs, new air-breathing cruise missiles or long-range bombers. Stalemate.

As talks in these two areas dragged on, questions about the ABM Treaty and defenses in general burst through: Specialists worried aloud about the erosion of the treaty as a result of developments in antisatellite weaponry and other kinds of missiles. A band of conservatives and scientists campaigned for ridding the world of MAD and for moving quickly toward a new age of space-based defenses. The technology was at hand, they argued. At the same time, the Reagan administration charged Moscow with violations of the ABM Treaty.

Deep inside Siberia, satellite photographs showed the construction of an enormous radar facility. The radar site near Krasnoyarsk had all the earmarks of an early-warning station, and by the ABM Treaty this could be deployed only along the Soviet periphery. Some administration experts claimed it was a battle-management radar, sited to serve as the hub of a nationwide ABM system. Moscow insisted that it was a space-tracking station, not a warning radar, and thus could be positioned anywhere. Democrats and Republicans alike felt that the placing of the Krasnoyarsk radar violated the treaty. But construction continued, and the matter festered.

Of almost equal concern, weapons developments in areas related to ABM's nipped away at the edges of the treaty. That was a major conclusion of a report by the Office of Technology Assessment, a research arm of the Congress. "The inherent limitations of language and the rapid pace of technology," the report said, "make it impossible to develop clear, unambiguous and objective standards by which to measure all possible research programs" covered by the treaty. Because the treaty only limited defenses against high-flying strategic, or long-range, missiles, Moscow moved sharply to develop ballistic-missile systems for use against medium-range missiles. These are sometimes known as antitactical systems, and the Reagan administration talked about developing its own antitactical missiles as well. ATBM systems, as they are called, could be effective in shooting down low-flying submarine-launched warheads, as well as tactical ballistic missiles, as they re-enter the atmosphere.

Antisatellite weapons, or ASATs, posed a challenge from another direction. Their purpose was to destroy targets, mainly satellites, in space. Though it is far more difficult to intercept an incoming warhead, the technologies are not dissimilar. Moscow had possessed a rudimentary ASAT capability for some years. Washington launched its own, superior one.

Into this lazy shower of weapons improvements and purported treaty violations and weapons improvements, Mr. Reagan's March 1983 speech struck like an X-ray laser. In a flash, the arms-control landscape was transformed. No more were there just two stagnating pools, medium-range and strategic forces; suddenly there was a powerful third force to worry about, this one far more complex than all offensive talks combined. Moscow would not budge on offense without first settling defense. Agreement seemed hopeless. Yet, paradoxically, the introduction of defenses into the bargaining equation was liberating as well. Two years later, Soviet leaders would begin to show greater flexibility on the offensive forces front. That story unfolded in the months before Reykjavik.

■

The immediate issue in 1983 was the legality of Star Wars, an issue that inevitably persisted. Article V of the ABM Treaty states, "Each party undertakes not to develop, test or deploy ABM systems or components which are sea-based, air-based, space-based or mobile land-based." This does not preclude research, which both sides have conducted all along, nor does it set firm lines between research and development. But according to the negotiating history and testimony to Congress at the time of ratification, research could be carried on short of producing and testing engineering mockups of such ABM components as interceptors and radars. There was but one exception to this limited definition of testing—the technology that existed at the time of the treaty, namely kinetic-energy weapons, where missiles attacked other missiles.

At first, Reagan administration officials contended the treaty presented no obstacles for Star Wars research. Those research programs called for testing what they called "subcomponents," not "components," and were thus permitted. Their proposal to Moscow set legal issues aside and asked Soviet leaders to join them in discussing how to make the transition from offense to defense. This was the essence of what Reagan said to Gorbachev when they met for the first time in Geneva in October 1985. Gorbachev said no and charged that Star Wars was illegal.

Pentagon and State Department lawyers then found a "loophole" in the treaty. Research and testing limits, they argued, did not apply to exotic technologies which did not exist at the time of the treaty, technologies such as laser and particle-beam weapons. For their authority, the lawyers cited Agreed Statement D of the treaty. It reads: "In order to insure fulfillment of the obligation not to deploy ABM systems and their components except as provided in Article III of the Treaty, the Parties agree that in the event ABM systems based on other physical principles and including components capable of substituting for ABM interceptor missiles, ABM launchers or ABM radars are created in the future, specific limitations on such systems and their components would be subject to discussion in accordance with" other treaty articles. In effect, the administration claimed to be able to do anything with respect to futuristic systems short of actual deployment.

Though the administration insisted that this new and broad interpretation of the treaty was correct, Mr. Reagan said he would continue to act in accordance with the traditional or strict interpretation. But he did not say how long he would restrain himself. Strict versus broad interpretation burst into the center of the debate and became a sword hanging over the whole arms-control question.

To reach its new reading of the treaty, the administration did a good deal of historical and textual scrambling. It essentially ignored the fact that treaty

negotiators told the Senate during the ratification debate that Agreed Statement D did not open the door to testing of exotic technologies. It ignored
the beginning words of the statement itself which stated: "In order to insure
fulfillment of the obligation not to deploy ABM systems and their components
except as provided in Article III. . . ." It ignored the fact that the two sides
had been acting for years as if the strict interpretation of the treaty held true.

Instead, administration lawyers and leaders concentrated on the fact that
during the talks leading up to the treaty it was Soviet negotiators who wanted
the agreed statement, so as not to preclude developing future technologies.
They noted the fact that Soviet negotiators never flatly or even directly
accepted the American interpretation of the statement as barring new technologies. They cited statements by Soviet leaders after the treaty had been
signed reiterating the irksome Soviet stance. In sum, the administration was
prepared to use the loophole which the Nixon administration tried to close—
and thought it had closed—as the opening to a future of space-based defenses.

The lines were drawn and the negotiations with Moscow bogged down
again. But in every bargaining process there is always another angle, and
the Reagan White House found one in time. Moscow, in addition to insisting
on the strict interpretation, had asked for a commitment not to withdraw
from the ABM Treaty for fifteen to twenty years. The administration grabbed
at this opening gambit as a way to open negotiations again.

Initially, Reagan countered with five years. Then, in a July 25, 1986,
secret letter to Gorbachev, he proposed a seven-and-a-half-year hiatus before
deploying his Strategic Defense Initiative. Under the treaty, either side could
withdraw six months after notification. In the key paragraph, Reagan wrote
that the United States would continue for five years to research, test and
develop S.D.I. "which is permitted by the Antiballistic Missile ABM Treaty."
The passage was silent about what was permitted and to which interpretation,
broad or strict, the United States would adhere. If, at the end of the five-
year research period, the defensive technologies are demonstrated to be feasible, the United States and the Soviet Union would undertake two years of
talks on how to manage a "transition period" from offenses to an era of
defenses. If the two sides agreed to make the transition, Reagan would pledge
to share "the benefits of the system," a reformulation of his original idea of
giving Moscow access to the technology itself. If the two sides failed to agree,
either side could proceed to deploy S.D.I. unilaterally after giving the required six-months' notice. The American President also proposed the total
elimination of ballistic missiles during this period.

Soviet and American officials who planned the summit in Reykjavik saw these moves as promising but wanted them in the background when the two leaders met. Better for them to focus on lesser issues where they could produce agreement, such as medium-range missiles, and then announce it to the world. But when the two leaders found themselves facing each other across history, they went for more—much more.

Reagan reaffirmed his proposal to eliminate ballistic missiles in ten years. Gorbachev increased the ante and called for eliminating all long-range nuclear forces—bombers and missiles alike. Reagan assented. Then they came to S.D.I. They agreed to more or less split the difference between the Soviet fifteen-year hiatus and Reagan's seven and a half and ended up with ten. But Gorbachev also demanded that during this period "testing of all space elements of antiballistic missile defense in space [be] prohibited except for research and testing in laboratories." No deal. The moment passed.

For some, the lost agreement was a tragedy. The nearly impossible goal of a world without nuclear weapons seemed within reach, a nightmare about to vanish. For others, particularly strategic experts, it was a blessing. They saw nuclear weapons as the great equalizer and ultimate deterrent against the numerically superior Soviet conventional forces. No nuclear weapons meant no deterrence to them and to many European leaders as well.

Reagan and Gorbachev continued to play out their bargaining hands. Mutual recriminations followed Reykjavik, and many predicted that negotiations were finished for the duration of the Reagan administration. But the doomsday sayers were too quick off the mark.

Beginning in November 1986, the President fell into a political swoon. Revelations that his administration had been involved in an arms-for-hostages swap with Iran, and that some of his subordinates had used the profits from these transactions to supply arms to the Nicaraguan rebels, led to a serious erosion of his power in Washington. At first glance, it seemed that the Iran-contra affair doomed arms control. In a curious way, however, it had the opposite effect.

Moscow quickly seemed to come around to its earlier view that it would be better to deal with Reagan, a strong conservative who could deliver congressional approval of an arms pact, rather than waiting for an unknown successor. Even if the Soviets could not obtain a signed and sealed agreement with Ronald Reagan, an agreement in principle would bind—and strengthen— whoever would follow him: The beginnings of a pact with Reagan could undercut subsequent political opposition from the right wing. Such considerations dovetailed naturally with Gorbachev's first priority: the remaking and resuscitation of the Soviet economy, on which his political survival would depend. For that, he would require a stable international environment and a period of toned-down competition with the United States.

Thus American politics and Soviet reforms both militated in favor of new compromises on arms control. In early 1987, the Soviet leader came very close to Reagan's position on medium-range forces in remarkable ways. In the first place, Mr. Gorbachev unlinked agreement in this area from agreement on strategic and space-based weapons. Second, he accepted Reagan's plan for zero-zero medium-range missiles in Europe, asking only that the Soviet Union be permitted 100 SS-20s in Asia, with Washington having rights to deploy an equal number in the United States. Third, he announced he would invite on-site inspections to verify compliance with the treaty.

By the fall, the two sides were on the verge of an even farther-reaching treaty. They agreed to *eliminate* all medium-range missiles. And, after Washington pressed the issue, they agreed to destroy all shorter-range Soviet missiles as well. The U.S. had no such weapons. The result promised the total elimination of all missiles on the Eurasian land mass with a range of between 300 and 3,000 miles. Effectively, the pact, finally signed on December 8, required the Soviet Union to scrap almost 2,000 missile warheads as against some 300 for the United States.

Back in 1981, no one anticipated that Moscow would accept such a treaty. It would be too favorable to the United States, the experts predicted. But even Moscow's virtually complete capitulation to the administration's terms didn't seem to satisfy American and European conservatives. They argued that the removal of the American missiles would leave a gap in the United States deterrent. They scoffed at the fact that these missiles were put in Europe to counter the Soviet SS-20, which the prospective pact would eliminate. Conservative leaders and experts also charged the pact would leave the West without a nuclear response in Europe, though over 2,000 American nuclear weapons and bombs would remain on European soil. The critics also maintained that the so-called double zero treaty would put NATO at an even greater disadvantage against Soviet conventional forces. But whatever Moscow's superiority here, it was no different from what it was before the American missile deployments began.

The hand-wringing notwithstanding, the general expectation was that the Senate would approve the double zero treaty. Soviet and American officials also expected the agreement would be signed at a summit meeting in Washington by mid-November 1987. When Secretary of State Shultz headed off to Moscow in late October, it seemed that all was on track. But suddenly the Star Wars issue intervened, once again, to derail the process. A few weeks before the Shultz trip, the Soviet side introduced new flexibility into its position. Soviet negotiators were no longer insisting on restricting Star Wars tests to the laboratory. Instead, they offered President Reagan a choice: Either accept a strict interpretation of the ABM treaty banning all tests of space-based systems, or discuss what Star Wars activities could and could not be carried out in space. Mr. Reagan would have none of it. Mr. Shultz and others tried to persuade him to compromise but failed. And so the Secretary of State told the Soviet leader in Moscow that the United States position was unchanged—cut strategic offensive arms but no restrictions on defenses.

From that March day when Mr. Reagan hurled his Star Wars vision at the world, nothing was quite the same. The vision would either stop cold the process of reaching arms-control accords or present new and greater opportunities for them. Opportunities for the United States were enhanced by the fact that Moscow would find it very difficult to compete with Washington in Star Wars technology. For Moscow, high technology dangerously diverts its already scarce resources away from more pressing economic concerns. Competition among nations in the state-of-the-art technology required for space-based defenses would be even more challenging and expensive. At a time when Gorbachev would want to use these limited resources for domestic economic growth, the cost would be even more enormous.

And compete Moscow must. Though Soviet experts, like most of their American counterparts, maintained that offenses could always overcome defenses, it would be too risky to stand aside and concede on space-based weapons. The United States could derive other, nonspace-related but militarily important benefits from the research. Gorbachev, almost from the outset, did not shy away from making concessions on offense to try to head off this competition. He, in effect, proposed to cut Soviet ICBMs by half, including the heavy ICBMs so feared by Washington. He made other important concessions as well. But the question of whether in the end the Soviet Union and the United States could find common ground on Star Wars seemed destined to shape the future of arms control.

14

THE CASE
FOR STAR WARS

President Reagan, of
course, presented the most compelling argument in
favor of attempting the almost impossible feat of building a full-scale defense
to protect the population against ballistic missiles fired in any number from
any direction on earth, through space and down at any selected target. Again,
to state simply, he held out the alluring promise that a defensive shield might
end the threat of nuclear weapons, a nuclear sword of Damocles hanging
over mankind for nearly a half century. In his Star Wars speech, the President
painted a breathtaking vision: "What if free people could live secure in the
knowledge that their security did not rest upon the threat of instant U.S.
retaliation to deter a Soviet attack, that we could intercept and destroy strategic
ballistic missiles before they reached our own soil or that of our allies?" he
asked. "I call upon the scientific community in our country, those who gave
us nuclear weapons, to turn their great talents now to the cause of mankind
and world peace, to give us the means of rendering these nuclear weapons

impotent and obsolete." Here was a promise, he said, for "changing the course of human history."

It was a marvelous vision, of a world free from the fear of instantaneous extinction. Although the Star Wars program did not seek explicitly to defend the nation against *all* nuclear weapons—it was not aimed at low-flying cruise missiles or bombers, for example—it did hold out hope that the most dangerous of these weapons, the intercontinental missiles capable of reaching their targets in half an hour, could be neutralized. And once that had happened, administration officials often said, then perhaps additional defensive technologies or new arms-control agreements could eliminate all other offensive nuclear weapons as well. "A security shield can one day render nuclear weapons obsolete and free mankind from the prison of nuclear terror," the President said three years later in his State of the Union address on February 4, 1986.

The vision proved enormously popular early on to many politicians and citizens desperately eager to escape the nuclear menace. "If we can create an effective ballistic-missile defense, the American people no longer need fear a nuclear holocaust," Senator William Armstrong, Republican of Colorado, told the Senate Armed Services Committee in May 1983. "We can lift that fear from the lives of all of our people without relying for our security on the goodwill and humanitarianism of leaders who have butchered innocents from Afghanistan to Poland, or on the promises of totalitarian leaders who have never kept such promises in the past."

Proponents cited many other reasons for pursuing a full-scale defense and many reasons why even a more limited defense would be valuable in its own right. Their chief arguments:

■ Star Wars would give the President an option for responding to an apparent Soviet nuclear strike without launching a massive retaliatory nuclear attack.

■ Star Wars, which would destroy offensive weapons and not people, is a far more moral and ethical way to protect the country than the traditional "mutual assured destruction" policy, which seeks to deter Soviet attack by threatening to destroy hundreds of millions of innocent civilians in a retaliatory strike.

■ Even a limited Star Wars defense could protect our ballistic-missile force and other military installations against attack, thus enhancing their deterrent value and making a nuclear strike by the Soviet Union less likely.

■ A limited Star Wars defense could also protect the population against small-scale missile attacks that might be launched by an erratic dictator, a terrorist group or a small nuclear power.

■ Star Wars, even if imperfect, would limit the amount of damage and reduce the number of people killed in a nuclear attack, a goal so worthy that it should be pursued even if the prospects for total success are small.

■ Star Wars will help achieve a breakthrough in arms control. Indeed, its very existence brought the Soviet Union back to the arms-control negotiations in Geneva in 1985 and prodded the Soviets into offering unprecedented proposals to eliminate nuclear arms at the pre-summit meeting in Reykjavik in October 1986.

■ A Star Wars defense would serve as insurance against cheating should the superpowers agree to eliminate nuclear missiles or weapons. In fact, it may prove impossible to reach a disarmament agreement without such defensive insurance.

■ Technology is advancing so rapidly that a Star Wars defense, once considered a hopeless impossibility, is now at least conceivable, if not inevitable.

■ Star Wars research will yield spinoff scientific and technological advances that will provide great benefits to the civilian economy and to other military programs.

■ Star Wars research is needed as a hedge against the possibility that the Soviet Union, which is aggressively studying ballistic-missile defenses itself, might achieve a technical breakthrough and deploy its own large-scale defensive system.

■ A Star Wars defense is needed to offset Soviet advantages in conventional military forces and the huge Soviet buildup in nuclear ballistic missiles. Star Wars offers a particularly promising new arena of military competition because it plays to American strengths in high technology.

■ The Strategic Defense Initiative will bleed the Soviet economy dry by forcing the Soviets to develop expensive countermeasures or costly defensive programs. By contrast, the American economy is far better able to support an expensive research and development program.

■ Star Wars may accelerate changes in the nature of Soviet society by forcing the Soviet leadership to allow more open exchange of information in an effort to keep up with the fast pace of scientific developments.

Nobody really knows how an American President would respond to indications that the Soviets had launched a nuclear strike against the United States. Would a President believe the reports he was getting, and launch a doomsday strike in return? Or would he be paralyzed with uncertainty, and wait until destruction was all about him?

"An effective strategic defense shield would provide the President with a third option if he is confronted by a nuclear attack—an option between doing nothing out of fear of an apocalypse, and doing something that might bring on nuclear war," said Ernest Lefever, president of the Ethics and Public Policy Center, at a September 10, 1986, reception celebrating publication by the center of a book on the Strategic Defense Initiative. "The question is: Who would deny the President this third option?" Indeed, two prominent conservative analysts of strategic policy, Keith B. Payne and Colin S. Gray, wrote in the spring 1984 issue of *Foreign Affairs* that a Star Wars defense would be a far more credible deterrent to Soviet attack than the current threat of nuclear retaliation. "Would an American President actually invite national self-destruction by unleashing U.S. nuclear forces in response to a limited Soviet attack?" they asked. "A solely offensive-oriented deterrent must lack credibility vis-à-vis most threats . . . but there would be no doubt concerning the credibility of a defensive deterrent being used."

Henry A. Kissinger, former Secretary of State, wrote in the *New York Post* on September 9, 1985:

> The policy on which Western defense has been built throughout the postwar period—the equating of security with the threat of massive nuclear devastation—is clearly losing relevance. . . . The specter of apocalyptic casualties deprives the threat of action of credibility. In those circumstances, democratic publics will sooner or later retreat to pacifism and unilateral disarmament. . . . Strategic defense is the only new idea that points away from the excessive reliance on nuclear weapons which threatens strategy with paralysis and arms control with triviality.

President Reagan repeatedly described his dream of a defensive system as far more moral than the current policy of deterrence through the threat of massive atomic retaliation. "Isn't it worth researching to see if there isn't some weapon that is more humane and moral than saying that the only defense we have in the nuclear age is that if they kill tens of millions of our people, we'll kill tens of millions of theirs?" he told a press conference at the White House on January 9, 1985. "What could be more moral than a system designed to save lives rather than avenge them?" he asked at a space luncheon two months later.

The theme was reiterated by other administration officials as well. Defense Secretary Weinberger called it "far more moral and noble . . . to try and destroy weapons rather than people." A defensive system is "not only prudent," he said, "it is far more in keeping with our democratic ideals than a mutual suicide pact." S.D.I.O. director General Abrahamson likened his program to the forces of good in the movie *Star Wars*, whose name later became commonly applied to the Strategic Defense Initiative. "We're not on the Dark Side," he told a symposium in October 1984.

"That is not Darth Vader here, I hope," a reference to the villain of the movie. "We really do have the Force with us," General Abrahamson said, referring to the mysterious power for good depicted in the movie. And many proponents argued that the nation's leaders had a moral imperative to provide citizens with the best possible defense against nuclear attack instead of leaving them helpless and unprotected as they are now.

However, the morality of strategic defense is actually far more complex than the administration implies. The Catholic Bishops' Pastoral Letter on War and Peace, issued on May 3, 1983, raised serious questions about the morality of nuclear deterrence but made no direct mention of strategic defense. Subsequently, the Reverend J. Bryan Behir, a key adviser to the drafting committee, hedged a bit when asked by *Arms Control Today*, a publication of the Arms Control Association, whether strategic defense was not something the bishops could endorse. The answer depends, he said, on such issues as the risks that would be run, the technical feasibility, the consequences to the strategic balance, the economic costs, and the impact on such arms-control treaties as the Anti-Ballistic Missile Treaty, which "was a significant milestone" in constraining the arms race.

Similarly, Henry Shue, a senior research associate at the Center for Philosophy and Public Policy at the University of Maryland, acknowledged that S.D.I. "packs a powerful moral appeal" because "what is more moral than self-defense, less moral than massive retaliation against civilians?" But he argued that "defensive weapons are not inherently more moral than offensive weapons"; it all depended on their purposes and the goals achieved. "The moral case for S.D.I. will not have been made until it has been shown why it will lead to the elimination of retaliation rather than to a spiral of offensive/defensive arms races," he said. Moreover, the great cost of S.D.I. "may be the ultimate moral argument against S.D.I." because "it competes with all the other good we could certainly do."

But proponents of strategic defense remained convinced that it is better to defend than to attack. In January 1986, Defense Secretary Weinberger took on critics from the arms-control community who "claim to have moral qualms" about strategic defense because "maintaining a balance of terror, they say, is the more moral course of action. . . . I often hear that arms control is more ethically justifiable than attempting to strengthen deterrence through defensive weapons. . . . recent history shows that arms control has hardly been a raving success. . . . There is nothing moral about a situation in which the strength of the democratic nations is slowly eroded. . . . Moreover, why is it moral to allow the Soviets to develop a defensive shield while we sit back and do nothing? And why is it immoral to research the possibility of creating options for a safer future, options which may lessen the risk of war?"

Freeman Dyson, a physicist who has long been active in arms-control issues, voiced the moral yearnings of many citizens in his 1984 book, *Weapons and Hope*. "Old-fashioned ethics say that self-defense is good and mass murder is evil," he wrote. Yet the strategic doctrine of deterrence "brings us into a world of upside-down logic which considers weapons of self-defense evil and weapons of mass murder good," he lamented. Although many experts reject the old-fashioned ethics as naïve and impractical, Dr. Dyson added that he would "stubbornly struggle . . . to be faithful to the old-fashioned ethics and look for an evolution of our strategic doctrines that will allow old-fashioned ethics to be once again relevant and practical."

■

Even a limited strategic defense that would protect only missile silos or offer a partial, but not leakproof, defense of population centers could greatly increase stability and make nuclear war less likely, according to Star Wars advocates. Such a partial defense would greatly complicate any Soviet plans to launch a first strike, would ensure that some of our retaliatory missiles would survive any Soviet attack and would thus enhance our current policy of nuclear deterrence. "You can have a most effective defensive weapon even if it isn't 100 percent" effective, President Reagan said in a 1985 interview with *The New York Times*. "If S.D.I. is, say, 80 percent effective, then it would make any Soviet attack folly. Even partial success in S.D.I. would strengthen deterrence and keep the peace."

Richard DeLauer, Under Secretary of Defense for research and engineering, said in a magazine interview in 1983, "We don't need a perfect defense; just one to raise doubts so the Soviets won't shoot at all." It was such considerations that led Henry Kissinger to change his mind on Star Wars, about which he had initially been less than enthusiastic. In a September 1984 article for the *Washington Post*, he wrote: "Even granting—as I do—that a perfect defense of our population is almost certainly unattainable, the existence of some defense means that the attacker must plan on saturating it. This massively complicates the attacker's calculations. Anything that magnifies doubt inspires hesitation and adds to deterrence. The case grows stronger if one considers the defense of intercontinental ballistic missile launchers. A defense of the population would have to be nearly 100 percent effective, while a defense that protected even 50 percent of land-based missiles and air bases would add hugely to deterrence. The incentive for a first strike would be sharply, perhaps decisively, reduced if an aggressor knew that half of the opponent's ICBMs would survive any foreseeable attack."

Many critics contended, however, that a Star Wars system would actually have the opposite effect—making a relatively stable world more dangerous. They argued that the presence of vast arsenals of nuclear weapons had thus far frightened the superpowers into abstaining from reckless behavior, thereby preventing the outbreak of nuclear war anywhere in the world. If a Star Wars defense system were now deployed, they said, it might provoke Soviet fears that the defense would be used to shield a first strike, and those fears might actually trigger a Soviet preemptive strike, unleashing the very nuclear holocaust the Star Wars defense was designed to prevent.

But Star Wars advocates answered, in turn, that they were unwilling to trust their long-term safety to the current balance of retaliatory terror, which could lead to annihilation at a single slip. "We are resting our future upon a nuclear deterrence system concerning which we cannot tolerate even a single serious malfunction," Colin Gray, president of the National Institute for Public Policy, told the House Armed Services Committee. "Thirty-nine years into the nuclear age it is uncertain whether the absence of bilateral nuclear war should be attributed more to luck than to sound policy. The question is: For how long should we expect this system of reciprocated nuclear retaliatory threats to work satisfactorily? You may be confident that stability reigns today, but how confident can you be for the next fifty or one hundred years?"

Might not a limited defensive system that would collapse under the weight of a massive Soviet nuclear attack nevertheless prove highly effective against the much smaller attacks that could be launched by lesser nuclear powers, an erratic dictator, a terrorist group or an accidental firing in the Soviet Union?

A White House publication entitled "The President's Strategic Defense Initiative" asserted in January 1985 that strategic defenses could provide insurance against either accidental ballistic-missile launches or launches by some future irrational leader in possession of nuclear-armed missiles. "While such events are improbable," it said, "they are not inconceivable." Kenneth L. Adelman, director of the Arms Control and Disarmament Agency, asked in an August 1985 speech: "What about a capability against accidental launch? Would we not all be better off if the President had the option of pushing a second button—one that could destroy incoming missiles—rather than only the button that would destroy people?"

"It's a critical issue that must be addressed," General Graham, director of High Frontier, told an October 7, 1986, press conference. "Not guarding this country against accidental launch is unconscionable."

Many experts on both sides of the Star Wars debate of the 1980s agreed that one of the most powerful arguments in favor of developing and deploying some kind of ballistic-missile defense is that, however leaky and unreliable it may be, it will almost certainly save some lives, a goal that most would agree is good. Whereas many critics of Star Wars insist that no defensive system will ever be leakproof and that the United States would thus be devastated by whatever warheads got through, the advocates of Star Wars say some reduction of the damage is better than no reduction.

Edward Teller expressed it this way: "Without a good defensive system, a billion people might die in a large-scale war. Defense might reduce that number to 'only' 100 million. This statement is grotesque and appalling, but the point is that 900 million lives could be saved. Without such a defense, the survival of the United States and of freedom around the globe is unlikely."

Similarly, General Graham commented that "should deterrence ever fail (and we all hope that it never does), defenses would provide protection for the American people at whatever level allowed by the technology of the day. This is why the S.D.I. makes sense to so many of us today, just as air defense made so much sense to Churchill and many others before and during World War II. It is also why the Anti-Ballistic Missile Treaty, which outlawed defense and, as a consequence, encouraged an offensive buildup, makes so little sense today."

Critics of Star Wars have insisted that missile defense could not prevent catastrophic damage to American cities. But nuclear weapons analyst Keith B. Payne argued in his book *Strategic Defense: Star Wars in Perspective* that an American defense might actually divert Soviet weapons away from the cities. "In the Soviet view, nuclear weapons should concentrate on military objectives, such as destroying enemy nuclear forces. The gratuitous destruction of population centers does not appear to play a role in Soviet military doctrine." The most likely Soviet response to a Star Wars defense would be to concentrate its retaliatory weapons on military targets to be certain some would get through, Dr. Payne wrote. "There would be some level of urban damage. But the level of civil destruction would be less than if the Soviets concentrated their warheads against U.S. cities . . . and considerably less than in our current state of defenselessness. If deterrence ever fails, defenses would help reduce the resultant level of destruction—even if they were not perfect."

Although leaders of the traditional arms-control community in the United States have warned that Star Wars is bound to trigger a new arms race in both offensive and defensive weapons, the advocates of Star Wars assert the opposite, namely that a Star Wars defense can serve as an important catalyst for truly effective arms control. They argue that traditional arms-control efforts have thus far largely failed. Instead of reducing the levels of destructive power in the world's arsenals, arms-control agreements have allowed the number of nuclear warheads possessed by the two superpowers to soar to about 50,000. Even major cuts in these totals, on the order of 50 percent or more, would still leave the world hostage to an immense level of destructive power. But the very existence of the S.D.I. program will, its advocates contend, force the Soviets to undertake meaningful arms-control negotiations and encourage both superpowers to reduce their nuclear arsenals because the intercontinental missiles that carry nuclear warheads will no longer be useful.

"By making missiles less effective, we make these weapons more negotiable," President Reagan told the National Space Club on March 29, 1985. "If we're successful, the arms spiral will be a downward spiral, hopefully, to the elimination of them." General Abrahamson told a military magazine that S.D.I. was intended to build a climate in which people on both sides feel secure enough to reduce their arsenals. Although Defense Secretary Weinberger repeatedly emphasized that Star Wars was not a bargaining chip that could be traded for deep reductions in Soviet nuclear arsenals, proponents contended that the Star Wars program prodded the Soviets to return to arms-control negotiations in Geneva after walking out in 1983, and stimulated the sweeping Soviet proposal at Reykjavik to eliminate all nuclear weapons. "President Reagan's Strategic Defense Initiative is the best thing that ever happened to arms control," Richard Sybert, a special assistant to the Secretary of Defense and a White House fellow, wrote in the *Los Angeles Times*. "It brought the Soviets back to the bargaining table in Geneva and moved them at last to show flexibility in their proposals. It has prompted the first, long overdue Soviet proposal for a real cut in offensive missiles."

After the collapse of the Reykjavik talks, where the two superpowers came close to major agreement, Secretary of State Shultz said the fact that they came as close as they did was owed to the very existence of the Star Wars program.

Perhaps a more controversial contention of the Star Wars advocates is that there is no way of achieving the complete elimination of nuclear missiles or other nuclear weapons without a defensive shield to guard against cheating. "Truly deep reductions in offensive nuclear arsenals would be feasible only in the event of heavy deployment of strategic defensive systems," wrote Keith Payne and Colin Gray in *Foreign Affairs*. "The United States could never verify strict Soviet compliance with a possible [arms reduction] regime that mandated reductions in offensive forces down to the low hundreds of weapons. But, with strategic defenses deployed, the superpowers could be confident that cheating would have to be conducted on a massive scale before it could provide a capability sufficient to yield important military or political advantage."

Without such protection against cheating, in the opinion of George Keyworth, the White House science adviser when Star Wars was first proposed, the world disarmed would be at the mercy of any state or faction that had concealed only a handful of weapons. But, he said, heavily defended countries could nonetheless realistically enter into treaties to reduce nuclear forces to near zero. "The scale of cheating necessary to provide an arsenal capable of successfully engaging several layers of active defenses would be so large as to be impractical within the context of normal intelligence-gathering capabilities." Henry Kissinger called arms control the most compelling argument in favor of S.D.I. A breakthrough in arms control, he said, requires reductions of the numbers of warheads on a scale inconceivable so long as the strategic balance depends entirely on offensive weapons.

And Freeman Dyson said, "If we can ever achieve drastic disarmament on earth, a deployment of appropriately designed space weaponry may help us to push the negotiated reduction of nuclear arsenals all the way to zero." Such space weapons would not have to nullify a full-scale onslaught by today's missile forces, he said, but only much smaller threats such as residual nuclear forces concealed in violation of an arms-control treaty, or embryonic nuclear forces developed by a country that decided to violate the treaty, or forces belonging to smaller countries that had never signed the treaty. Space forces which could defeat these smaller threats are not beyond the realm of technical possibility and might well be effective enough to help stabilize the world against backsliding into nuclear terror, Dyson contended.

Administration officials from President Reagan on down argued consistently that the swift pace of technological advance has made a Star Wars defense attainable, if not almost inevitable. The U.S. conclusion, after examining the feasibility of ABM systems in the late 1960s, that defense could be easily overcome by a buildup of offense, was based on technology far less advanced than that imagined for the 1990s. Paul Nitze, a top arms-control negotiator for the administration, told the North Atlantic Assembly on October 15, 1985, that technology has come a long way since the conclusions of the 1960s were drawn and that it may well be possible in the future to

Key proponents of the Strategic Defense Initiative: George Keyworth, left, the President's Science Adviser, and Lieutenant General James Abrahamson, his S.D.I. Director. They appear here before a Senate Foreign Relations Committee meeting.
AP/WIDE WORLD PHOTOS

reverse them. "Great strides have been made in effectiveness and reduced cost in many areas relevant to ballistic-missile defense, such as microelectronics, data processing and sensors."

A key judgment that needed technologies were, indeed, becoming available was made by the "Defensive Technologies Study," a major review of the technical prospects for strategic defense that was carried out by some fifty scientists and engineers headed by then former NASA administrator James Fletcher. The study concluded in 1984 that advances during the previous two decades made the job of ballistic-missile defense seem more feasible. Perhaps the most important, many scientists said, were technologies that might make it feasible to destroy enemy missiles in the boost phase, shortly after lift-off, when they are most vulnerable and have not yet had a chance to deploy their large load of nuclear warheads and decoys. In the 1960s, the Fletcher panel noted, the only technologies available were for terminal defenses that would intercept incoming warheads on the way down to their targets: "There were no credible concepts for boost-phase intercept" that would destroy missiles shortly after lift-off. But the panel listed the new approaches now being developed—the lasers, particle beams, kinetic energy weapons—that might make boost-phase interception feasible. The Fletcher panel also pointed to advances in sensors and hit-to-kill vehicles that made it more feasible to detect and destroy warheads in mid-course or at high altitudes on the way down, using precise guidance and homing technologies to achieve a kill rather than nuclear explosions that might damage the defense itself. And the panel cited extraordinary gains in computer capacity and signal processing that made the previously impossible job of managing a multilayered defense now seem potentially doable.

The Fletcher report's overall judgment on computers was later found overly optimistic, however, and scaled down into a computer-software program that would direct smaller clusters of Star Wars defense, rather than becoming one giant instruction panel for the worldwide missile shield. A follow-up panel's judgment was that the model described in the Fletcher report and initially proposed by the aerospace companies would demand too much sophistication from the software and would not allow for adequate testing. Dr. Fletcher later wrote of his panel's investigation that "the technological challenges of strategic defense are great but not insurmountable. In the 'Defensive Technologies Study,' we took an optimistic view of the emerging technologies and concluded that 'a robust, multitiered ballistic-missile defense system can eventually be made to work.'"

Star Wars advocates often argued that, as a side benefit, the program would produce rich rewards in terms of jobs, industrial contracts and technical advances that would revolutionize the civilian economy, health care and a range of military activities outside of the Star Wars program. "The technology of swords and the technology of plowshares have much in common," Dr. John P. McTague, deputy director of the White House Office of Science and Technology Policy, told a conference on "Commercializing Strategic Defense," held in Austin, Texas, in November 1985. Others expressed the same idea. Edward Teller wrote in *Defense Science* magazine: "Much of our work in developing defensive arms can be used with little or no modification in the civilian economy." General Abrahamson testified before the Senate armed services subcommittee on strategic and theater nuclear forces: "I would like to mention, at least briefly, the potential for spinoff and civilian application of the S.D.I. research. We think this promise is great throughout all parts of the program. I am personally concerned that we do not miss the splendid opportunity to capitalize on the results of the research of the Strategic

Defense Initiative and apply it across all facets of our economy and society."
And President Reagan, while campaigning in 1986 on behalf of Republican
candidates for the Senate, said in Colorado Springs, in a speech supporting
Representative Ken Kramer, that "our strategic defense initiative will open
the door to a new technological age. Just as America's space program created
new jobs and industries, S.D.I. could open whole new fields of technology
and industry, providing jobs for thousands right here in Colorado, and improving the quality of life in America and around the world."

Spinoffs were predicted in a wide range of military and civilian areas,
including electronics, computers, artificial intelligence, transportation, space
applications, health care, energy production and storage, materials and scientific instrumentation, to name a few. The railguns, electromagnetic sling-
shots that would fire nonexplosive weapons at high speed to destroy a target
on impact, might be used against tanks as well as ballistic missiles. The
techniques used to harden Star Wars electronics against nuclear and radiation
attacks could protect other military and civilian electronics in the same way.
The computers under investigation for Star Wars, requiring enormous speeds
and the ability to surmount defects in the software, would be valuable throughout
the economy. The sensors and precision guidance techniques designed to
locate targets for the Star Wars system could also locate objects anywhere
on earth with high accuracy. An X-ray laser perfected for Star Wars could
also make three-dimensional images of a virus. Energy devices developed
for Star Wars would be useful elsewhere. And a wide range of miniaturized
technologies developed for Star Wars battle stations might benefit the civilian
space program as well. Furthermore, at a time when federal funds are drying
up, the Star Wars program offers support for basic research at the nation's
universities.

Critics retorted that far greater benefits could be achieved if the billions
of dollars spent on Star Wars were directly spent on civilian research rather
than on military projects which might or might not have spinoff uses in the
civilian world. But the proponents response was that without Star Wars the
money might not be spent and the advances might not be made.

Experts on both sides of the debate are in accord that some degree of
research into defensive systems is needed just to keep up with the Soviet
Union, which has historically been more interested in ballistic-missile defenses than the United States.

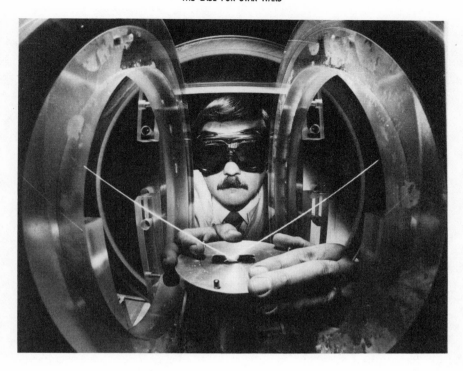

Star Wars spin-off: An IBM engineer explores ways to use lasers that store vast amounts of information on magneto-optic rings.
AP/WIDE WORLD PHOTOS

"Readiness to deploy advanced ballistic-missile defense systems is a necessary part of a U.S. hedge against the increasingly ominous possibility of one-sided Soviet deployment of such systems," said the 1983 Future Security Strategy Study, a group headed by Fred S. Hoffman which analyzed the potential role of strategic defenses for the administration. "Such a Soviet deployment, superimposed on the present nuclear balance, would have disastrous consequences for U.S. and allied security." Secretary of Defense Weinberger told NBC Reports on September 8, 1984: "This is not an option that we have whether we do this or not. The Soviets are working on it very hard—have been since 1967—and if they should get it first, then this would be a far more perilous world than it is now. . . . it would be very dangerous if they could render our missiles impotent and we did not have a similar capability. So, I think we have to work on it."

A group of twelve former Soviet scientists, now teaching or doing research in the United States, warned in an open letter to the President that the Soviet Union was aggressively pursuing its own version of advanced Star

Wars. "The Soviet scientific community and government leaders believe that effective strategic defenses are technically possible and doable," the defectors said. "The Soviet Union has been intensely working on its own version of S.D.I. since the 1960s and puts much more of its effort and resources into its Star Wars program than does the United States. . . . The Soviet Communist leaders can be expected to continue working on their Star Wars system, either overtly or covertly and with high priority, no matter what they say or what they sign or what the United States does."

Although the Defense Department maintained that the United States was ahead of the Soviet Union in most of the technological areas needed for advanced military systems, including Star Wars, some advocates disputed this conclusion. Dr. Teller told the Senate appropriations subcommittee for defense on May 9, 1986, that with respect to strategic defense, "the Soviets are ahead in all areas, in my opinion, where we can check." When the Defense Department says that "we are ahead" of the Soviet Union, he said, "the fact is that we are equal. When they say we are equal, the Soviets are ahead. When they say the Soviets are ahead, the fact is that they are far ahead." Dr. Teller cited Soviet achievements in high-intensity optic lasers, X-ray lasers, and rocket development as examples of their prowess. "We are ahead in one field only," he said, "computers."

Proponents of Star Wars believe a new strategic defense system is needed to offset what they consider a threatening Soviet buildup of nuclear ballistic missiles and other military forces. The Defense Department's June 1986 report to Congress on the Strategic Defense Initiative contended that, since 1969, the Soviet Union had built five new classes of intercontinental ballistic missiles and upgraded these seven times, whereas the United States had built only one new missile and upgraded it once. "The alarming growth, both in quantity and quality, of Soviet ballistic missiles is yielding a prompt hard target force capable of rapidly and significantly degrading our land-based retaliatory capability," the report said.

"We should make no mistake about the fact that Soviet offensive and defensive capabilities pose real threats to the security of the West," Paul Nitze told the American Defense Preparedness Association on March 18, 1986. "Our work in S.D.I. is, in large part, a reaction to the unabated growth of this threat, especially during the last twenty years. Through S.D.I., we seek both new capabilities and a new approach to rectify the deteriorating strategic balance."

Some advocates of strategic defense suggested that the technical competition itself, the race between the superpowers to develop new space defenses on a previously unimaginable scale, would wreck the Soviet economy, thereby enhancing the relative strategic position of the United States. In a strategy paper proposing prompt deployment of a defensive system in space using existing technologies, the High Frontier project, headed by General Graham, suggested that an American strategic defense program would "confront the USSR with precisely the sort of armaments competition that the Soviet leadership most fears and is most anxious to avoid" and would "severely tax, perhaps to the point of disruption, the already strained Soviet technological and industrial resources."

"The United States wants to economically tire the Soviet Union, to exhaust the Soviet Union economically, by encouraging the arms race," Mr. Gorbachev charged in a radio broadcast after the meeting in Iceland.

However, when asked if the Star Wars program was designed to force the Soviets into a competition that they could neither afford economically nor succeed at technically, Air Force major Peter Worden, a special assistant to the Star Wars director, said, "There are certainly those who have raised that issue, but I will say that is not, emphatically not, the administration policy." Similarly, Assistant Secretary of Defense Richard Perle told a press conference on October 14, 1986, that the administration was not trying to break the Soviet economy. "On the contrary," he said, "the elimination of offensive ballistic missiles, together with the other reductions down to levels that were discussed in Geneva, would relieve the burden on the Soviets to continue to invest funds in strategic weapons."

A few Star Wars advocates suggested that high-technology competition between the two superpowers to develop strategic defenses would inevitably cause beneficial changes in Soviet society. They argued that the need to share technical information among scientists would force the closed Soviet system to allow greater communication and that the increasing spread of computers would also foster more open communications.

"S. D. I. would force the Soviet scientific and technological security system to change dramatically," a columnist asserted in the August 1985 issue of *Defense Science & Electronics*. "It is likely that the Soviets also would have to begin relying more heavily on evaluations of technical expertise as a basis of promotion rather than merely party loyalty." That, in turn, could ultimately weaken the Communist Party itself. "Perhaps S.D.I. is a major destabilizing factor as the Soviets claim," the magazine said, "but the major effect of that destabilization is not upon world peace, but rather upon the Soviet scientific community and the Soviet government itself."

Despite the obvious difficulties of the task they have undertaken, Star Wars officials believe that the reasons for forging ahead far outweigh the qualms expressed by critics. In a speech to the U.S. Space Foundation on June 23, 1986, Defense Secretary Weinberger noted that President Reagan had asked "that we relegate nuclear missiles to the dustbin of history."

"I'm optimistic about our ability to overcome vexing problems," he said. "What is most puzzling to me is the self-defeating pessimism that afflicts the critics of strategic defense. Why shouldn't we try to discover if a defense against nuclear missiles is possible? Why should this be such a forbidden agenda for anybody to even think about? . . . why shouldn't we seek to transcend the mutual suicide pact that we have locked ourselves into?"

15

WHY OPPONENTS
SAY IT IS BAD

Most of the public
debate about the Strategic Defense Initiative seeks to
resolve itself on the issues of scientific and technical feasibility.* In a sense,
much of the debate has been sterile. Persuasive arguments can be made for
or against a specific technology. Early experiments are sometimes described
by Pentagon officials as "dramatic breakthroughs," while derided by Star
Wars critics as poorly conducted or fraudulent. In fact, it is probably too
early to know if missile defense is technically feasible. Although S.D.I.
program managers sometimes freely admit that they are aiming at eventual
deployment, the program as it was originally conceived was one simply to
investigate the feasibility questions most often debated.

* A distinction exists. Even if a ballistic-missile defense concept is scientifically
feasible, for the foreseeable future it still might not be possible to do the necessary
engineering to make a device workable, or to produce it at acceptable cost, or to
integrate it with associated components—all elements of technical feasibility.

Most of the public and most members of Congress are scarcely aware of a different debate. This is an argument on the strategic worth of ballistic-missile defense and on its actual military desirability—or possible lack of military utility. However, debate on those subjects appears to be more advanced than that on feasibility. Strategic questions are, at this stage, more amenable to analytical tools. Mathematical modeling can tell more now about the possible advantages and disadvantages of Star Wars than is known about whether it can be built. Although it has received little notice for it, the S.D.I.O. has devoted considerable attention to these questions. It has engaged in extensive "war-gaming" exercises and something called "exchange modeling," in which the effect of nuclear exchanges in different circumstances is studied.

But in studying the strategy and tactics of missile defense, some analyses have raised doubts about the most fundamental thesis on which President Reagan's program rests, which is that defense against ballistic missiles must inherently be a good thing. This would be a common-sense conclusion: If a defense could stop only a few nuclear warheads from exploding on the United States, would it not be worth the effort and cost?

That might be true, some experts say, if nuclear war had become inevitable. The critics are not sure, even in that horrifying circumstance. Those who believe that prevention of even limited nuclear war is the only worthwhile method of avoiding its disastrous and probably widespread consequences tend to be less than enthusiastic about Star Wars.

How can nuclear-missile defense possibly be bad for the United States? One element of the answer is the assumption of most analysts that the Soviet Union will develop and deploy its own missile defense system if the United States builds Star Wars, even if President Reagan's somewhat ambiguous promises to share the technology are never honored. Despite its technological inferiority, the Soviet Union has managed to match the United States after relatively small time spans at each milestone of the nuclear arms race, from the atomic bomb to the hydrogen bomb to accurate multiple warheads on missiles.

When analytical methods are applied to hypothetical scenarios involving *mutual* possession of missile defenses by the two countries, a U.S. defense may be less attractive than political advocates of Star Wars have portrayed it. In 1985, in a major study of S.D.I. issues, a panel of experts for the congressional Office of Technology Assessment, or O.T.A., offered several examples. Some of their work drew on analytical studies conducted by the Rand Corporation, an Air Force think tank. One important conclusion was drawn about the ramifications of a possible Soviet first strike and American retaliation. "If the Soviets also have defenses," the panel said, "their defenses will reduce the number of U.S. weapons that survive and penetrate to their targets." This would degrade and reduce American nuclear retaliatory capacity, the deterrent on which strategy will continue to depend until defenses become nearly perfect.

The O.T.A. analysts imagine this scenario: If, with 5,000 warheads, the Soviet Union attacked the United States ICBM arsenal today, when neither side has any missile defense, it could expect to destroy almost all of the 2,800 reentry vehicles mounted on the American ICBMs. However, the United States could retaliate with 4,500 RVs fired from submarines, which are believed to be invulnerable to any Soviet first strike. The result would be that 4,500 retaliatory warheads penetrate the Soviet Union and explode there. If, on the other hand, both sides had missile defenses capable of destroying 4,000 incoming RVs, the United States defense would "save" 2,240 ICBM RVs that would survive the attack by 5,000 Soviet warheads. The United States would then be able to launch a retaliatory attack of 4,500 submarine-launched RVs and the surviving 2,240 land-based ICBM RVs, a total of 6,740 RVs. But because the Soviets had an equivalent ballistic-missile defense capable of destroying 4,000 incoming RVs, only 2,740 American warheads—not 4,500, as in the previous scenario—would explode on Soviet soil: a 39 percent reduction in U.S. retaliatory power and a commensurate reduction in the destruction which Soviet military planners would have to take into account in considering a preemptive strike in the first place. Few senior officers in the Pentagon would take such a degradation in United States striking power lightly. "Thus," wrote the O.T.A. panel, "equal defenses on both sides would increase the number of United States reentry vehicles surviving the attack." So far so good. But, the analysts added, the defense systems would result in a reduction of "the number that survive and penetrate to their targets."

General Abrahamson has told congressional committees several times that the United States must have a missile defense that is better than the Soviet Union's. Is this just a form of military insurance based on the principle that numerical superiority is inherently good? Apparently not. Glenn Kent, a retired Air Force general and strategist who now works at Rand, pointed out the statistical analysis that led the O.T.A. report to make the following conclusion: "As long as the number of RVs the Soviets attack our silos with exceeds the number of U.S. ICBM RVs—which is quite possible with today's forces—adding defense to both sides in equal increments will decrease the number of U.S. RVs that survive *and* penetrate the Soviet defense [emphasis added by the authors of this book]."

To correct the loss of retaliatory capacity was thought to require a U.S. advantage in defensive capability of approximately two to one. Star Wars advocates argued that in these circumstances the United States defense would decrease the "confidence" of Soviet leaders in achieving their attack goals and destroying their full set of high-priority targets, and that the defense would thus discourage war. Given present forces, this may not be mathematically sound. Even given a preferential defense, in which U.S. defensive assets were heavily allocated to save a relatively small number of key targets, the Soviet Union should be able to allocate its attacking RVs in ways that would permit few, if any, to survive.

That is only one difficulty with the proposition that any level of defense is automatically, inherently good. In the previous scenario, at least part of the Soviet Union's numerical advantage grew out of striking first. It may also suggest that in such circumstances, U.S. officials will pay a price for sticking with the presently declared policy that the United States will never launch a preemptive strategic—that is, long-range—attack of its own (the United States has long reserved the option of limited first use of tactical, or short-range, nuclear weapons). The O.T.A. panel wrote that an attempt by the United States to make a transition from the present strategy of deterrence by threatened retaliation to defense should not make the world significantly more dangerous than it is now.

The panelists conceded that extremely effective defenses that could protect almost all strategic military targets, such as ICBM fields and urban centers, would probably provide a very stable situation in which there would be little incentive for or likelihood of nuclear war. However, even that attractive prospect poses difficult problems. "This level of protection," the report said, "could probably only be reached by a combination of defense deployments and negotiated deep reductions of offenses." Many other people share this view. Similar statements have been made by General Abrahamson and senior administration officials such as arms-control adviser Paul Nitze and former White House national security adviser Robert C. McFarlane. The declared policy of the Soviet Union is that it will not agree to such reductions but will, to the contrary, increase its offensive forces as one way of countering Star Wars.

Still another problem, some critics assert, is a tendency for proponents of Star Wars to view the introduction of missile defenses as a static event, rather than a dynamic process in which an adversary will make every effort to chip away at the protective umbrella. In the fall 1984 issue of *International Security*, Charles L. Glasser, a fellow at the John F. Kennedy School of Government at Harvard, furnished an example of such an argument. "First," he wrote, "there could be no guarantee that perfect defenses would remain perfect. . . . the far more likely course of events is that a world of perfect defenses would decay into a world of imperfect defenses. A nuclear situation in which both superpowers were invulnerable to nuclear attack would be extremely sensitive to even small improvements in the ability of one country's offense to penetrate the adversary's defense."

The present strategic situation in which both sides have huge and, in fact, redundant nuclear arsenals capable of great overkill is hardly a happy situation. However, it is one which is not sensitive to small changes or surges in offensive weapons; if the Soviet Union managed to add 200 more warheads it makes little practical difference. In a world of defenses, however, even a small increase in weapons capable of penetrating the defense would be highly significant. Thomas H. Karas, a space policy analyst and the director of the 1985 O.T.A. report, made another point in an interview: "An interesting question is: Did we feel secure in the early 1960s when the Soviets had a small number of inaccurate warheads that could only be used against cities? That is essentially what S.D.I. is offering the prospect of returning to."

Glasser also touched on the troubling question of whether defense can be counted on to discourage nuclear risk-taking. "If a change in the nuclear situation would reduce the damage of a nuclear attack but would also increase the probability of the attack, then the change might not increase U.S. security," he said. Moreover, to reach a world of extremely capable defenses, the United States would have to make what Mr. Nitze called the "tricky" transition from an offense-dominated strategy to one dominated by defenses. During that transition there is expected to be a prolonged period in which both sides would have modestly capable defenses while retaining large offensive missile arsenals. If one side strikes first, the argument goes, the other side will only be able to make a "ragged," limited retaliatory attack with its surviving nuclear forces. A modest defense would be more effective in dealing with such a ragged response than in coping with a full-scale attack by an undamaged enemy. "At this level," the O.T.A. report said, "a significant and extremely dangerous possibility is that the Soviets might calculate that a first strike against U.S. retaliatory forces combined with Soviet defenses could keep damage from a U.S. retaliatory strike to a relatively low level. If the Soviets similarly calculated that the United States could strike first and defend successfully against their retaliation, that would be an additional incentive for the Soviets to attack preemptively."

How realistic is such analysis? It is interesting to note that it is not really different from the words President Reagan's speechwriters provided him for a passage in his 1983 Star Wars speech: "I clearly recognize that defensive systems have limitations and raise certain problems and ambiguities. If paired with offensive systems, they can be viewed as fostering an aggressive policy, and no one wants that." In his interview with Soviet journalists on October 31, 1985, President Reagan himself said, "If someone was developing such a defensive system and going to couple it with their own nuclear weapons— yes, that could put them in a position where they might be more likely to dare a first strike." He told the *Baltimore Sun* in 1986 that he thought it would be "the most dangerous thing in the world" for one side to deploy defenses without consultation with the other and "to be seen as having the capacity for a first strike."

Strategists have sometimes discussed the possibility that a cold-blooded attempt to achieve a goal, such as "victory," is not the only plausible motive for nuclear war. Soviet, or American, leaders might in a crisis consider using nuclear weapons as a precursor attack, to fend off the possibility of a severe loss or unlimited damage to their nation. "In time of crisis we would not want the Soviet leadership to calculate that its least bad option was to start a nuclear war," the O.T.A. report said. Thus, goes the reasoning, moderately capable defenses raise for the first time the possibility that a first strike, combined with missile defense, might keep damage from a retaliatory strike to low levels. That is an incentive, rather than a disincentive, for nuclear conflict.

The already troubling problem of the survivability of Star Wars defenses also seems to be related to incentives to initiate conflict. If both Soviet and American defenses are vulnerable to a precursor or "defense suppression" attack, then there would be an obvious temptation to knock out the other side's defenses in a surprise blow. If this left one side with even a partially effective defense, that side could count on suffering significantly lower net damage in a nuclear conflict that it would in today's world of deterrence by threat of mutual destruction.

In the nuclear war era, the question of relative military advantage in combat has always been less important than the problem of avoiding the possibility of nuclear war in the first place.

Proponents of Star Wars say that it will enhance "strategic stability," opponents that it will be highly destablizing, "stability" being generally taken to mean a situation in times of crisis in which no country would see the advantages of attacking first as outweighing the disadvantages. President Reagan and some other advocates of Star Wars have also stressed that ballistic-missile defense is morally superior as a strategy to the policy of MAD, or mutual assured destruction. Mutual assured destruction became U.S. policy during the period 1961 to 1968, when Robert S. McNamara was Secretary of Defense. McNamara, who opposed building an extensive antiballistic-missile system, believed that nuclear war could be deterred more effectively if each side had an unimpeded ability to inflict "unacceptable" levels of damage on its adversary.

Although MAD is scoffed at by advocates of S.D.I., it has not been declared U.S. strategy for many years. Since the mid-1970s, declared official policy has been called a "countervailing" strategy, a war-fighting strategy in which the United States would seek to control the level of nuclear violence and to end the conflict on "favorable" terms. However, many critics believe that the actual possibility of conducting protracted, controlled nuclear war is close to zero and that, in fact, assured destruction remains the bedrock of the deterrence policies of both the United States and the Soviet Union. Although Reagan administration officials tend to be highly critical of assured destruction, some strategists believe that it is a stable strategy and has kept the peace for more than forty years. As long as destruction is mutually assured, neither side can make an attack without suffering devastation itself. This limits the incentives for nuclear war, and, as the O.T.A. analysts said, it makes the probable outcome of a nuclear war fairly certain: In a crisis "neither leader would rationally perceive that the advantage in firing first outweighed the imperative to make every possible effort to avoid nuclear war altogether."

In a period of transition from such an offense-dominated world to a defense-dominated world of Star Wars, a number of outcomes become possible and uncertainty is markedly increased. With medium levels of defense, each side may have the capability to attack first and then defend itself from retaliation as well as possible. One element of recent American thinking, as illustrated in strategy proclaimed in 1979 by President Jimmy Carter, is an emphasis on targeting most nuclear weapons to military targets. The hope is that the Soviet Union, too, would avoid a policy of targeting urban areas and the civilian population as such (although no one doubts that collateral damage to civilians would be great even if weapons were aimed only at military targets). But at some relatively crude levels of defense, critics have said that the United States would be denied the chance of destroying many purely military targets. A retaliation strategy in which cities became the primary targets might conceivably result.

There are other important differences between what might work technologically and what will work effectively in military and strategic terms. Such terms as "good defense" and "effective" seem to have clear, generally understood meanings, until they are subjected to analysis. In political terms, the most alluring aspect of S.D.I. has been the suggestion that it can eventually be made into what Secretary of Defense Weinberger calls a thoroughly reliable defense that would stop almost all nuclear warheads—he has said "all" at times—and would thus protect the civilian population from both the psychological terror of anticipated war and the horrors of a nuclear battle.

However, there are many reasons to doubt that even a "very good" defense would do this. If the United States did have a 99 percent effective defense it would not protect 99 percent of the United States population: A 99 percent effective defense, which many experts believe is implausible in the first place, would only destroy 99 percent of Soviet reentry vehicles; the remaining 1 percent could still do nearly unimaginable damage to American society. The O.T.A. report, for instance, described a hypothetical scenario in which the Soviet Union possessed 9,000 RVs, which is close to the size of the 1986 Soviet arsenal. Faced with a 99 percent defense, Soviet planners could theoretically target 100 RVs on each of the ninety most populous metropolitan areas in the United States. There would thus be a high probability that most would be struck by one warhead.

In a more elaborate analysis, the O.T.A. analysts discussed several different scenarios to arrive at worst-case expectations with which U.S. strategic planners would have to deal. The O.T.A. team disclaimed their work as a precise prediction of what U.S. casualties would actually be.

The analysts noted that the Soviet planners could allocate or distribute their weapons in an effort to produce either three pounds per square inch of overpressure or five pounds per square inch of overpressure—the downward thrust of energy from a nuclear airburst—on their targets. Studies by other government agencies have concluded that such pressures are enough to collapse a brick house. A 1979 study by the same agency predicted that most people exposed to five pounds per square inch would be killed or seriously wounded. It predicted that about half of those subjected to two or more pounds per square inch would be killed. These would be instant deaths. Actual casualties would be higher because of radioactive fallout and ground-water contamination and other nuclear weapons effects felt outside the immediate attack area. The 1985 O.T.A. report concluded that only forty nuclear detonations of 750 kilotons each, exploded at 2,000 feet, would be required to produce an overpressure of three pounds per square inch over a total area of 2,000 square miles and only eighty detonations would be required to produce five pounds per square inch over the same area. The most populous 2,000 square miles of the United States contains about seventeen million people. According to the report, "If the Soviets were intent on killing Americans, it would require an extremely capable defense to keep casualties 'low.' A defense that permitted 1 percent of the Soviet weapons through might result in casualties well in excess of 10 million. It would appear that keeping casualties below one million would require a defense that could stop in excess of 99.9 percent of the Soviet attack." In another calculation, the O.T.A. panel put the worst-case limit of deaths at 26 million for a 99 percent effective defense in circumstances in which the Soviets knew exactly how effective the American defense was and allocated their weapons in the most efficient manner.

Such calculations underline one of the problems of ballistic-missile defense: An effective defense for a nation's own strategic weapons, such as missile silo fields, is very different from an effective defense for its population. In the case of missile silos, some attrition is acceptable. The strategic aim is only to assure the survival of enough missiles to mount a retaliatory attack. It is virtually impossible to define, or to get agreement on, the question of what constitutes "acceptable" civilian deaths. In silo defense, a difference between 40 and 50 percent effectiveness is small. In city defense, the difference between 90 percent and 99.9 percent effectiveness is a hundredfold increase in the number of weapons reaching cities.

In an article in the March 1986 issue of *Arms Control Today*, the chief negotiator of the ABM Treaty, Gerard C. Smith, argued that even a 95 percent effective defense would, at present arsenal levels, permit "some 500" ballistic-missile warheads, "not to mention bomber and cruise-missile weapons, to hit our country. No responsible official could suggest that, with such a system in place, nuclear war was any more acceptable than it is today.

The leading critics: Hans Bethe (*above*), Nobel Prize Laureate, and John Pike (*left*), Associate Director of Space Policy. "It would be terribly comfortable for the President and the Secretary of Defense if there were a technical solution" to nuclear arms control, says Dr. Bethe. "But there isn't any."

BETHE PHOTO: © NEW YORK TIMES PICTURES/ F. FRANDSIN
PIKE PHOTO: MARTY KATZ

The only way to protect our country from nuclear war is to prevent nuclear war."

Hans Bethe said in an interview with *The New York Times* soon after the Star Wars speech that President Reagan seemed to be seeking a technological solution to the nuclear dilemma, but that only a political solution was possible.

Still another strategic problem posed by missile defense is the question of whether it will make conventional war more likely. The U.S. policy of retaliation is coupled with another policy known as "extended deterrence." This doctrine holds that the United States, under the policy of "flexible response," retains the option of using nuclear weapons first in case a massive Soviet attack on Western Europe cannot be contained or turned back by conventional armies and conventional forces. It has always been assumed that the United States would first employ small, tactical nuclear weapons and would attempt to maintain something called escalation dominance if the Soviet Union responded by using some of its own tactical nuclear weapons. But in the end the United States retains the implied threat that it would use its strategic, or long-range, nuclear missiles if nothing else could prevent Soviet conquest of Western Europe.

The credibility of this policy has often been called into question. Henry Kissinger, for example, has told the Europeans they should never believe the Americans would actually use long-range nuclear missiles in this way. In fact, many American citizens seem to be unaware that the option even exists. However useful as the policy may be as a brake on possible conventional warfare by the Soviet Union, as a long line of United States officials have argued, it might still become the first casualty of Star Wars. If the Soviet Union also deploys ballistic-missile defenses, some analysts argue, the policy of extended deterrence collapses. While the Soviet defense probably could not insure against serious damage from U.S. warheads, it might offer good protection for purely military targets. In those circumstances, critics say, the United States would be limited to an attack on the Soviet civilian population and cities, something it would be unlikely to do because of the near certainty of a retaliatory attack on the U.S. population.

Senator Sam Nunn, the Georgia Democrat who is chairman of the Senate Armed Services Committee, has said that one little-considered aspect of S.D.I. is that it might force the United States and the NATO allies to consider the necessity of making very large new expenditures on conventional weapons and to increase the size of standing armies to deter military adventurism by the Soviet Union.

The proponents of Star Wars turn this argument around. They contend that the nuclear threat on which extended deterrence rests has not been believable for many years. While it may have been credible when the United States enjoyed a clear nuclear superiority over Russia, they argue, it became less and less useful as the Soviet Union attained nuclear parity with the United States. In a report to Congress in 1985, the Pentagon said: "In effectively countering ballistic-missile threats against the U.S., such defenses would strengthen the credibility of U.S. extended deterrence and NATO's flexible response strategy by reducing U.S. vulnerability to attack." Weinberger told the German-American Roundtable at Bonn in December of that year that Star Wars would strengthen the "coupling" of the United States and Europe and "would help deter conventional aggression."

One view is that Star Wars should be designed to conform to a clear national strategy; another, that strategy should conform to the technological advances that emerge from the S.D.I. laboratories. In any case, it is difficult to fashion a coherent strategy unless the Star Wars program has a coherent, clearly understood goal.

Senator Nunn supports a research program on ballistic-missile defense technologies. However, he is also one of many observers who have been complaining since 1983 that the Reagan administration has failed to make public an unequivocal, clear goal for the program. Salesmanship may play a role in this. The most appealing goal for Star Wars is complete protection of the American public. President Reagan and some other officials, such as Defense Secretary Weinberger, have repeatedly stressed this objective. However, when critical scientists and politicians raise troubling questions about the feasibility of a "people defense," administration officials tend to fall back and to say that the goal is much more modest.

As late as 1986, in a speech to the high school in Glassboro, New Jersey, Mr. Reagan called his program an effort "that might one day enable us to put in space a shield that missiles could not penetrate—a shield that could protect us from nuclear missiles just as a roof protects a family from rain." But earlier, in an interview with the *Wall Street Journal* on February 8, 1985, Reagan said, "Oh, I've never asked for 100 percent. . . . the other fellow would have the knowledge that if they launched a first strike, that it might be such that not enough of their missiles could get through, and in return we could launch the retaliatory strike." Then, only six weeks later, the President said in a speech to the National Space Club: "We are not discussing a concept just to enhance deterrence, but rather a new kind of deterrence," and added that the program was seeking "a shield that could prevent nuclear weapons from reaching their targets."

Weinberger said in 1983 that Reagan was not talking about "partial" defenses but sought something to "ensure that no missiles could get through." More formal and therefore supposedly more serious was the unclassified version of the National Security Decision Directive 172 of May 30, 1985, made public in its nonsecret form in June 1985: "The purpose of the defensive options we seek is clear—to find a means to destroy attacking ballistic missiles before they can reach any of their targets." But that same directive added that "for the foreseeable future, offensive nuclear forces and the prospect of nuclear retaliation will remain the key element of deterrence." When Senator John Glenn, Democrat of Ohio, asked General Abrahamson at a hearing in early 1985 if the hope would be to "protect the whole population," the general answered, "Yes, sir." But less than a year earlier, Abrahamson had told the House Appropriations Committee, "Nowhere have we stated that the goal of the S.D.I. is to come up with a 'leakproof' defense." In 1985 the Defense Department told Congress in a report that "with defenses, the U.S. seeks not to replace deterrence, but to enhance it."

At times these conflicting signals seem almost incomprehensible, or blatantly cynical. But if there is a reason for them it may lie in the inability of officials themselves to anticipate what form Star Wars will take. Dr. Gerold Yonas, who was then the chief scientist for the program, was quoted at a symposium in October 1984 as saying that "coming up with a clear concept that can be explained to the public is extremely difficult. What this program is pursuing is not really even a concept yet."

But despite the contradictions made by administration spokesmen, outsiders have used available evidence to draw their own, usually more pessimistic, conclusions. "Pursuit of defenses able to protect the U.S. population and all of its allies in the face of a determined Soviet effort to overcome them does not appear to be a goal of the Strategic Defense Initiative program," the O.T.A. report said. It cited the 1985 report by the Pentagon to Congress that said Star Wars seeks "to exploit emerging technologies that may provide options for a broader-based deterrence by turning to a greater reliance on defensive systems."

The O.T.A. report does not seem to be an example of determined or isolated pessimism. Retired Air Force Major General John Toomay, who was deputy chairman of the Fletcher panel, wrote in the summer 1985 *Daedalus* that "no imaginable set of defenses can prevent a determined and resourceful enemy from detonating nuclear weapons in our country." One point often raised is that a sound decision on Star Wars would require that policymakers carefully consider alternative policies that might achieve roughly the same goals. In other words, deployment of Star Wars should be no more costly or risky than alternative means, if they exist, of achieving the same goals. Specifically, to what extent can arms control and such measures as making American missiles more survivable by making them mobile achieve the goals now being sought in a missile-defense program?

Take as a starting point an S.D.I. defense that is hypothetically capable of destroying 50 percent of all ballistic-missile RVs in the Soviet weapon inventory. If feasible, such a defense would offer no meaningful protection to urban population centers. S.D.I.O. officials agree on that. But they and other advocates of ballistic-missile defense use the "enhanced deterrence" rationale to argue that such a defense would improve the overall American strategic situation, partly by reducing possible damage to the U.S. ICBM force. Those who advocate arms control as the best approach argue, however, that the United States could achieve almost exactly the same result, at much lower monetary costs, by concluding a verifiable treaty with the Soviet Union to reduce the warhead totals of both nations by 50 percent. A modifying word is useful here because if the missile defense were preferential rather than random selective—that is, allocated unevenly to improve chances of hitting key targets—a 50 percent effective defense would probably save at least a few more key American facilities than the 50 percent negotiated reduction in warheads. However, in broad terms the treaty may seem not only cheaper but also a far simpler and more attractive policy.

Until the Reagan administration entered office, the United States had sought to solve the problem of ICBM vulnerability primarily through a plan to shuttle each ten-warhead mobile MX missile between clusters of protective shelters. Strategists argued that the Soviet Union would have had to allocate 9,200 warheads to an attack on MX if it took the apparently prudent step of using two warheads for each shelter. President Reagan and Defense Secretary Weinberger killed this "race course" plan soon after taking office. Under pressure from Congress and a panel of non-government strategists convened in 1984 under the chairmanship of President Ford's former national security adviser Brent Scowcroft, the Reagan administration did agree in 1984 to begin development of the small, mobile single-warhead missile dubbed Midgetman. However, influential officials in the Pentagon have made clear they are dubious about and hostile to Midgetman, and would prefer to make it a less mobile, perhaps immobile—but more powerful—missile with at least three warheads.

Toward the end of the 1980s, there seemed to be a growing body of opinion among some Star Wars critics as well as proponents in favor of modifying the broad goal of population protection and a sophisticated, multilayered defense to a goal that might be more attainable in the near future.

Many in Congress expressed a desire for rapid deployment of a limited defense, perhaps one focused almost entirely on protecting U.S. missile silos. However, there was, from the start, strong resistance to that kind of limitation of S.D.I. among those closest to the President. Mr. Keyworth, the former White House science adviser, told a group of military contractors that if Star Wars were limited to defending weapons "the President's vision is lost." And in his annual report to Congress in February 1986, Mr. Weinberger said, "The defense that will evolve from the research program will not be intended to defend our strategic weapons systems." However, by late 1986 officials were more and more stressing that because a multilayered, complex defense would have to be deployed in stages, an intermediate or initial system meant primarily to defend strategic military targets was a possible approach to future Star Wars management programs.

These overall strategic questions about—and objections to—Star Wars have not been lost on the managers of the program and on its most committed supporters. Their response, however, has for the most part been regarded by the critics as ambiguous. General Abrahamson and John L. Gardner, who until 1986 was the S.D.I.O. official in charge of systems analysis, said that Star Wars officials and contractors had conducted their own analysis and that it was more sophisticated than that done by outsiders. They contended that their war games and analytical studies showed that some levels of mutual defense would not result in a net military disadvantage to the United States. Mr. Gardner told *The New York Times* that with any level of defense, from modest to good, "deterrent posture is improved." But critics point out that these government officials have declined to describe the studies in any detail to the public or to congressmen, or even to discuss the logical process by which these conclusions were reached. They cite secrecy as one reason.

One specialist in Soviet affairs, who works intermittently for the government, was invited along with several of his colleagues to participate in one such war game, played against employees of military contractor corporations usually selected for analytical work by S.D.I.O. This specialist said: "We found we were playing against defense contractor personnel and others who know nothing about Soviet doctrine. It took our whole team, the Red Team, less than twenty minutes to agree that our first counter to Star Wars would be to increase offensive missile numbers. Their team, the Blue Team, said, 'No, that is not how the Soviets think.' Every step we took surprised them."

At some point, it is likely that Congress will insist on being informed about the analytical processes used by S.D.I.O. In the meantime, Peter Sharfman, the manager of international security programs for the Office of Technology Assessment, commented that no one can have much confidence in any war game unless he knows the rules, especially those called the "measure of merit."

In war games, the measure of merit is simply the rule or set of rules that describes the winning course of action. A less-than-enthusiastic veteran of such war-gaming said that the Pentagon has been known to play United States–Soviet Union war games in which the measure of merit was defined as having the most remaining nuclear warheads at the close of the game: "With that kind of rule, the game-winning strategy is for the United States not to respond at all to a Soviet nuclear attack. Because by doing nothing, you end up with more nuclear warheads. However, that is not the winning strategy in a real war. Games can often merely reflect bad assumptions by those who devise them."

Star Wars officials were regarded as more forthcoming in their rebuttal of arguments that ballistic-missile defense might increase the incentives for the Soviet Union to engage in nuclear war. Their argument was that the Soviets would only wish to attack key strategic military targets, and that if defense reduces their confidence that such targets can be destroyed, the possibility of war becomes very remote. These Star Wars officials reject the idea that the Soviets would attack cities and the population or that a moderately capable defense would force Moscow to change its strategy to a cities-only targeting plan. "It would be irrational," said General Abrahamson in an interview. George Keyworth said in 1985 that if the Soviets cannot hit military targets, nuclear weapons "have been made obsolete since they have lost their military potential."

The critics are not so sure. During the battle of Britain, Hitler and Goering shifted the force of German air raids from the British Spitfire fields and radar installations to London. Attacks on civilian populations have been a part of war for thousands of years. The real question, the critics said, remained this: Even if we can have missile defense, are we sure we want it?

16

THE FUTURE
OF STAR WARS

The future of weap-
onry and warfare suggested by this book, which is
rooted in hundreds of interviews, stacks of private studies and federal documents, and years of reporting and reflection in science, technology, politics,
economics and military affairs, is that Star Wars is both impossible and
inevitable. Given the current size of the Soviet arsenal aimed at the United
States, some 10,000 warheads strong, a space-based defense has no chance
of working as envisioned by President Reagan. For the foreseeable future,
man and his technology, however great, cannot hope to create a shield that
would save the nation's cities and citizens. Even the slightest breach of it
during a full-scale nuclear attack would bring an unprecedented rain of
destruction and death. Even so, President Reagan's original vision contains
an important truth: Antimissile technology has made vast strides over past
decades and will continue to do so. In the twenty-first century, the beams
of exotic weapons will flash ever brighter, over longer distances, with ever

greater precision, raising new doubts about the future of the land-based ballistic missile, a lumbering, old fire-breathing giant that might well be headed for extinction.

But the bomb itself cannot be uninvented. Its progeny are likely to be with us forever. What is changing, and will continue to change at an accelerated pace in the next century, is the way these weapons are delivered to targets. Long before President Reagan's call to arms, the land-based intercontinental ballistic missile had been losing status as a delivery system to hard-to-locate submarine missiles, to low-flying cruise missiles fired from land, sea and air, and to portable battlefield bombs. Today, a Soviet submarine off the East Coast can drop a warhead in Washington, D.C., in a little more than five minutes. In the future, as technology advances, bombs will become ever smaller and easier to conceal. A danger indicated by this trend is the potential for nuclear blackmail and terrorism. Suitcase bombs could be planted in New York, in Washington, in military bases across the nation. Worse, this threat will always be greater for the West than the East, since open societies are inherently more vulnerable to sudden nuclear assault.

Given inevitable shifts in the machinery of warfare, and the impossibility of population defense, what is the fate of Star Wars in the years ahead? What impact will it have on the uneasy peace that has marked superpower relations for the past four decades? As Mikhail S. Gorbachev came to America in early December 1987 to sign the intermediate nuclear forces treaty banning intermediate- and shorter-range, land-based missiles, Star Wars lurked in the background. Was it not Star Wars that brought Mr. Gorbachev to the conference table? Is it not Star Wars that will eventually make all nuclear missiles impotent and obsolete, as Mr. Reagan has contended? Or is there some far different future for the world and for this notion of developing incredibly sophisticated, fast and effective weapons to place in space?

Glimmers of what the future may hold can be found in the thoughts of private scientists and military experts as well as recent trends in technology and policy. Among the questions most readily addressed:

■ Is Star Wars a research program or a virtual commitment to the deployment of weapons in space?

■ If President Reagan's goal of rendering nuclear weapons obsolete is unattainable, is a less ambitious goal—such as a partial defense that would protect American missiles and bombers but not the public—desirable, even though it would enhance the status of nuclear weapons?

■ Is Mr. Reagan's stated goal in fact a desirable objective, or do nuclear weapons play an essential role in preventing war between the superpowers?

■ What impact will Star Wars ultimately have on arms control?

■ Does the program have enough political appeal to survive the departure of President Reagan, its strongest booster?

■ How would a future President manage the precarious business of actually deploying a defensive system?

■ Is the arming of the heavens inevitable, given the nature of man and international rivalries?

As to the first question, whether the Star Wars program is one of research or deployment, it is clear that the program has gained vast momentum leading toward the building and fielding of antimissile arms even though the endeavor was originally billed as pure research. From the start, critics feared that, fueled by an ever larger array of military contractors, lobbyists, technologists and congressmen, the program would steamroll to the point that it could not be stopped. Still, a reversal is possible if history is any guide. In the mid-1970s, the nation spent $5.7 billion to build and deploy a ground-based system to defend American missiles. It was quickly scrapped, however, when judged too expensive and ineffective.

Originally, General Abrahamson said the judgment was up to America's elected representatives, calling it "the most complex decision Congress will ever have to make." He described a process by which Congress would be asked to make a series of graduated decisions based on the validation of technology, realistic cost estimates and an honest analysis of production hurdles and time schedules. Moreover, it was official administration policy that any proposed system must meet the twin criteria of being survivable against enemy attack and "cost-effective at the margin." This meant that it should be cheaper for the United States to add a unit of defense than for the Soviet Union to add a comparably effective unit of offense.

But by the end of the Reagan administration, much of this scenario was crumbling or had crumbled. The Secretary of Defense proclaimed that he did not know the meaning of "cost-effective at the margin." General Abrahamson himself had told *The New York Times* in 1986 that "affordability" was a better yardstick than cost-effectiveness. The cost of missile defense, he said, was not purely an economic question because the United States was seeking to "change Soviet behavior" in the nuclear age, to influence a watershed change in international affairs. Further, although he had promised to give Congress estimates of what Star Wars "should" cost, he failed to do so. It was a figure that, at that point, no one could really provide with any accuracy.

There was more. Instead of pursuing an orderly evaluation process involving the nation's elected representatives, a unilateral push for Star Wars deployment was made by the executive branch in the final days of the Reagan era. Starting in late 1986, antimissile advocates inside and outside the administration pressed for "near-term" deployment, saying the program was losing political momentum because its research goals were too distant. In October 1986, such influential Star Wars advocates as Edward Teller, Lowell Wood, Representative Jack Kemp and Eugene V. Rostow urged President Reagan to act quickly and decisively. "We are deeply concerned," they wrote, "that an S.D.I. research program which has no definite consequences for defense of America and its Allies within the next ten years will not be politically sustainable." In January 1987, Secretary of Defense Weinberger told an aerospace conference that "we are now seeing opportunities for earlier deployment of the first phase of strategic defense." It would be imperfect, he said, insisting that additions to the first phase would ultimately lead to more complete protection. That same month, Attorney General Edwin Meese III acknowledged the importance of political factors in the push, saying the system should be deployed as soon as possible "so it will be in place and not tampered with by future administrations."

The rudimentary system was to have none of the lasers, particle-beam weapons or other futuristic arms that gave rise to Star Wars in the first place. Instead, in a vision similar to that of General Graham's long-since-rejected High Frontier idea, it was to rely on small homing rockets launched from the ground and from space-based battle stations using in large part existing technology. Kinetic-energy warheads would zoom from these rockets to destroy targets by smashing into them. For the space-based part of the system, the Pentagon envisioned some 3,000 weapons.

To achieve the "near-term" goal, the Pentagon in fiscal 1987 began a vast reordering of priorities, taking funds from exotic research and putting them into the development of kinetic-energy weapons. Leading Star Wars scientists publicly denounced the shifts, saying they slowed research on lasers and particle beams and upset long-term planning for research, personnel and facilities. Expressing his "frustration," Dr. William Barletta of Livermore Laboratory told the authors that the antimissile program "has the flavor of having a new twist in priorities every few years. That does not aid the cause of serious, stable research. The surprises keep you in a state of perpetual soul-searching." Dr. Sidney Drell, deputy director of the Stanford Linear Accelerator Center in California, and many other private physicists warned that a full-throttle program aimed at developing early technologies could in the long run "lock out" better ideas.

■

The Pentagon's "near-term" push also revealed a vast number of associated challenges that would have to be met if Star Wars were to move from the drawing board to the heavens. One was a way to get arms into space. In December 1986, the Pentagon asked Congress for funds to speed research on an immense new space truck that would be ready in the early 1990s. Known as the heavy-lift vehicle, it would be capable of lifting 100,000 to 150,000 pounds into low orbit—more than twice the capacity of the shuttle or the largest American rocket then envisioned. At a news conference, Defense Secretary Weinberger said the need for such a vehicle "has become more and more apparent in recent months" as the Pentagon studied plans, amid disruptions in the American space program caused by the *Challenger* disaster, for lofting antimissile weaponry into space.

Prompted by these considerations of Star Wars deployment, the Pentagon also eyed the proposed space station of the National Aeronautics and Space Administration as a potentially crucial adjunct to deployment—a move that upset Congress and potential foreign partners in the space station. The space station, meant to go into operation in the mid-1990s, was originally seen as a permanently manned base for civilian research. But in December 1986, talks on possible participation by Japan, Europe and Canada broke down when the Pentagon insisted that any agreement permit military use. Then, in April 1987, Defense Secretary Weinberger touched off a furor by telling Secretary of State George Shultz that the United States "must be prepared to go forward alone" if its allies were unwilling to give the Defense Department broad latitude to "conduct national security activities." What might these be? Publicly, the Pentagon in referring to Star Wars spoke only of research. But a study prepared for the Air Force by the American Institute of Aeronautics and Astronautics suggested the station might also be used as a depot to fuel antimissile weapons—chemical lasers and other Star Wars devices needing huge amounts of combustible fluids—and as a service station to repair arms and turn space junk into decoys and armor. The study also said manned military activity in orbit might be so extensive early in the next century that it would require an altogether new space station dedicated to the Department of Defense.

The Pentagon, while making no public declarations about plans for Star Wars deployments, had in fact secretly decided to undertake that enormous task, according to a fifty-eight-page congressional report released in March 1987 by Senators William Proxmire of Wisconsin and J. Bennett Johnson of Louisiana. It found the Pentagon had "a highly classified program which is developing a blueprint for deploying strategic defenses in the near term." The report, based on secret data from industry contractors and the Pentagon, said deployments were to begin by 1994, around the same time the space station would be ready. Remarkably, the report found that the effectiveness of the entire system would be no greater than 16 percent. In other words, five out of every six Soviet warheads would pass through the antimissile net untouched and proceed toward targets in the United States.

Not only Congress greeted the Pentagon's rush with skepticism. So did the nation's top physicists. In April 1987, the American Physical Society, the nation's largest professional society of physicists, published an exhaustive, 424-page report based on an eighteen-month study of the Pentagon's own secret data. It found that so many breakthroughs were needed for overall Star Wars development that no deployment decision should even be considered for another decade or more—in other words, until after the presidencies of both Ronald Reagan and his successor. Such a timetable meant that anti-missile deployments, if deemed worthwhile, should wait until the twenty-first century. The physicists who made the study included Nobel laureates and some of the world's leading authorities on particle beams and lasers. Their assessment focused on exotic arms rather than kinetic weapons. But the physicists found that the survival of any space-based antimissile system against enemy attack was "highly questionable," noting at the same time that Soviet countermeasures "may be less difficult and costly to develop."

All of which raises the second question: If the stated objective of rendering nuclear weapons obsolete turns out to be unattainable, is a less ambitious goal still desirable? Many of the administration's experts and study groups have stressed that a partial defense that ensured the survival of American missiles and bombers from preemptive enemy attack would be a good thing because it would mean they could unleash a devastating retaliatory blow on any aggressor. (The U.S. strategic arsenal, like the Soviet one, currently contains about 10,000 warheads.) Of course, such a rationale turns Mr. Reagan's original idea on its head, the goal of partial defense becoming a means to enhance the retaliatory power of nuclear weapons rather than doing away with it. So, too, it undercuts the ethical high ground claimed by many Star Wars advocates, some of whom nonetheless try to have it both ways. After faulting the "cruel policy" of mutual assured destruction, Robert Jastrow, author of *How to Make Nuclear Weapons Obsolete*, notes in his book that the antimissile protection of offensive forces would mean retaliatory strikes could "reduce all the major Soviet cities to rubble in thirty minutes."

Star Wars supporters see no conflict between the two goals. They say that President Reagan has always held that the nation will continue to rely on the threat of nuclear retaliation to deter attacks until an effective defense is ready. A partial defense, they say, would be perfectly acceptable for this purpose and a valuable way station on the road to an overall defense. But Star Wars critics say the ultimate destination is simply a dream. They add that no partial defense of land-based missiles and bombers is needed, since half of America's nuclear deterrent is carried on submarines deep in the ocean.

Is a partial shield needed because American land-based missiles are in danger of being knocked out by increasingly accurate Soviet missiles? Is there, in fact, a "window of vulnerability"? Harold Brown, the former Defense Secretary, said that, under some circumstances, a defensive system might be needed to protect American missiles, but that at present they face no danger and are likely to be secure for the rest of the century. The issue of whether land-based missiles are open to assault raises a host of topics unrelated to Star Wars. For instance, other ways to protect them include dispersal, hardening and mobility. Some experts say such passive techniques are cheaper, safer and easier to achieve than any antimissile system.

Perhaps the biggest problem with partial defense is that it contains a hidden danger acknowledged by both defenders and detractors of Star Wars. In his 1983 speech, President Reagan alluded to the peril: "I clearly recognize that defensive systems have limitations and raise certain problems and ambiguities. If paired with offensive systems, they can be viewed as fostering an aggressive policy and no one wants that." What he meant was that a nation that struck first with its nuclear weapons could use a partial shield to mop up an enemy's ragged retaliation. Even a nation with benign intent and a partial shield might be tempted to strike quickly during an international crisis, since its antimissile system would never stop a massive attack but might easily halt a weak retaliatory blow after a large, preemptive strike. In other words, a shield might raise the risk of war. This dark side of Star Wars is unique to space-based systems, which try to protect whole nations, including both missiles and cities. In contrast, old-fashioned ground-based systems have little strategic ambiguity. They are good mainly for defending missiles, and if so used have no potential for increasing the feasibility of waging a nuclear war.

Is it wise to protect nuclear weapons, or is it better to strive, as President Reagan suggested, for their complete elimination? Clearly, the goal of abolishing nuclear arms strikes a resonant chord among many people who live in fear that some day the thousands of existing weapons will be fired. Even some leading critics of the President's proposed system say that if they really thought it would work, they would be all for it. But other arms-control experts say the fear of nuclear weapons has preserved the peace between East and West for the last four decades. And while these experts say they are eager to see the overwhelming size of the world's arsenals reduced, and delivery systems made as stabilizing as possible, they are reluctant to give up nuclear weapons entirely unless something they consider a better guarantor of the peace is at hand.

One respected arms-control analyst, Thomas C. Schelling, of the John F. Kennedy School of Government at Harvard, questioned "whether the President's dream is a good one" and "whether we should wish away deterrence as the foundation of peace." In a 1985 lecture, later published in *Foreign Affairs*, he pointed to "forty years of living with nuclear weapons without warfare" as evidence that such weapons are helping to avoid nuclear war. "I go further than that," he added. "A prudent restraint from aggressive violence that is based on acknowledgment that the world is too small to support a nuclear war is a healthier basis for peace than unilateral efforts to build defenses. I feel safer in an environment of deterrence than I would in an environment of defense."

Whatever the faults or merits of Star Wars, the threat that the United States might erect an expensive space-based system of orbiting arms has clearly produced great diplomatic leverage for the West. In 1985 it brought the Russians back to the negotiating table in Geneva, and in 1986 and 1987 prodded them into offering sweeping proposals to eliminate nuclear arms.

What impact will Star Wars ultimately have on arms control? President Reagan and other advocates suggest the program will continue to have a beneficial impact—by spurring the Soviets to negotiate in good faith, by making offensive missiles useless and thus easier to trade away in arms-control agreements, by giving the two superpowers the confidence that they will be safe even after discarding their nuclear deterrents. But critics say any buildup of defensive systems would set off another arms race, pointing to history to buttress their claim. The first and only actual deployment of missile defenses, in the 1970s, led to the development of today's most feared offensive weapon in the arsenals of the superpowers: the MIRVs, or multiple independently targetable reentry vehicles, designed to overwhelm defenses by releasing many warheads from a single missile. The critics suggest that an American Star Wars system would inevitably force the Soviets to develop more and better offensive weapons and would also spur the Soviets to expand their own defensive system, thereby causing the American military to lose faith in its own deterrent weapons and seek to expand its own arsenal. In short, it would trigger an endless cycle of spending.

During the October 1986 summit meeting in Reykjavik, Soviet leader Gorbachev absolutely refused to go through with massive cuts in offensive weapons unless the Star Wars program was sharply restricted, whereas Mr. Reagan absolutely refused to eliminate nuclear missiles unless he could retain a Star Wars defense. If neither side were to change its position, the Star Wars program would seem fundamentally at odds with an arms-control agreement that would eliminate the threat of strategic nuclear weapons. Clearly, the question of arms control is complicated by a paradox of no small dimensions. Yet the paradox might prove useful.

In the future it seems likely that the Soviet Union, fearful of the West's industrial might as applied to fielding Star Wars weaponry, would be willing to agree to large missile cuts if deployment were put off, in effect conceding the West's upper hand at this stage in history and allowing a restructuring of its strategic arsenal along lines agreeable to Washington. But only if there were no deployment. Russia's insurance policy against a deployed Star Wars system, as Soviet officials have repeatedly stressed, would be the production of more missiles, decoys and other countermeasures to overwhelm it. In short, from the standpoint of reducing the size of the world's arsenals, Star Wars would work if deployment were rejected and fail if it were placed in operation. However frustrating, the paradox might provide powerful negotiating leverage for decades to come. If the West stays strong in its technical and industrial base, it could weigh whether to abandon the antimissile limitations imposed by the ABM Treaty every five years or so, with its pledge to renew the limits allowing the Star Wars bargaining chip to be "sold" to the Soviets again and again.

◼

Does the Star Wars program have enough political appeal to survive the departure of President Reagan, its biggest fan? The answer is clearly yes. It will remain in one form or another, if only as a hefty research program. Even before the Star Wars speech, the Pentagon was spending about a $1 billion a year to investigate lasers and particle beams for antimissile defense. During the Reagan era, the momentum of Star Wars remained intact despite the explosion of the space shuttle *Challenger* and the death of its seven crew members, a disaster that illustrated as no critic ever could the difficulties and dangers of trying to achieve ambitious goals in space. It also grounded the nation's shuttle fleet for more than two years, temporarily ending shuttle-related Star Wars tests. On the other hand, the political appeal of Star Wars has risen with the dazzling series of diplomatic coups it has induced. More-over, in light of ongoing Soviet work in conventional and exotic antimissile arms, it seems unlikely that Congress would allow the research quest to be abandoned altogether, no matter who occupied the White House, Repub-lican or Democrat. To do so would give the Soviets hope of achieving a nuclear first strike with no fear of retaliation. Defense Secretary Weinberger reacted to such a scenario in December 1983, saying unilateral Soviet de-velopment of an effective defense "would be one of the most frightening prospects I could imagine."

As Star Wars moves forward, it may change direction in a way already suggested by Congress. In a major shift, a majority of the Senate Armed Services Committee, traditionally a strong supporter of military programs, urged in 1986 that the Star Wars program put greater emphasis on the modest goal of defending military targets. "The major emphasis" should be on shielding strategic forces and not on "comprehensive, nationwide population protection," the committee said, saying the more ambitious goal was for the moment unrealistic. Whether Star Wars research will culminate in spec-tacular tests in space, or in quiet research in the laboratory, is an issue that will probably be decided by some future occupant of the White House and by future East-West negotiations. Plans were set in motion for several Star Wars tests to be done in the late 1980s and early 1990s that would revolve around laser tests aboard the space shuttle. Whether real science or stunts,

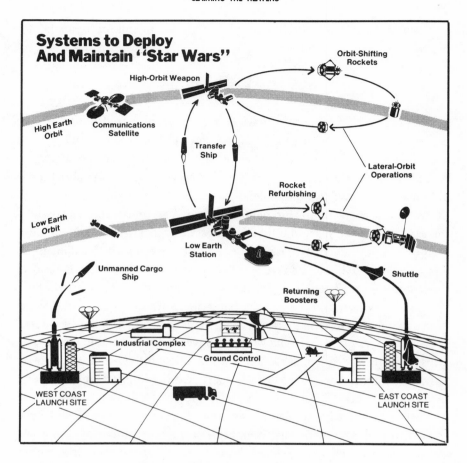

The Plan: Drawing based on official U.S. view of support for the anti-missile system.
THE NEW YORK TIMES COMPANY

or a politic combination of the two, these tests are meant to demonstrate the ability of the technology to find and track moving targets as a weapon would.

In one shuttle mission being designed primarily by Lockheed Missiles & Space Company, a top Star Wars contractor, laser beams fired through a window of the European-built Spacelab are to strike a large mirror mounted in the shuttle's payload bay, and then be reflected toward satellites and rising rockets. For the near future, however, Congress is likely to prohibit space experiments like this one that are so advanced that they would raise any question about American compliance with the ABM Treaty, just as it has limited tests of an antisatellite weapon the Pentagon wants to develop. But beyond this, Congress is simply in no mood for Star Wars deployment when a workable strategy for it has yet to be decided upon, despite already heavy investment in it. In 1987, a congressional report found that while significant Star Wars progress had been achieved, there had been no breakthroughs. "More importantly," it said, "the progress made in the program in the past year does not appear to serve as a compelling justification for near-term deployment."

The quest for exotic antimissile arms can take many forms other than the one championed by the Reagan administration. Even if funding levels remain unchanged, Star Wars could strengthen rather than weaken the structure of science by emphasizing a trend toward more basic research, a move which would allow greater freedom of scientific speech and publication, and by shifting secret work on weaponry away from universities. The 1985 study by the congressional Office of Technology Assessment noted that alternative programs "can differ greatly from the S.D.I. in emphasis, direction, and level of effort. Moreover, research programs having different perceived and intended purposes—even if they have similar technical content—can have very different consequences." For instance, it said, a program could still be large but directed "so that it does not either prematurely compromise the ABM Treaty by encouraging Soviet exploitation of technical ambiguities, or stimulate the Soviets to begin deploying ballistic-missile defenses and enhanced offensive forces at a time more advantageous to them than to us."

If Congress, the White House, and the American public one day agreed that a Star Wars system should be built and deployed, an undertaking whose initial cost has been estimated to range between $100 billion and more than $1,000 billion, how would the transition be managed? With difficulty, according to both detractors and defenders of Star Wars. Unless both sides deployed comparable systems simultaneously, the side with no defense—or one it perceived as inferior—might become terrified and start shooting at the emerging antimissile arms of the other before they could be deployed.

President Reagan himself put his finger on this problem when he announced, in a statement later much ridiculed, that he would be willing to share with the Soviet Union any antimissile technologies that are developed by his program. The White House subsequently played down this offer, apparently realizing that the new system, if it works, will embody the nation's most sophisticated computers, sensors and high-technology arms—items that could be used not just in a defensive system but in a variety of offensive ways as well.

Indeed, little thought has been given to the transition problem. Paul Nitze, the Reagan administration's top arms-control adviser, said in a speech that the period of transition from offense to defense might take decades and "could be tricky" to manage. The kind of cooperation required between the super-powers has never occurred in recent diplomatic history, in the view of both proponents and opponents of Star Wars. Some critics doubt such cooperation is likely. Others suggest that if the superpowers were to decide to work that closely together they should simply agree to get rid of their nuclear arsenals altogether and avoid the enormous expense of building defenses.

■

If Star Wars as envisioned is so ineffective, so ambiguous and so dangerous to deploy without an unlikely accord between East and West, is it in fact nothing but an illusion that can do little but stir debate among the educated public? Far from it. Despite ups and downs, praise and blame, hype and hoopla, Star Wars is clearly more than a political ploy. On a technical level, it is a vast scientific venture that will have repercussions for decades to come. No less should be expected from the biggest research project of all time. Even if it fails to render nuclear weapons impotent and obsolete, it will enhance the accuracy of long-distance, targeted destruction—maybe not to the point that it can intercept 10,000 Soviet warheads, but surely some smaller numbers of weapons.

A limited shield that could stop only small nuclear attacks might prove indispensable in the dangerous years ahead as the traditional confrontation between East and West expands worldwide to include Third-World nations. Already the deadly art of mating ballistic missiles to atomic warheads has spread to the far corners of the globe, even as the superpowers turn from fixed land-based missiles to more advanced systems of delivery. All told, six nations are known to have exploded nuclear weapons: the United States, the Soviet Union, China, Britain, France and India. Three nations are thought to have a secret nuclear capability: Israel, South Africa and Pakistan. And six nations are known to be taking steps to acquire the bomb: Argentina, Brazil, Iran, Iraq, Libya and North Korea.

Clearly, no antimissile system could stop a suitcase bomb. But it might defeat a terrorist missile, such as the one sought by Libyan leader Colonel Muammar al-Qaddafi. Indeed, the threat of terrorist and Third-World mis-siles is considered so great that in 1987 the United States and six allies—Britain, France, West Germany, Italy, Japan and Canada—agreed to strong controls on the export of missiles and missile technologies that can be used to deliver nuclear arms. Unfortunately, such steps are belated. Rockets of various types and ranges have already been acquired by Argentina, Brazil,

India, Taiwan, Indonesia, Israel, Egypt, Syria, and North and South Korea.

In addition to thwarting space-age terrorism, a limited defense could counter the threat posed by those missiles fired accidentally by a nation because of technical failures or, more chilling, because a rogue military commander had decided to unleash the bomb. The workable basis for such a shield might be found in the $1 billion free-electron laser facility under construction in New Mexico, if it lives up to scientific hopes. Its beam could be bounced off a mirror in geosynchronous orbit to offer limited protection for the nation. As such, it would clearly offer no broad protective capability against a massive nuclear attack. Moscow, with its conventional missile intercepters, already has the ability to stop stray warheads.

Are such limited goals worth our time, effort and expense? It is easy to develop a cavalier attitude about the bomb when size estimates of arsenals are rounded to the nearest thousand weapons, easy to forget the agony of Hiroshima and to forget that today a single nuclear warhead has the ability to make that tragedy seem small by comparison.

A large part of the Star Wars debate, and this book, has revolved around the issue of whether it is feasible to eliminate the threat of nuclear weapons. The essence of that debate is defense. The word itself has a simple, intuitive meaning—to guard against attack, to keep from harm and danger.

But there are other dimensions to the debate, beyond defense, that are seldom articulated, and a few that are hard to fathom. One of the most fundamental issues concerns the psychological drive for superiority. It is human nature to want to feel superior to others. In the twentieth century, this urge has helped fuel the race for all kinds of new machinery, whether fancy cars to impress the neighbors or advanced arms to intimidate enemies. The thrill of getting the upper hand with technology is clearly evident in Ronald Reagan's early movie *Murder in the Air*. There Reagan, as secret agent Brass Bancroft, warms to the task of keeping a death ray out of Communist hands. "Well," he says, "it seems the spy ring has designs on the greatest war weapon ever invented which, by the way, is the exclusive property of Uncle Sam." That kind of exclusivity is the hallmark of military superiority.

Is a race to arm the heavens inevitable, given the nature of man and international rivalries? Although some psychological forces might fuel that drive, there are others that work against such an outcome. Since the dawn of the space age, many people have felt that man's final frontier, the edge of the rest of the universe, should be a preserve used exclusively for peaceful purposes. Several international treaties, to which the United States is signatory, foster this goal. Even so, space is already a realm of considerable military activity, though of the passive kind. For decades both superpowers have used satellites for early warning of nuclear attack, intelligence gathering, and long-range communications. Such operations, it is generally agreed, have a stabilizing effect on world tensions because they enable each side to verify the other's compliance with arms-control treaties.

The question then is not whether space should be militarized—it already is—but whether it should be weaponized. Many civilian experts say we should bar our terrestrial arms race from expanding to the heavens, arguing that nations will be forced to engage in an ever-expanding arms race that would rob treasuries of funds for pressing problems on earth. In contrast, many military planners and their political allies, reciting maxims of seapower, airpower and the foot soldier's "high ground," tend to take for granted the strategic value of space and its ultimate exploitation by the superpowers. They believe that its weaponization cannot be avoided and advocate the development of new arms and defenses that, if deployed, would fulfill their prophecy. History, they contend, is on their side.

A few months before the Star Wars speech, Ronald H. Stivers, then Assistant Deputy Under Secretary of Defense for policy, remarked on the allure of space for the military. "History," he said, "teaches us that each time a new medium is opened to man it is exploited to gain a military advantage. The course of world affairs has repeatedly been altered by the nation which first grasped the advantages offered by developing the military potential of the newest medium." The American advantage in lofting Star Wars weaponry into space was elaborated by General Graham, who once headed the Defense Intelligence Agency before he went on to direct the High Frontier group advocating space-based antimissile systems. In the forward to the group's 1982 report, General Graham recalled his search for "a technological end-run on the Soviets" and said it had "led inexorably to space." He continued: "The ability of the United States to miniaturize components gives us great advantages in space where transport costs-per-pound are critical. Today a pound of U.S. space machinery can do much more than a pound of Soviet space machinery. It also happened that the technologies immediately available for military systems—beyond intelligence, communication and navigation-aid satellites—are primarily applicable to ballistic-missile defense systems."

Although today the Star Wars debate is cast in terms of antimissile defense, the issue clearly goes much further, involving elements of psychological superiority and the threat of offensive strikes. In private, some Star Wars advocates say the system can be viewed as exclusively offensive, given that a leaky shield would work best for fending off a foe's ragged retaliation after a first strike. But they argue that the West—which is fundamentally pacific, is tired of building nuclear missiles, and is interested mainly in making money and satisfying creature comforts—needs to hold that threat over the Soviet Union, which is backward, paranoid and expansionist. Star Wars critics, ignoring this social critique, say a space-based antimissile system is a poor way to gain the upper hand since it would tip the balance of terror and probably provoke nuclear war. Hans Bethe, the Nobel Prize–winning physicist, summed up the danger this way: "It is difficult to imagine a system more likely to induce catastrophe than one that requires critical decisions by the second, is itself untested and fragile, and yet is threatening to the other side's retaliatory capability."

Despite decades of military endeavor to gain the high ground of space, a period during which tens of billions of dollars have been spent on the development of space arms, none of the envisioned weapons has ever been deployed. If recent history is any guide, the weaponization of space is not, in fact, inevitable. Indeed, the quest for space-based systems to shoot down enemy missiles goes back a quarter century to the Eisenhower administration, which launched a crash program of antimissile research that eventually cost billions of dollars and involved thousands of the nation's best scientists. "Project Defender," created in 1959, was to develop exotic antimissile arms. Its scientists soon proposed to destroy a Soviet missile early in its flight with a ballistic missile boost intercepts, called Bambi. The system was to consist of hundreds of space-based battle stations using infrared sensors to track the fiery exhaust of enemy missiles. The Bambi interceptor itself, propelled by rockets, was to simply smash into the rising enemy missile. The whole idea was not unlike the kinetic-energy arms currently proposed by the Pentagon for the first phase of its Star Wars system.

But as a way to keep the peace, Bambi and its progeny were rejected time and again over the decades—by Presidents Eisenhower, Kennedy, Johnson, Nixon, Ford and Carter. It was Ronald Reagan who embraced the idea of basing weapons in space, saying the technology was finally ripe and the military imperative finally clear. But as his term in office came to a close, knowledgeable critics still insisted, as they had all along, that Reagan and his antimissile supporters would fail to end the age of vulnerability. "These people want to eliminate the danger of nuclear weapons by technical means," Dr. Bethe said in an interview. "I think this is futile. The only way to eliminate it is by having a wise policy. That means going back to the policy of the six Presidents preceding Reagan. We need to try to understand the other fellow and negotiate and try to come to some agreement about the common danger. That is what's been forgotten. The solution can only be political. It would be terribly comfortable for the President and the Secretary of Defense if there was a technical solution. But there isn't any."

The advocates of Star Wars will keep searching for that technical solution. The scientists will continue their quest. The twenty-first century will no doubt be very different from the one that preceded it. New military technology will evolve from billions of dollars of new research. The days of the large, lumbering nuclear missile are probably numbered. The chances are that soldiers of the future will fire powerful lasers at enemy targets. What is unclear, and will probably remain that way for years to come, is whether the new weapons will be defensive or offensive, whether they will make the world safer or more dangerous, whether they will render nuclear weapons impotent and obsolete or will simply add costly impetus to the arms race.

APPENDIX

Treaty Between the
United States of America and the
Union of Soviet Socialist Republics
on the Limitation of
Anti-Ballistic Missile Systems

The United States of America and the Union of Soviet Socialist Republics, hereinafter referred to as the Parties,

Proceeding from the premise that nuclear war would have devastating consequences for all mankind,

Considering that effective measures to limit anti-ballistic systems would be a substantial factor in curbing the race in strategic offensive arms and would lead to a decrease in the risk of outbreak of war involving nuclear weapons,

Proceeding from the premise that the limitation of anti-ballistic missile systems, as well as certain agreed measures with respect to the limitation of strategic offensive arms, would contribute to the creation of more favorable conditions for further negotiations on limiting strategic arms,

Mindful of their obligations under Article VI of the Treaty on the Non-Proliferation of Nuclear Weapons,

Declaring their intention to achieve at the earliest possible date the cessation of the nuclear arms race and to take effective measures toward reductions in strategic arms, nuclear disarmament, and general and complete disarmament,

Desiring to contribute to the relaxation of international tension and the strengthening of trust between States,

Have agreed as follows:

Article I

1. Each Party undertakes to limit anti-ballistic missile (ABM) systems and to adopt other measures in accordance with the provisions of this Treaty.

2. Each Party undertakes not to deploy ABM systems for a defense of the territory of its country and not to provide a base for such a defense, and not to deploy ABM systems for defense of an individual region except as provided for in Article III of this Treaty.

Article II

1. For the purpose of this Treaty an ABM system is a system to counter strategic ballistic missiles or their elements in flight trajectory, currently consisting of:

(a) ABM interceptor missiles, which are interceptor missiles constructed and deployed for an ABM role, or of a type tested in an ABM mode;

(b) ABM launchers, which are launchers constructed and deployed for launching ABM interceptor missiles; and

(c) ABM radars, which are radars constructed and deployed for an ABM role, or of a type tested in an ABM mode.

2. The ABM system components listed in paragraph 1 of this Article include those which are:

(a) operational;

(b) under construction;

(c) undergoing testing;

(d) undergoing overhaul, repair or conversion; or

(e) mothballed.

ARTICLE III

Each Party undertakes not to deploy ABM systems or their components except that:

(a) within one ABM deployment area having a radius of one hundred and fifty kilometers and centered on the Party's national capital, a Party may deploy: (1) no more than one hundred ABM launchers and no more than one hundred ABM interceptor missiles at launch sites, and (2) ABM radars within no more than six ABM radar complexes, the area of each complex being circular and having a diameter of no more than three kilometers; and

(b) within one ABM system deployment area having a radius of one hundred and fifty kilometers and containing ICBM silo launchers, a Party may deploy: (1) no more than one hundred ABM launchers and no more than one hundred ABM interceptor missiles at launch sites, (2) two large phased-array ABM radars comparable in potential to corresponding ABM radars operational or under construction on the date of signature of the Treaty in an ABM system deployment area containing ICBM silo launchers, and (3) no more than eighteen ABM radars each having a potential less than the potential of the smaller of the above-mentioned two large phased-array ABM radars.

ARTICLE IV

The limitations provided for in Article III shall not apply to ABM systems or their components used for development or testing, and located within current or additionally agreed test ranges. Each Party may have no more than a total of fifteen ABM launchers at test ranges.

ARTICLE V

1. Each Party undertakes not to develop, test, or deploy ABM systems or components which are sea-based, air-based, space-based, or mobile land-based.

2. Each Party undertakes not to develop, test, or deploy ABM launchers for launching more than one ABM interceptor missile at a time from each launcher, not to modify deployed launchers to provide them with such a capability, not to develop, test, or deploy automatic or semi-automatic or other similar systems for rapid reload of ABM launchers.

Article VI

To enhance assurance of the effectiveness of the limitations on ABM systems and their components provided by the Treaty, each Party undertakes:

(a) not to give missles, launchers, or radars, other than ABM interceptor missiles, ABM launchers, or ABM radars, capabilities to counter strategic ballistic missiles or their elements in flight trajectory, and not to test them in an ABM mode; and

(b) not to deploy in the future radars for early warning of strategic ballistic missile attack except at locations along the periphery of its national territory and oriented outward.

Article VII

Subject to the provisions of this Treaty, modernization and replacement of ABM systems or their components may be carried out.

Article VIII

ABM systems or their components in excess of the numbers or outside the areas specified in this Treaty, as well as ABM systems or their components prohibited by this Treaty, shall be destroyed or dismantled under agreed procedures within the shortest possible agreed period of time.

Article IX

To assure the viability and effectiveness of this Treaty, each Party undertakes not to transfer to other States, and not to deploy outside its national territory, ABM systems or their components limited by this Treaty.

Article X

Each Party undertakes not to assume any international obligations which would conflict with this Treaty.

Article XI

The Parties undertake to continue active negotiations for limitations on strategic offensive arms.

Article XII

1. For the purpose of providing assurance of compliance with the provisions of this Treaty, each Party shall use national technical means of

verification at its disposal in a manner consistent with generally recognized principles of international law.

2. Each Party undertakes not to interfere with the national technical means of verification of the other Party operating in accordance with paragraph 1 of this Article.

3. Each Party undertakes not to use deliberate concealment measures which impede verification by national technical means of compliance with the provisions of this Treaty. This obligation shall not require changes in current construction, assembly, conversion, or overhaul practices.

ARTICLE XIII

1. To promote the objectives and implementations of the provisions of this Treaty, the Parties shall establish promptly a Standing Consultative Commission, within the framework of which they will:

(a) consider questions concerning compliance with the obligations assumed and related situations which may be considered ambiguous;

(b) provide on a voluntary basis such information as either Party considers necessary to assure confidence in compliance with the obligations assumed;

(c) consider questions involving unintended interference with national technical means of verification;

(d) consider possible changes in the strategic situation which have a bearing on the provisions of this Treaty;

(e) agree upon procedures and dates for destruction or dismantling of ABM systems or their components in cases provided for by the provisions of this Treaty;

(f) consider, as appropriate, possible proposals for further increasing the viability of this Treaty; including proposals for amendments in accordance with the provisions of this Treaty;

(g) consider, as appropriate, proposals for further measures aimed at limiting strategic arms.

2. The parties through consultation shall establish, and may amend as appropriate, Regulations for the Standing Consultative Commission governing procedures, composition and other relevant matters.

Article XIV

1. Each Party may propose amendments to this Treaty. Agreed amendments shall enter into force in accordance with the procedures governing the entry into force of this Treaty.

2. Five years after entry into force of this Treaty, and at five-year intervals thereafter, the Parties shall together conduct a review of this Treaty.

Article XV

1. This Treaty shall be of unlimited duration.

2. Each Party shall, in exercising its national sovereignty, have the right to withdraw from this Treaty if it decides that extraordinary events related to the subject matter of this Treaty have jeopardized its supreme interests. It shall give notice of its decision to the other Party six months prior to withdrawal from the Treaty. Such notice shall include a statement of the extraordinary events the notifying Party regards as having jeopardized its supreme interests.

Article XVI

1. This Treaty shall be subject to ratification in accordance with the constitutional procedures of each Party. The Treaty shall enter into force on the day of the exchange of instruments of ratification.

2. This Treaty shall be registered pursuant to Article 102 of the Charter of the United Nations.

DONE at Moscow on May 26, 1972, in two copies, each in the English and Russian languages, both texts being equally authentic.

For the United States
of America

For the Union of Soviet
Socialist Republics

RICHARD NIXON

L. I. BREZHNEV

Agreed Statements, Common Understandings, and Unilateral Statements

1. Agreed Statements

[The document set forth below was agreed upon and initialed by the heads of the Delegations on May 26, 1972; letter designations added.]

AGREED STATEMENTS REGARDING THE TREATY
BETWEEN THE UNITED STATES OF AMERICA
AND THE UNION OF SOVIET SOCIALIST REPUBLICS
ON THE LIMITATION OF ANTI-BALLISTIC MISSILE SYSTEMS

[A]

The Parties understand that, in addition to the ABM radars which may be deployed in accordance with subparagraph (a) of Article III of the Treaty, those non-phased-array ABM radars operational on the date of signature of the Treaty within the ABM system deployment area for defense of the national capital may be retained.

[B]

The Parties understand that the potential (the product of mean emitted power in watts and antenna area in square meters) of the smaller of the two large phased-array ABM radars referred to in subparagraph (b) of Article III of the Treaty is considered for purposes of the Treaty to be three million.

[C]

The Parties understand that the center of the ABM system deployment area centered on the national capital and the center of the ABM system deployment area containing ICBM silo launchers for each Party shall be separated by no less than thirteen hundred kilometers.

[D]

In order to insure fulfillment of the obligation not to deploy ABM systems and their components except as provided in Article III of the Treaty, the Parties agree that in the event ABM systems based on other physical principles and including components capable of substituting for ABM interceptor missiles, ABM launchers, or ABM radars are created in the future, specific limitations on such systems and their components would be subject to discussion in accordance with Article XIII and agreement in accordance with Article XIV of the Treaty.

[E]

The Parties understand that Article V of the Treaty includes obligations not to develop, test, or deploy ABM interceptor missiles for the delivery by each ABM interceptor missile of more than one independently guided warhead.

[F]

The Parties agree not to deploy phased-array radars having a potential (the product of mean emitted power in watts and antenna area in square meters) exceeding three million, except as provided for in Articles III, IV and VI of the Treaty, or except for the purposes of tracking objects in outer space or for use as national technical means of verification.

[G]

The Parties understand that Article IX of the Treaty includes the obligation of the US and the USSR not to provide to other States technical descriptions or blue prints specially worked out for the construction of ABM systems and their components limited by the Treaty.

2. Common Understandings

Common understanding of the Parties on the following matters was reached during the negotiations:

A. LOCATION OF ICBM DEFENSES

The U.S. Delegation made the following statement on May 26, 1972:

Article III of the ABM Treaty provides for each side one ABM system deployment area centered on its national capital and one ABM system deployment area containing ICBM silo launchers. The two sides have registered agreement on the following statement: "The Parties understand that the center of the ABM system deployment area centered on the national capital and the center of the ABM system deployment area containing ICBM silo launchers for each Party shall be separated by no less than thirteen hundred kilometers." In this connection, the U.S. side notes that its ABM system deployment area for defense of ICBM silo launchers, located west of the Mississippi River, will be centered in the Grand Forks ICBM silo launcher deployment area. (See Agreed Statement [C].)

B. ABM TEST RANGES

The U.S. Delegation made the following statement on April 26, 1972:

Article IV of the ABM Treaty provides that "the limitations provided for in Article III shall not apply to ABM systems or their components used for development or testing, and located within current or additionally agreed test ranges." We believe it would be useful to assure that there is no misunderstanding as to current ABM test ranges. It is our understanding that ABM test ranges encompass the area within which ABM components are located for test purposes. The current U.S. ABM test ranges are at White Sands, New Mexico, and at Kwajalein Atoll, and the current Soviet ABM test range is near Sary Shagan in Kazakhstan. We consider that non-phased array radars of types used for range safety or instrumentation purposes may be located outside of ABM test ranges. We interpret the reference in Article IV to "additionally agreed test ranges" to mean that ABM components will not be located at any other test ranges without prior agreement between our Governments that there will be such additional ABM test ranges.

On May 5, 1972, the Soviet Delegation stated that there was common understanding on what ABM test ranges were, that the use of the types of non-ABM radars for range safety or instrumentation was not limited under the Treaty, that the reference in Article IV to "additionally agreed" test ranges was sufficiently clear, and that national means permitted identifying current test ranges.

C. MOBILE ABM SYSTEMS

On January 29, 1972, the U.S. Delegation made the following statement:

Article V(1) of the Joint Draft Text of the ABM Treaty includes an undertaking not to develop, test, or deploy mobile land-based ABM systems and their components. On May 5, 1971, the U.S. side indicated that, in its view, a prohibition on deployment of mobile ABM systems and components would rule out the deployment of ABM launchers and radars which were not permanent fixed types. At that time, we asked for the Soviet view of this interpretation. Does the Soviet side agree with the U.S. side's interpretation put forward on May 5, 1971?

On April 13, 1972, the Soviet Delegation said there is a general common understanding on this matter.

D. STANDING CONSULTATIVE COMMISSION

Ambassador Smith made the following statement on May 22, 1972:

The United States proposes that the sides agree that, with regard to initial implementation of the ABM Treaty's Article XIII on the Standing

Consultative Commission (SCC) and of the consultation Articles to the Interim Agreement on offensive arms and the Accidents Agreement,* agreement establishing the SCC will be worked out early in the follow-on SALT negotiations; until that is completed, the following arrangements will prevail: when SALT is in session, any consultation desired by either side under these Articles can be carried out by the two SALT Delegations; when SALT is not in session, *ad hoc* arrangements for any desired consultations under these Articles may be made through diplomatic channels.

Minister Semenov replied that, on an *ad referendum* basis, he could agree that the U.S. statement corresponded to the Soviet understanding.

E. STANDSTILL

On May 6, 1972, Minister Semenov made the following statement:

In an effort to accommodate the wishes of the U.S. side, the Soviet Delegation is prepared to proceed on the basis that the two sides will in fact observe the obligations of both the Intertim Agreement and the ABM Treaty beginning from the date of signature of these two documents.

In reply, the U.S. Delegation made the following statement on May 20, 1972:

The United States agrees in principle with the Soviet statement made on May 6 concerning observance of obligations beginning from date of signature but we would like to make clear our understanding that this means that, pending ratification and acceptance, neither side would take any action prohibited by the agreements after they had entered into force. This understanding would continue to apply in the absence of notification by either signatory of its intention not to proceed with ratification or approval.

The Soviet Delegation indicated agreement with the U.S. statement.

3. Unilateral Statements

The following noteworthy unilateral statements were made during the negotiations by the United States Delegation:

* See Article 7 of Agreement to Reduce the Risk of Outbreak of Nuclear War Between the United States of America and the Union of Soviet Socialist Republics, signed September 30, 1971.

A. Withdrawal from the ABM Treaty

On May 9, 1972, Ambassador Smith made the following statement:

The U.S. Delegation has stressed the importance the U.S. Government attaches to achieving agreement on more complete limitations on strategic offensive arms, following agreement on an ABM Treaty and on an Interim Agreement on certain measures with respect to the limitation of strategic offensive arms. The U.S. Delegation believes than an objective of the follow-on negotiations should be to constrain and reduce on a long-term basis threats to the survivability of our respective strategic retaliatory forces. The USSR Delegation has also indicated that the objectives of SALT would remain unfulfilled without the achievement of an agreement providing for more complete limitations on strategic offensive arms. Both sides recognize that the initial agreements would be steps toward the achievement of more complete limitations on strategic arms. If an agreement providing for more complete strategic offensive arms limitations were not achieved within five years, U.S. supreme interests could be jeopardized. Should that occur, it would constitute a basis for withdrawal from the ABM Treaty. The United States does not wish to see such a situation occur, nor do we believe that the USSR does. It is because we wish to prevent such a situation that we emphasize the importance the U.S. Government attaches to achievement of more complete limitations on strategic offensive arms. The U.S. Executive will inform the Congress, in connection with Congressional consideration of the ABM Treaty and the Interim Agreement, of this statement of the U.S. position.

B. Tested in ABM Mode

On April 7, 1972, the U.S. Delegation made the following statement:

Article II of the Joint Text Draft uses the term "tested in an ABM mode," in defining ABM components, and Article VI includes certain obligations concerning such testing. We believe that the sides should have a common understanding of this phrase. First, we would note that the testing provisions of the ABM Treaty are intended to apply to testing which occurs after the date of signature of the Treaty, and not to any testing which may have occurred in the past. Next, we would amplify the remarks we have made on this subject during the previous Helsinki phase by setting forth the objectives which govern the U.S. view on the subject, namely, while prohibiting testing of non-ABM components for ABM purposes: not to prevent testing of ABM components, and not to prevent testing of non-ABM components for non-ABM purposes. To clarify our interpretation of "tested in an ABM mode," we note that we would consider a launcher, missile or radar to be "tested in an ABM mode," if, for example, any of the following events occur: (1) a launcher is used to launch an ABM interceptor missile, (2) an interceptor missile is flight tested against a target vehicle which has a flight trajectory with characteristics of a strategic ballistic missile flight trajectory, or is flight tested in conjunction with the test of an ABM interceptor missile or an ABM radar at the same test range, or is flight tested to an altitude inconsistent with interception of targets against which air defenses are deployed, (3) a radar makes measurements on a cooperative target vehicle of the kind referred to in item (2) above during the reentry portion of its trajectory or makes measurements in conjunction with the test of an ABM interceptor missile or an ABM radar at the same test range. Radars used for purposes such as range safety or instrumentation would be exempt from application of these criteria.

C. No-Transfer Article of ABM Treaty

On April 18, 1972, the U.S. Delegation made the following statement:

In regard to this Article [IX], I have a brief and I believe self-explanatory statement to make. The U.S. side wishes to make clear that the provisions of this Article do not set a precedent for whatever provision may be considered for a Treaty on Limiting Strategic Offensive Arms. The question of transfer of strategic offensive arms is a far more complex issue, which may require a different solution.

D. No Increase in Defense of Early Warning Radars

On July 28, 1970, the U.S. Delegation made the following statement:

Since Hen House radars [Soviet ballistic missile early warning radars] can detect and track ballistic warheads at great distances, they have a significant ABM potential. Accordingly, the United States would regard any increase in the defenses of such radars by surface-to-air missiles as inconsistent with an agreement.

APPENDIX B

President Reagan's
"Star Wars" Speech

March 23, 1983

. . . Thus far tonight I have shared with you my thoughts on the problems of national security we must face together. My predecessors in the Oval Office have appeared before you on other occasions to describe the threat posed by Soviet power and have proposed steps to address that threat. But since the advent of nuclear weapons, those steps have been directed toward deterrence of aggression through the promise of retaliation—the notion that no rational nation would launch an attack that would inevitably result in unacceptable losses to themselves. This approach to stability through offensive threat has worked. We and our allies have succeeded in preventing nuclear war for three decades. In recent months, however, my advisors, including in particular the Joint Chiefs of Staff, have underscored the bleakness of the future before us.

Over the course of these discussions, I have become more and more deeply convinced that the human spirit must be capable of rising above dealing with other nations and human beings by threatening their existence. Feeling this way, I believe we must thoroughly examine every opportunity for reducing tensions and for introducing greater stability into the strategic calculus on both sides. One of the most important contributions we can make is, of course, to lower the level of all arms, and particularly nuclear arms. We are engaged right now in several negotiations with the Soviet Union to bring about a mutual reduction of weapons. I will report to you a week from tomorrow my thoughts on that score. But let me just say I am totally committed to this course.

If the Soviet Union will join us in our effort to achieve major arms reduction we will have succeeded in stabilizing the nuclear balance. Nevertheless it will still be necessary to rely on the specter of retaliation—on mutual threat, and that is a sad commentary on the human condition.

Would it not be better to save lives than to avenge them? Are we not capable of demonstrating our peaceful intentions by applying all our abilities and our ingenuity to achieving a truly lasting stability? I think we are—indeed, we must!

After careful consultation with my advisors, including the Joint Chiefs of Staff, I believe there is a way. Let me share with you a vision of the future which offers hope. It is that we embark on a program to counter the awesome Soviet missile threat with measures that are defensive. Let us turn to the very strengths in technology that spawned our great industrial base and that have given us the quality of life we enjoy today.

Up until now we have increasingly based our strategy of deterrence upon the threat of retaliation. But what if free people could live secure in the knowledge that their security did not rest upon the threat of instant U.S. retaliation to deter a Soviet attack; that we could intercept and destroy strategic ballistic missiles before they reached our own soil or that of our allies?

I know this is a formidable technical task, one that may not be accomplished before the end of this century. Yet, current technology has attained a level of sophistication where it is reasonable for us to begin this effort. It will take years, probably decades, of effort on many fronts. There will be failures and setbacks just as there will be successes and breakthroughs. And as we proceed we must remain constant in preserving the nuclear deterrent and maintaining a solid capability for flexible response. But is it not worth every investment necessary to free the world from the threat of nuclear war? We know it is!

In the meantime, we will continue to pursue real reductions in nuclear arms, negotiating from a position of strength that can be ensured only by modernizing our strategic forces. At the same time, we must take steps to reduce the risk of a conventional military conflict escalating to nuclear war by improving our non-nuclear capabilities. America does possess—*now*— the technologies to attain very significant improvements in the effectiveness of our conventional, non-nuclear forces. Proceeding boldly with these new technologies, we can significantly reduce any incentive that the Soviet Union may have to threaten attack against the United States or its allies.

As we pursue our goal of defensive technologies, we recognize that our allies rely upon our strategic offensive power to deter attacks against them. Their vital interests and ours are inextricably linked—their safety and ours are one. And no change in technology can or will alter that reality. We must and shall continue to honor our commitments.

I clearly recognize that defensive systems have limitations and raise certain problems and ambiguities. If paired with offensive systems, they can be viewed as fostering an aggressive policy and no one wants that.

But with these considerations firmly in mind, I call upon the scientific community who gave us nuclear weapons to turn their great talents to the cause of mankind and world peace; to give us the means of rendering these nuclear weapons impotent and obsolete.

Tonight, consistent with our obligations under the A.B.M. Treaty and recognizing the need for close consultation with our allies, I am taking an important first step. I am directing a comprehensive and intensive effort to define a long-term research and development program to begin to achieve our ultimate goal of eliminating the threat posed by strategic nuclear missiles. This could pave the way for arms control measures to eliminate the weapons themselves. We seek neither military superiority nor political advantage. Our only purpose—one all people share—is to search for ways to reduce the danger of nuclear war.

My fellow Americans, tonight we are launching an effort which holds the promise of changing the course of human history. There will be risks, and results take time. But with your support, I believe we can do it.

GLOSSARY OF TERMS, ABBREVIATIONS AND ACRONYMS*

ABM   Antiballistic missile, a defense missile designed to intercept an offensive missile.

ASAT   Antisatellite weapons, weapons designed to destroy earth-based satellites.

BM   Ballistic missile, an unmanned missile that is propelled into space by one or more rocket engines and returns to earth without orbiting the planet.

* Some definitions were adapted from *Star Wars: A Defense Expert's Case Against the Strategic Defense Initiative* by Dr. Robert M. Bowman; *Strategic Nuclear Arms Control Verification: Terms and Concepts*, by Richard A. Scribner and Kenneth N. Luongu, and *Strategic Defense Initiative: Some Arms Control Implications*, by Jeffrey Boutwell and Richard A. Scribner, both works published by the American Association for the Advancement of Science.

BMD   Ballistic-missile defense.

BPI   Boost-phase intercept, the destruction of a ballistic missile during the initial stage of flight while its engines are still running.

BUS   Shorthand term for post-boost vehicle that holds and eventually dispenses the warheads in space.

CHAFF   Bits of metal or other materials dispersed around incoming warheads to confuse radar by reflecting multiple signals.

CRUISE MISSILE   An unmanned missile propelled by an air-breathing engine that operates entirely within the earth's atmosphere and maintains thrust throughout its flight. Current U.S. systems are considered to be more technologically advanced, of smaller size, and equipped with better guidance systems than the Soviets'. Current U.S. cruise missiles are subsonic. Cruise missiles may be launched from land, sea, and air.

DARPA   Defense Advanced Research Projects Agency.

DECOYS   Balloons and other light objects made to appear like warheads to radar and other sensors, confusing defensive systems.

DIRECT ENERGY WEAPONS   These intense energy "beam" weapons use the most exotic technologies currently being considered for BMD applications. Included are chemical lasers and free electron lasers, nuclear-bomb-powered X-rays, neutral and charged particle beams, and microwave weapons. They could be earth- or space-based, and their potential strategic missions include defense against, or destruction of, aircraft, missiles, and satellites.

DIRECT ASCENT   A type of ASAT that does not need to go into orbit with its target, but attacks from below immediately after being launched.

EMP   Electromagnetic pulse, an intense burst of radio frequency created by a nuclear explosion.

ENDOATMOSPHERIC   Refers to antiballistic missile systems that operate within the atmosphere, from the earth's surface to about 300,000 feet altitude.

EXOATMOSPHERIC   Refers to antiballistic missile systems that operate outside the atmosphere. Theoretically an "exo" defense can destroy many reentry vehicles (RVs) targeted on the same site because of the long flight times of RVs outside the atmosphere and the large battlespace.

EXCALIBUR   Code name for a series of underground tests of a device to produce beams of X-rays from a nuclear explosion.

GALOSH ABM SYSTEM   The one antiballistic system allowed the U.S.S.R. under the ABM treaty. It has been deployed around Moscow.

HARDEN   To protect military facilities, such as missile silos, against nuclear attack by using reinforced concrete or by burying the facilities deep beneath the earth's surface.

HARD-POINT DEFENSE   Defense of specific military assets—such as missile silos, bomber bases, command-and-control facilities—as opposed to "soft targets"—e.g., cities, transportation systems, agricultural assets.

HOE   Homing Overlay Experiment. An army program to develop a ground-based high-altitude interceptor for a BMD point defense system.

ICBM   Intercontinental ballistic missile.

INF   Intermediate nuclear forces. Designation of a series of U.S.-Soviet talks to limit intermediate-range ballistic missiles, particularly in Europe.

INTELSAT   International Telecommunications Satellite Organization.

INTERCEPTOR   In the context of antisatellite weapons, the warhead and maneuvering or homing apparatus. In the context of the ABM Treaty, an interceptor missile deployed to counter strategic ballistic missiles or their elements in flight trajectory.

INFRARED SCANNER   An imaging sensor deployed on a satellite or aircraft that can detect heat radiation. Infrared scanners can penetrate cloud cover, nighttime darkness, and camouflage. These scanners can detect underground silos and discriminate among test missiles by the way their propellants burn.

IR   Infrared. A portion of the electromagnetic spectrum with wavelengths shorter than visible light. Such radiation is given off by all objects, even in the dark. The intensity depends on the temperature of the object.

KINETIC-ENERGY WEAPONS Weapons that use high-speed aimed projectiles with built-in homing devices to destroy their target. Examples include interceptor missiles, ASAT projectiles, and hypervelocity railguns.

LASER Light amplification by stimulated emission of radiation; it is electromagnetic waves marching in coherent step, unlike the directionless, choppy waves of a stormy sea.

LOW Launch on warning.

MHV Miniature homing vehicle. This is the kill mechanism of the new U.S. ASAT launched on a two-stage rocket by the F-15 fighter. The MHV is a cylinder about a foot in diameter. It contains IR sensors to detect the heat of its target, a ring of thrusters to enable it to maneuver for a direct hit, and computers to perform the necessary calculations and control the thrusters. It kills by direct impact with the target satellite.

MIDGETMAN A small single-warhead mobile ICBM under development by the U.S. Air Force for deployment in the 1990s. The Snowcroft Commission recommended Midgetman as a way of backing away from destabilizing MIRVs.

MINUTEMAN A three-stage second-generation U.S. ICBM. Currently, 450 Minuteman IIs are deployed with single warheads, and 550 Minuteman IIIs were deployed in the early 1960s but are no longer in operation. Minuteman IIs and IIIs are being modernized.

MIRV Multiple independent-target reentry vehicles. More than one warhead on each ICBM.

NORAD North American Aerospace Defense Command.

OUTER SPACE TREATY According to this treaty, nuclear or other weapons of mass destruction cannot be placed in orbit around the earth, installed on the moon or any other celestial body, or otherwise stationed in outer space. It also limits the use of the moon and other celestial bodies exclusively to peaceful purposes and expressly prohibits their being used for establishing military bases, installations, or fortifications, testing weapons of any kind, or conducting military maneuvers. Verification is carried out by space tracking systems. The treaty, signed by the U.S., the U.S.S.R., and eighty-seven other countries, was ratified by the U.S. in 1967.

OTA Office of Technology Assessment. An arm of Congress.

PASSIVE DEFENSE Defense of population or military facilities by protective shelters, hardening, dispersal, mobility, or other means.

PAYLOAD For missiles, the total weight of the warheads, shroud, penetration aids, post-boost vehicle, and activating devices.

PERSHING II New U.S. intermediate-range ballistic missile stationed in Europe.

PHASED-ARRAY A type of radar that steers the beam electronically rather than mechanically.

POINT DEFENSE The use of antiballistic missile weapons to defend a limited geographic area, such as a missile silo, against attacking missiles.

RAILGUN A kinetic weapon meant to destroy ballistic missiles, post-boost vehicles, reentry vehicles, and satellites. As currently proposed, the electromagnetic railgun would be deployed on orbiting platforms. The gun operates by converting electrical energy to magnetic pressure, firing guided projectiles at or near the speed of light.

RV Reentry vehicle. The portion of a ballistic missile that carries the nuclear warhead. So named because it reenters the earth's atmosphere in the terminal phase of the missile's flight.

SAFEGUARD The modification of the Sentinel ABM system announced by President Nixon in March 1969. The system was designed to protect U.S. ICBM sites. It was deployed near Grand Forks, North Dakota, in 1975 and deactivated in 1976.

SALT Strategic arms limitation talks. Bilateral negotiations between the U.S. and the U.S.S.R. that began in Helsinki in 1969 following preliminary discussions between President Johnson and Premier Kosygin at Glassboro, New Jersey, in June 1967. The aim of the SALT process was to move toward lower numbers of nuclear weapons by first establishing parity in forces and equal aggregate totals and then moving to reductions in arsenals. Throughout the SALT negotiations, verification issues played a key role.

SALT I The first set of strategic arms limitation talks produced two agreements that were ratified in 1972, one permanent, and one of five years' duration limiting offensive arms. These were followed by an accord signed in Vladivostok in 1974 setting the framework for the SALT II negotiations.

SALT II   This treaty, which was signed in 1979 and was to last through 1985, set limits on the number of U.S. and Soviet strategic offensive nuclear missiles, warheads, launchers, and delivery vehicles, and constrained the deployment of new strategic offensive arms on both sides. The SALT II agreement was signed by President Carter and General Secretary Brezhnev in Vienna in June 1979, and President Carter sent it to the Senate for its advice and consent to ratification. The treaty was withdrawn from Senate consideration in 1980, after the Soviet invasion of Afghanistan, and was never ratified by the U.S.

SENTINEL   An American ABM system approved by President Johnson that was designed to protect cities against small-scale nuclear attack, such as the one from the People's Republic of China. It became the Safeguard system in the late 1960s.

SILO   A fixed vertical structure either above ground or in the ground housing an ICBM and its launch support equipment. A silo includes the power supply, communications equipment, and environmental control equipment.

SPARTAN   An exoatmospheric nuclear-warhead-carrying antimissile that was part of the old U.S. ABM system.

SPRINT   An endatmospheric nuclear-warhead-carrying antimissile that was part of the old U.S. ABM system.

SS-17   A cold-launched fourth-generation Soviet ICBM with high accuracy that became operational in 1975. It can carry four MIRVed warheads. The missile has a range of about 10,000 km, and has targeting flexibility. There were 150 deployed as of April 1984, some with single warheads.

SS-18   A very accurate cold-launched fourth-generation Soviet ICBM. The SS-18 has a range of 11,000 km and can carry ten MIRVed warheads. As of April 1984 there were 308 deployed.

SS-19   A very accurate fourth-generation Soviet ICBM that became operational in 1974. With a range of 10,000 km, the SS-19 can carry six MIRVed warheads. It has targeting flexibility, enabling it to be aimed at either North America or Eurasia. As of April 1984, there were 360 deployed, some with single warheads.

SS-20   The newest Soviet MIRVed intermediate-range ballistic missile. Currently, over 300 of these accurate missiles, first deployed in 1977, are stationed in the U.S.S.R. They are primarily deployed west of the Ural Mountains and are targeted on Western Europe. Some are also deployed in the eastern Soviet Union with Asian targets.

STRATEGIC   Long range.

SLBM   Submarine launched ballistic missile. A ballistic missile carried by and launched from a submarine.

TACTICAL   Short range.

TERMINAL INTERCEPTION   The destruction of ballistic missile warheads after they reenter the atmosphere and approach their targets on earth. This phase generally lasts from thirty to a thousand seconds.

THEATER NUCLEAR WEAPONS   A nuclear weapon, usually of longer range and larger yield than tactical weapons, that can be used in major regional operations. Many strategic nuclear weapons can be used in theater operations, but not all theater weapons are designed for strategic use. The Soviet SS-20 and the U.S. Pershing II are considered theater nuclear weapons.

THROW WEIGHT   The maximum weight of warheads plus the guidance unit and penetration aids that can be derived by a missile over a particular range and in a stated trajectory.

TITAN II   A two-stage single eight-to-ten-megaton U.S. ICBM. Deployed in the early 1960s in substantial numbers, the Titan force is currently being deactivated. As of March 1984, thirty-three Titans were deployed in hardened silos in Arizona and Arkansas.

INDEX